THE ATHENIAN TRIREME

THE ATHENIAN TRIREME

The history and reconstruction of an
ancient Greek warship

J. S. MORRISON AND J. F. COATES

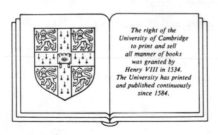

The right of the
University of Cambridge
to print and sell
all manner of books
was granted by
Henry VIII in 1534.
The University has printed
and published continuously
since 1584.

CAMBRIDGE UNIVERSITY PRESS

Cambridge

New York   New Rochelle   Melbourne   Sydney

Published by the Press Syndicate of the University of Cambridge
The Pitt Building, Trumpington Street, Cambridge CB2 1RP
32 East 57th Street, New York, NY 10022, USA
10 Stamford Road, Oakleigh, Melbourne 3166, Australia

First published 1986
Reprinted 1986, 1987 (twice), 1988 (twice)

Printed in Great Britain at the University Press, Cambridge

British Library cataloguing in publication data

Morrison, J.S.
The Athenian trireme
I. Triremes   2. Ships – Reconstruction
I. Title   II. Coates, J.F.
6238'21   VM75

Library of Congress cataloguing in publication data

Morrison, J.S. (John S.), 1913–
The Athenian trireme.
Bibliography.
Includes indexes.
1. Triremes. 2. Navigation – Greece – Athens – History.
3. Athens (Greece) – History, Naval.
I. Coates, J.F. (John F.) II. Title.
VM 16.M66   1986   623.8'21'0938   85-26984

ISBN 0 521 32202 2 hard covers
ISBN 0 521 31100 4 paperback

CONTENTS

LIST OF ILLUSTRATIONS

MAPS

PREFACE

In the collection of material for this book, and in the scientific and technical work for the design of the ship which is its *raison d'être*, the authors have received generous help from a wide range and a large number of individuals and institutions. We have done our best to acknowledge this help in the Introduction, List of Illustrations and footnotes to the text, but realise that we cannot here give just recognition to much that has been of vital importance to us.

More widely we wish to thank those in this country who with us have founded and who have given support and backing to the Trireme Trust. Our Greek friends deserve particular mention: Mr George Dracopoulos, Captain A.I. Tzamtzis of the Hellenic Maritime Museum, Mr H.E. Tzalas of the Hellenic Institution for the Preservation of Nautical Tradition, whom we first met at Greenwich in April 1983, Admiral E. Makris, whom we met subsequently in Piraeus, and last but by no means least Commodore I. Kolliniatis and Commander S. Platis, with whom we have had the pleasure of working closely towards the realisation of what is likely to prove the fastest oared ship afloat. Collectively they have been successful in securing Greek financial backing for building the trireme, and are now bringing it about. We thank them all for their confidence, collaboration and friendship.

We acknowledge with gratitude the award by the Leverhulme Foundation of an Emeritus Research Fellowship to JSM which has helped very greatly in the assembly of material, and in travel, connected with the book.

Lastly we wish to thank Cambridge University Press and its skilful and sympathetic staff whose efficient labours have made it possible for the book and the ship to be launched together.

J.S. Morrison
J.F. Coates

xi

ABBREVIATIONS

anc.   ancient
Arch. Eph.   *Archaiologike Ephemeris* (*Eph. Arch.* before 1860)
C.   Cape
CP   *Classical Philology*
CQ   *Classical Quarterly*
CR   *Classical Review*
FGrH   *Die Fragmente der Griechischen Historiker:* F. Jacoby, 1957–8
GOS   Morrison and Williams (1968): *Greek Oared Ships*
IG   *Corpus Inscriptionum Graecarum*
IJNA   *International Journal of Nautical Archaeology*
JEA   *Journal of Egyptian Archaeology*
JHS   *Journal of Hellenic Studies*
LSJ   Liddell–Scott–Jones: *Greek-English Lexicon*
MM   *The Mariner's Mirror*
mod.   modern
pr.   promontory
RA   *Revue Archéologique*
SI   Système International
SIG   *Sylloge Inscriptionum Graecarum*
t.t.   technical term

The initials JSM and JFC are used to refer to the two authors.

INTRODUCTION

The idea of building a full-scale replica of a trieres, or Greek trireme as it is better known in English, the first and most famous of the standard oared warships of the ancient Mediterranean, first took shape in 1981. Roddi Williams and I were beginning work on a book about the later oared warships of the Hellenistic and Roman navies, and had asked John Coates to join us. He had recently retired as Chief Naval Architect for the Ministry of Defence, and was interested in marine archaeology. We were aware that the weakness of *Greek Oared Ships 900–322 BC* (1968) had been its neglect of the architectural and engineering aspects, and we could see that in the explanation of the nature of the later (and larger) ships these considerations would have a vital part to play.

At this point, Charles Willink, a classical scholar whom I had known at Trinity, telephoned to say that he had been having dinner with Frank Welsh, a banker and writer, and Edwin Woolf, a Liverpool solicitor who had recently spent a year as a Visiting Senior Member at Wolfson, my most recent College at Cambridge. The idea had còme up of making a reconstruction of a trireme, and he asked if I was interested. I telephoned John Coates, warning him that if we did agree to undertake such an enterprise most of the work would fall on him. It so happened that he and I, as might have been foreseen, had just reached the conclusion that before we could approach the design problems of the later ships we should need as a starting-point to develop in more detail the design of the trieres; for it was beginning to appear that the design of the later ships was likely to have been based on that of the trieres. Early design work on the trieres had already been started, so we were in the mood to agree to undertake the project, and we did so.

The first public step was a press conference in the City of London in August 1982, at which the project was announced to the world, and a partial model of the proposed oarsystem was exhibited (fig. 1).

1. Model made by Sinclair Morrison in 1940 to demonstrate that the oars in each three-level unit of a trieres could be of the same length.

Seven years before, there had been a correspondence of record length in *The Times* (6 September–4 October 1975) on the subject of the trieres. We were not therefore surprised at the considerable attention the announcement aroused in this country as well as in continental Europe and in the USA. The trieres was clearly not only a matter of arcane interest to a few classical scholars, ancient historians and archaeologists. A much greater number of other people had had their curiosity stimulated, and frustrated, in their schooldays by reading about these famous and quite extraordinary warships, and finding no adequate explanation of how they were pulled by their huge crews of oarsmen. Rowing men, boatbuilders, scientists and Mediterranean yachtsmen all joined in, displaying very decided views on various aspects of the ship and its performance, and adding significantly to the body of relevant knowledge.

The press conference was followed in April 1983 by an Advisory Discussion. This was a 'live' version of the *Times* correspondence and so designated with the profitable outcome of the latter in mind. It was held at the National Maritime Museum at Greenwich under the auspices of the Director, Dr Basil Greenhill, and with the valuable and energetic assistance of Dr Sean McGrail and his department. During the previous winter John Coates and another naval architect, David Moss, had built a full-scale mock-up of the oarsystem which we were proposing for the reconstruction (fig. 2), while another friend of John Coates, Norman Gundry, made a 1.5 m model of the whole ship (fig. 2, foreground), both to be shown, with drawings, at Greenwich. All the people who were known to have an interest in the subject were invited to attend the discussion, and a good number, including a strong contingent from Greece and one or two from other continental European countries and from America, were able to come. We wanted to receive as many comments and suggestions as possible before, rather than after, the designs were finalised, and to have time to consider them.

The model and the working drawings were exhibited and explained, and the ancient evidence discussed. The mock-up of the oarsystem, with a pool alongside, was set up outside the Museum, and manned by a crew of oarsmen from Emmanuel College,

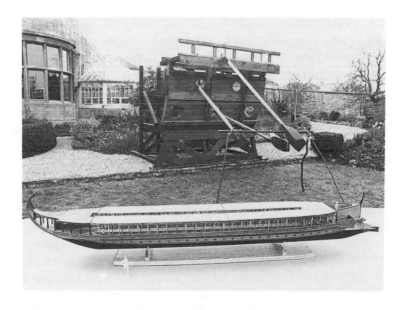

2. Full-scale mock-up of a trieres' oarsystem made by JFC and David Moss in 1982/3. In front, the model of the proposed replica made by Norman Gundry in 1982/3.

3. The mock-up demonstrated at the National Maritime Museum, Greenwich, April 1983.

Cambridge, who after some preliminary splashing settled down to a steady, if cautious rhythm (fig. 3). A naval onlooker[1] suggested that the uppermost oarsmen might more comfortably hold their oars with their inner hand under rather than above the oar (a position adopted in fact by the uppermost oarsmen of the open Roman trireme, Trajan's flagship, on Trajan's column (fig. 4)). There was some discussion of the steepness of the angle made with the water by the uppermost oars, which we were subsequently able to reduce. In general, both oarcrew and spectators expressed themselves satisfied with the system, although some doubts remained about the top oars.

For the structure of the hull we proposed to take as a model the third-century Phoenician oared ships[2] found by Miss Honor Frost off Marsala (anc. Lilybaeum) and also the fourth-century Kyrenia

1. Admiral Sir Simon Cassels KBE, The Admiral President of the Royal Naval College
2. Honor Frost (1973) and (1974b).

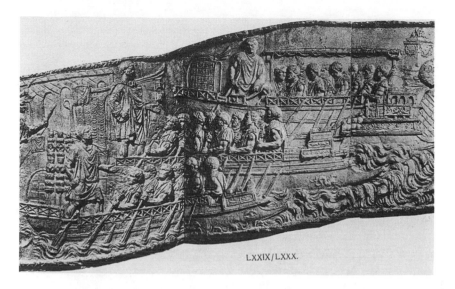

LXXIX / LXXX.

4. The three-level open trieres on Trajan's Column in Rome, early second century AD.

merchant ship (fig. 5).[3] It was fortunate that Richard Steffy was able to be present at the discussion. He was a member of the team from the Texas Institute of Nautical Archaeology which had raised the Kyrenia ship. He gave advice on the method of construction, and the discussion on this topic was particularly fruitful.

The Advisory Discussion at Greenwich was recorded and published by the National Maritime Museum in December 1984. It had attracted a good deal of attention in the press, and had resulted in an invitation from the *Daily Express* to exhibit the mock-up, the model and the working drawings at the Earl's Court Boat Show in January 1984. In September 1983 John Coates and Eric McKee,[4] who was advising the Trust as an expert in methods of wooden boat construction, visited Greece to study the work that was being done in a Piraeus boatyard on a replica of the Kyrenia merchant ship. John Coates was invited to give a lecture on the Trust's project to a Greek audience. In conversations with the President and Secretary General of the Hellenic

3. H.W. Swiny and M.L. Katzev (1973) and (1974).
4. See the Bibliography.

5. The Kyrenia merchant ship, fourth century BC.

Maritime Museum (Admiral E. Makris and Captain A. I. Tzamtzis), with the President of the Institute for the Preservation of Nautical Tradition (Mr Harry Tzalas) and with representatives of the Hellenic Navy, the Trust's representatives became aware that there was a great deal of active interest and substantial support for the project in various quarters in Greece, official and unofficial. Sadly, and to the detriment of the project, Eric McKee died suddenly, shortly after taking part in these promising discussions.

In Britain the promoters of the project had by now formed the Trireme Trust, with charitable status. Air Vice-Marshal Peter Turner, Bursar of Wolfson College, became its Treasurer, and a public appeal for contributions was made. A number of generous donations resulted, including a substantial gift from Mr Eddy Kulukundis and research grants from the Classical Faculty at Cambridge and a number of Cambridge Colleges. The exhibition of the mock-up and model at the Boat Show, the former with oars pulled by crews from Trinity, Magdalene and Corpus Christi Colleges, brought in some further contributions and widened the general interest in the project. Achievement of the Trust's aim began now to seem possible.

It was realised at the outset that before the building of the ship could be put in hand a good deal of preliminary experimentation would be necessary. Small models to test the run of planking at bow and stern would have to be made, and destruction tests carried out on the mortice-and-tenon joints by which the planks of the hull were fastened edge to edge. It was also seen to be necessary to build a piece of the hull to full scale to try out the ancient methods of construction, as attested by the discovered remains of ancient hulls, and to experiment in accurate detail with the seating and pulling arrangements for the oarsmen. Problems which drawings might not reveal could thus be identified and tackled in advance of the actual building of the ship. A Trial Piece built for these purposes would also serve as a useful guide for the future boatbuilders, and might ultimately find a place in a Maritime Museum, since it would be a section, accurate in all respects, of the built ship. Accordingly, in June 1984 a contract for building a full-scale Trial Piece, one-seventh as long (5.5 m) and slightly over half as broad (3.5 m) as the eventual ship, was placed with Coventry Boatbuilders at an initial cost of £30,000 (which eventually rose to nearly £40,000). In view of the favourable prospects which were developing in Greece the Trust thought it essential to press on with these essential preliminary stages, although funds from the appeal were not yet sufficient to cover them, Lloyd's Bank and the Co-operative Bank provided over-draft facilities.

In February 1984 Frank Welsh and I had visited Athens to talk to our Greek friends. They came forward with a firm proposal that the two ministries involved, Defence and Culture, and the National Tourist Organisation, should put up half the cost of building the ship (which they estimated at £300,000) if the Trust would put up the other half, in addition to the research and development costs already incurred and the cost of the Trial Place. On our return the Trust began to look for some more substantial sponsorship.

In June 1984 Frank Welsh went to Athens for the Poseidonia shipping exhibition, taking with him the Gundry model for display on the Hellenic Navy stand. He was then officially informed that the Hellenic Navy, having received assurances of full financial support from Greek sources, was prepared to go ahead with the building of the ship in Greece, the Trust providing the Trial Piece, detailed specifications and working drawings, and conducting the sea trials of the ship when completed. John Coates and I went to Athens at the end of June shortly after the public announcement there of the initiation of the project by the Hellenic Navy and the Trust in partnership. Mr George Dracopoulos, chairman of Empros Lines, offered free transport of the Trial Piece from Felixstowe to Piraeus and back.

By this time, after more than a year's work, John Coates had developed the design to the point where a specification could be written. As the Hellenic Navy wished to press ahead and invite tenders to build, he set about writing it. With substantial help from Dorian Dymoke, this 150-page document was completed, together with the building drawings, in time to meet the Hellenic Navy authorities again at the end of July. In consultation with John Coates, they immediately translated the specification into Greek and sent out invitations to tender for building the trieres in Greece.

During the winter of 1984/5 while the building contract was being negotiated in Greece, the Trial Piece was being constructed in Britain, rather slowly at first owing to the large amount of work involved in forming and fitting the keel and the thick lower strakes.

6. The Trial Piece at Coventry Boatbuilders, June 1985, with the Tzakakos brothers.

Commander Stavros Platis and Lieutenant Christos Leletzis of the Hellenic Navy visited Coventry to see the progress and to understand the problems of building an ancient ship. In May 1985 the building contract was awarded to the boat-building firm of the brothers Tzakakos of Kiratzini, a suburb of Piraeus. The two brothers are seen in fig. 6 in front of the Trial Piece at Coventry a few weeks later.

The stewards of the Henley Royal Regatta kindly agreed to a request from the Trust that the Trial Piece should be shown at the Regatta before being shipped out to Greece at the end of July. Their chairman Mr Peter Coni QC earned our gratitude for the helpful and efficient way he enabled us to carry out this rather unusual operation, financed by a generous grant from the Hellenic Foundation.

To be sure that all would be well at Henley, the Trial Piece was given a preliminary testing in the moat of Coombe Abbey near Coventry, where the fifteen oars were pulled with great enthusiasm and precision first by Warwick University Boat Club and then by Worcester Rowing Club. Since it was only a small part of the complete ship and asymmetrical along its length and across its breadth, the achievement by means of a number of steel drums of exactly the right position in the water demanded by the sophisticated oarsystem was a matter of delicate calculation and experiment. Fig. 7 shows how John Coates' sums and the Worcester Rowing Club's performance came right.

At Henley, publicity for exhibiting the Trial Piece was financed by grants from Global Asset Management and the Grocers' Company, and the whole event was organised with the greatest efficiency and enthusiasm by the Trust's Henley representative Rosie Randolph of Watlington. Our purpose at Henley was to interest and inform the international rowing community about the trireme and the building of the ship in Greece with a view to the recruitment of volunteer oarsmen and oarswomen for the sea trials in the autumn of 1986 or the spring of the following year. About 150 individuals and a number of rowing clubs put their names on the list. To these the Trial Piece gave some indication of what pulling a trieres would be like (fig. 8), and it did not seem to deter them. The exhibition also stimulated a very lively interest by many members of the public in the whole pro-

7. The Trial Piece pulled by the Worcester Rowing Club at Coombe Abbey, June 1985.

8. The Trial Piece at Henley Royal Regatta, July 1985.

ject. Some useful contacts were made and suggestions put forward in the area of fund-raising. These were important because the activities of the Trust were still being run almost entirely on credit.

After two weeks at Henley the Trial Piece was lifted from the river onto a truck and driven to Felixstowe, where one of Mr George Dracopoulos' Empros Line ships was waiting to take it to Greece. The first stage of the British part of the project had been completed.

Building the trieres herself had already started in Greece and we looked forward to her completion and commissioning there to be followed by sea trials under oar and under sail to fulfil the main aims of the project.

1

QUESTIONS AND ANSWERS

The Greeks called the standard warship of the classical period a *trieres*. The Romans called it a *triremis*, and English scholars have traditionally followed the Romans and called it a trireme.[1] But since the Greek ship is the theme of this book we shall use the term 'trieres' (plural 'triereis') throughout, except when we are speaking of the Roman vessel.

At the outset a number of questions require to be answered. Why is the trieres important? Why does a book need to be written on the subject? Why should the book be followed up by the design and making of a full-scale ship? And, finally, why has the definitive book not been written, and a satisfactory ship built, long ago, since the evidence has been available for a good many years?

The importance of the trieres

Oared warships, of which the trieres is the most famous, lie at the heart of the Greek, Hellenistic and Roman story as it unfolds from Homer to Constantine. In the seventh and sixth centuries BC, oared galleys took Greek colonists from their mother cities to all parts of the Mediterranean and the Black Sea. In 480 BC a great Persian armada was defeated by a much smaller Greek fleet in the narrow waters between Attica and the island of Salamis. Athens' ensuing maritime supremacy was founded on the crucial role which she played in that famous victory. The skilled use of the trieres enabled her to win, and for some decades to keep, the hegemony over some, at least, of her former Greek allies. In the fourth century larger oared ships – 'fours', 'fives', and 'sixes' – were built in Sicily at Syracuse to meet the growing seapower of Phoenician Carthage, and

---

1. Unlike the French (*trière*) and the Germans (*Triere*). The word 'trieres' probably means 'fitted with three' of something. Lionel Casson calls the ships of higher denomination 'fours', 'fives' etc.

'fours' and 'fives' were employed at the end of the century by Athens
and in the Levant. After the death of Alexander, his successors in the
late fourth and third centuries BC disputed among themselves the
command of the Eastern Mediterranean in fleets of increasingly
large denomination. Rome had to build fleets of 'fives' (quinqueremes) and accustom herself to their use in a war with Carthage
for the control of Sicily. In 31 BC at the sea battle of Actium, fought
in oared ships of a great variety of sizes, the young Octavian defeated
Antony and Cleopatra and gained the mastery of the Roman world as
the emperor Augustus.

To understand the naval confrontations of ancient history, on
which the future of western civilisation has so often turned, it is
essential to know as much as possible of the nature and potentials of
the vessels in which the two sides fought, as well as to form an idea of
the economic and social aspects of the organisation of fleets; and
knowledge of the trieres is basic to the understanding of the larger
ships. The trieres was the first type of oared warship to be pulled by
oars at three levels. No representation of an oared warship exists
showing oars at more than three levels. It seems likely, then, that the
types of larger denomination than three were pulled at three levels
and employed more than one man on each oar. (The 'four' is probably an exception, being pulled at two levels with two men to each
oar.) It follows that understanding of the trieres is important in relation not only to the deployment of that ship herself but also to the
deployment of the larger ships, which also were pulled by oarsmen at
three levels.

To Athens in the fifth and early fourth century BC the importance
of the trieres hardly needs to be emphasised. The fleet of 200 triereis
built shortly before the second Persian invasion, when she was
involved in a naval war with Aegina, enabled the Greeks successfully
to repel the invasion when it came. The entrance fee to the club of
naval powers was high, and we are told that Athens was only able to
afford it by using, at Themistocles' suggestion, the proceeds of a
lucky strike in the silver mines at Laurium. These ships were also,
Plutarch tells us (*Cimon* 12.2), specially designed by Themistocles
'for speed and quick turning', information which suggests that he
had his own ideas of trieres tactics. Only by understanding these tactics and the nature of the ships which employed them can we form an
idea of how the Greeks were able to defeat a fleet three times the size
of their own.

After the repulse of the Persian invasion a naval force under Athenian command proceeded to liberate the Greek cities of Asia Minor and the offshore islands, as well as part of Cyprus, and later invaded Egypt. In the last third of the fifth century Athens, now at war with her Peloponnesian allies, ensured her power at sea with a mastery of that special skill in fighting with triereis which was the despair of her rivals, and which, in the end, led her to overestimate the value of sea power against a continental league. In 415 an over-confident and ill-planned naval expedition to Sicily ended in disaster, and was a prelude to Athens' ultimate defeat by Sparta and her allies in 404, after some brave attempts to re-establish her naval command of the Aegean. Even after her defeat and surrender she managed with inadequate resources and varying success to cling to some semblance of maritime supremacy in the eastern Mediterranean for more than three-quarters of a century, in competition with strong Peloponnesian, Theban and ultimately Macedonian fleets, until her defeat at sea by a Macedonian-led Phoenician fleet off Amorgus in 322. A fitting epitaph for Athenian sea power is the proud reply put into the mouth of an Athenian traveller by a comic poet (Aristophanes, *Birds* 108) in the year of the Sicilian expedition. Asked for his country of origin he gives the answer: 'Where the fine triereis come from.' It was, it seems, the superior quality of her ships of which she boasted. This, very briefly, is the story of the Age of the Trieres,[2] and of the trieres as the weapon by which Athens achieved and maintained, and in which in the end she lost, her power and prosperity. The trieres was not only a battle weapon but also the means by which Athens deployed her military power quickly and for the most part effectively.

The need for a theoretical reconstruction

The trieres is important, first because her design is basic to the designs of all the subsequent ancient oared warships, and secondly because she played so significant a role in preserving the political and economic conditions in which Athens was able to make her great contribution to ideas of human society, to art, literature and

2. Lionel Casson entitles chapter 4 of his *Ships and Seamanship in the Ancient World* (1971) 'The age of the trireme'. Cf. Tarn (1930) p. 122: 'Down to the final destruction of Athenian sea-power at the battle of Amorgus in 322 the standard warship of the Mediterranean had been the trireme.'

philosophy. We need to know, and modern historians of Greece have not yet told us, how the trieres played that role, or rather how it was that the Athenians exploited more successfully than others the potential of the three-level oared ship as a naval weapon, and what that potential was. We want to know how she was used, to attempt to recognise the tactical purposes for which she was built, her strengths, and the limitations on her use which those strengths necessarily imposed. Fundamental questions need to be answered about the physical environment provided for her crew, the practice of pulling and sailing, her performance under oar and sail, the pay and recruitment of her crew, and the materials with which she was built. All this may be called the theoretical reconstruction of the trieres, and it needs to be set out as far as the evidence we have will allow.

There are two possible kinds of indisputable evidence for an ancient object: actual recognisable remains and a detailed description in contemporary literature. Neither exists for the trieres. Recent activities of underwater archaeologists in the Mediterranean have produced no remains of a trieres to give a whole or partial answer to questions about the hull-structure or oarsystem, although numerous remains of ancient merchant ships have been found, some of them deriving from the fifth and fourth centuries BC and offering a useful analogy for building a trieres' hull (below, p. 130). Nor do historians writing at the time when the trieres was the standard warship of contemporary fleets give the kind of detailed descriptions of her such as we have of the monster double-hulled 'forty' which Ptolemy Philopator built (below, p. 14) or of the Byzantine *dromon* (below, p. 10).

The enquirer must satisfy his frustrated curiosity by picking up information about the trieres from any contemporary source he can. First will be the narratives of the historians describing the actions and voyages of triereis at sea. These will give him a feel of what sort of ship the trieres was. The picture he gets will be supplemented by passing references to triereis or things connected with them in the poets – tragic and, in particular, comic – and even in the philosophers.

After literature, archaeology provides a variety of indirect information. The excavated remains of the Zea ship-sheds, built for triereis, give the maximum overall dimensions of the ship (37 metres long, 6 metres broad) (fig. 9). The surviving inventories of the Piraeus naval dockyards inscribed on stone and covering a number of years in the last third of the fourth century, provide a wealth of detailed information, in particular the length and number of the oars in the various categories. Finally there are the vase-paintings, reliefs and coins which can be claimed to represent the trieres, though no ship is labelled as such.

The intricate process of piecing together the clues from all these sources has the fascinating quality of a detective story and has attracted professional interest not only among classical scholars.

The foundations of the present investigation were laid in *Greek Oared Ships* in 1968, but although the general principles of the trieres' oarsystem there presented seem now to be generally accepted, a good deal more work remains to be done. The use of the ship in battle and moving from place to place has to be more closely studied, and the nature of the ship and her characteristics have to be deduced as ground rules for a theoretical reconstruction. These ground rules have then to be embodied in a detailed design which will satisfy the demands of the naval architect as well as those of the historian and archaeologist.

The need for a practical reconstruction

The next step is to build a trieres. One reason for doing this is the truth that the proof of this particular pudding is very much in the eating, since it must be borne in mind that a three-level oared ship is an elaborate and highly sophisticated phenomenon without parallel elsewhere in time or place. The picture of the trieres which can be pieced together in a book is by the nature of the evidence necessarily a fragile construction, resting on interpretations of difficult texts and puzzling representations. Working together, the joint authors of this book have for the first time brought to bear on the trieres problem three fields of knowledge: the learning of the scholar and traditional archaeologist, the more recent knowledge of ancient ship construction gleaned by underwater archaeologists, and the professional skill of the modern warship designer. In the light of that pooled expertise there is, apart from details, almost certainly only one practicable design for the trieres which conforms to the available evidence. That thesis has been strengthened during the

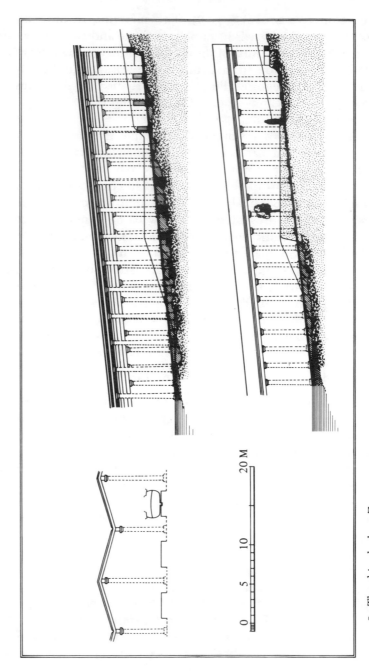

9. The ship-sheds at Zea.

development of the design as more detailed features have been worked out and found to knit together neatly, with the need for no more than minor adjustments to the main parameters. Thus we have on paper a ship which is not only a practical proposition but is also very likely to be in essentials the only possible solution to the trieres problem. Such a ship seems well worth building.

A reconstructed ship ought to accord with the known evidence about the original in dimensions, materials, construction, appearance and performance. If that is not completely possible, the exceptions should be defined and explained. Consequences or side effects of exceptions should be made clear.

The purposes of building a full-scale trieres need to be defined. Reconstruction of the past, by itself, in most cases hardly justifies the expense and effort involved. The best reason for making reconstructions of past artefacts is to improve our understanding of important aspects of history. As most artefacts are made for use, reconstructions can generally serve their main purpose only if they too work, and their performance can be assessed by proper measurements. An historically authentic working ship reconstruction can give us an insight into the realities of ancient seafaring, mercantile or naval, which would otherwise be unattainable. Another aspect of reconstructions, well expressed by Howard I. Chappelle (1936), the historian of American sailing ships, '. . . is that of learning to appreciate the intellect and ability of past generations. It is perfectly natural for each successive generation to look upon itself as far better equipped mentally than the ones before. If, however, one may judge by a comparison of naval architecture of the past with that of today as represented by modern sailing craft, there is little to support this self-admiration . . . men of earlier years had the same abilities and powers of reason and intellect that can be found in similar stations of life today.' The design of the trieres reconstruction has not only fully demonstrated Chappelle's point, but also borne witness to the very high level of craftsmanship in wood achieved in ancient times. The reconstructed ship will bring home to many that techniques of wood construction were as refined as those in stone and metal with which we have for a long time been familiar through numerous surviving examples of ancient architecture and sculpture.

The importance of ship reconstructions from the ancient

Mediterranean world is enhanced by three further facts. The first is that stone and metal played a role in the general constructive and manufacturing effort of those societies that was relatively minor compared with that of wood, though of course surviving relics would overwhelmingly and quite erroneously indicate the opposite. Secondly, ships represent solutions to more complex and testing structural problems than arise in land-based structures. Thirdly, among ships, those for war were developed to points nearest to the edge of technical feasibility at the time, regardless, it seems, of safety, expense or effort: they were, and indeed always have been, in modern terms, the high-technology products of their time.

The purposes of the reconstructed ship are three: (1) to prove that the reconstruction designed to the historical requirements and built in accordance with archaeological evidence will have a performance consistent with historical accounts; (2) to improve understanding of naval operations in the Mediterranean from the fifth to the third centuries BC; (3) to broaden appreciation of the technical, economic and naval achievements of Hellenic society and culture from the fifth to the third centuries BC by exhibiting the replica to the public in Greece with explanatory material. This purpose will, it is hoped, be amplified by housing the ship in a reconstruction of a Piraeus ship-shed of the fourth century BC, from which it will be launched for historical research and demonstration at sea; (4) to recreate one of the major artefacts of Hellenic civilisation and a unique ship-type of outstanding interest to naval historians and architects.

The history of the problem

The last question remains. Why was the problem not solved, and a reconstructed ship not built to everyone's satisfaction, long ago?

The historian Zosimus, writing in the fifth century AD, speaks (5.20.3–4) of the 'liburnians' which the Gothic chief Fravitta employed in the Aegean at the beginning of the century: 'These seem to be not less speedy than pentecontors[3] though far inferior to ships of the trieres kind, *the method of construction of the latter having been forgotten many years ago.*' Zosimus (2.22.3, 23.3) speaks of the last

---

3. Oared ships with 15 oarsmen a side at one or two levels were called triacontors (thirty-oared ships). Those with 25 oarsmen a side at one or two levels were called pentecontors (fifty-oared ships).

engagement in which triereis took part, the battle between Constantine and Licinius at the Hellespont in AD 323. On that occasion 200 of Licinius' triereis were defeated by 80 of Constantine's thirty-oared ships, a result which no doubt contributed to the trieres' final obsolescence.

The liburnian was originally a light warship with oars at two levels, invented as a pirate craft on the Dalmatian coast and subsequently much used in Roman fleets.[4] Vegetius, who was a contemporary of Zosimus, came to use the word for warships in general (*On Warfare* 2.1)

There are several kinds of liburnians, the smallest have one column or file (*ordo*: i.e. of oarsmen) a side, the slightly bigger ones have two a side, while those of the ideal size have three or four a side; sometimes they have five levels (*gradus*) a side. This should not seem strange to any one when in the battle of Actium much larger vessels are said to have run.

There are two things to be noted in connection with Vegetius' observations. First there is no evidence for ships being pulled at more than three levels, nor is such a thing feasible. Secondly, Vegetius was writing at a time when 'the method of building ships of the trieres kind had long been forgotten'. He reveals himself as the first of many writers on the subject to explain the ancient types of ships, 'threes', 'fours', 'fives', etc. in terms of the oared ships of their own time. He slips from columns or files (i.e. lines of oarsmen sitting one behind the other from stern to bow at one or more levels: figs. 20 and 26) quite unconsciously to speak of levels, as if the number of files and the number of levels of oarsmen in a ship were *necessarily* the same. He does this without noticing it because in the two-level liburnians (as in the warships in fig. 26) known to him there were in fact two fore-and-aft files of oarsmen, and one was above the other on each side of the ship. Quinqueremes, then, were for him, by the same

---

4. Appian (early second century AD), *Roman History* 10.1.3: 'The liburnian was named after a tribe of Illyrian pirates who roved the Ionian sea and islands in ships both fast and light . . . whence even now the Romans call their light swift ships with two oar-beats (*dikrotous*) liburnians.' For the meaning of *dikrotous* see Xenophon, *HG* 2.1.27–9 where of the Athenian triereis at Aegospotami, surprised on the beach by the Spartan admiral Lysander's unexpected attack, some were caught *monokrotoi* (i.e. with one file of oarsmen manned), some *dikrotoi* (i.e. with two files manned), and some entirely empty. See below p. 35 n.16.

mode of reckoning, ships with five fore-and-aft files of oarsmen on each side of the ship sitting *at five levels*. He has interpreted the quinquereme, quite absurdly, in terms of the ships he knew, although no representations of ships with more than three levels of oars in fact exist.

The warships of the Byzantine navy were called *dromons* ('runners'). We possess a building brief for them from the hand of the emperor Leo VI (19.7), who was writing at the end of the ninth century AD:

Let each of the dromons be long in proportion to her breadth and well proportioned with two oar-levels, the upper and the lower. Let each oar-level have at least twenty-five thwarts (*zyga*) on which the oarsmen will sit, so that all the thwarts are twenty-five above and twenty-five below, making fifty in all. And on each one of them let two oarsmen sit, one on the starboard side and one on the port side.

Leo's dromon is nearly as big as the Boeotian ships in Homer (*Iliad* 2.509–10); it is a large two-level ship with 50 oarsmen a side in two files of 25, each man pulling a single oar. There is no deck between the two levels of Vegetius' liburnians or of Leo's dromons, nor had there been a deck between the levels in the two-level pentecontor. The anonymous author of the *Itinerarium Peregrinorum*, however, who wrote in the twelfth century about the crusade of King Richard of England, appears to have known oared warships in which the two levels were separated by an actual deck. He tells (ch. 34) the story of the sea-fight between the Christians and Turks in the bay of Acre in the course of which Turks got possession of the upper deck of a *galea* and her oars and pulled in one direction, while the Christians, still in possession of the oars below, pulled in the other, and succeeded in winning this unusual kind of boat race. When the author comes to mention the ships of antiquity, with echoes of Vegetius, he, like Vegetius, interprets them in terms of the ships he knows, but the ships of his time are different from Vegetius'. They have a deck between the two levels of oars. The ships of the ancients, he says, accordingly 'rose level by level in distinct decks and some smote the waves with the beat of the longest oar, others with the beat of a shorter oar'. There is no need to trust the author of the *Itinerarium*'s account of how ancient ships were pulled, any more than Vegetius'. Both are reflections of the oared ships of their respective times.

In Renaissance Europe the general awakening of interest in the ancient world led to speculation about the nature of the oared ships which readers found mentioned in their texts. In 1514 the French humanist Budé, who was acquainted with the contemporary galleys of the western Mediterranean and Adriatic, wrote (1514, p. 135):

We read that among the ancient peoples there were not only ships of three files [i.e. of oarsmen] which are called triremes by our moderns, *triereis* by the Greeks (in these ships three oarsmen sit to each bench each pulling his own oar, so that the man who sits furthest inboard pulls the longest oar) but also quadriremes and quinqueremes and ships of six files of oarsmen.

The system of oars which Budé describes is the system known as *alla sensile*, developed in Venice in the Middle Ages, in which the oars at each bench were not only of different lengths but also nearly 36 ft (11.83 m) long. Molmenti (1906: Vol. 1, p. 131)[5] describes this system and the one that followed it:

The (Venetian) galley was propelled by oars, first of all two to a bench, then three or even four, so that they took the classical names of triremes and quadriremes. It was not until the middle of the sixteenth century that they adopted the single oar, forty or fifty feet long, rowed by four, five, six, seven, or even eight men.

The former system can be recognised as the *alla sensile* system, the latter as the *a scaloccio* (figs. 10(a) and (b)). It is clear that Budé, like the others before him, aided and abetted by the Venetians, who called their *alla sensile* galleys by the ancient names, has attributed the known contemporary *alla sensile* system, in the usual manner but again quite arbitrarily, to the ancient ships.

Sir Henry Savile, Queen Elizabeth's tutor in Greek and later Provost of Eton, saw the fallacy in the approach to the problem adopted by Budé and others. He writes (1581: p. 49 of the notes):

Now warships (*longae*) were sorted into their several kindes according to the number of bankes [i.e. benches] and oares placed one above the other, as I take it, though peradventure not directly. Some I know have concluded

5. Cf. Guilmartin (1974) p. 101: 'Starting about the middle of the fifteenth century there was a shift in the rowing system of the Mediterranean galleys from one where each oarsman pulled his own individual oar to one in which all the oarsmen on a bench pulled a single large oar'; p. 226: 'Before 1550 the standard Mediterranean warship was the *triremi alla sensile* of 24 banks', i.e. benches of three oarsmen (so 72 a side, 144 all told). For the length of the oars in *alla sensile* galleys see Jurien de la Gravière (1885) pp. 190–1. The gearing was 3.8 m (loom) : 8 m (outboard).

a

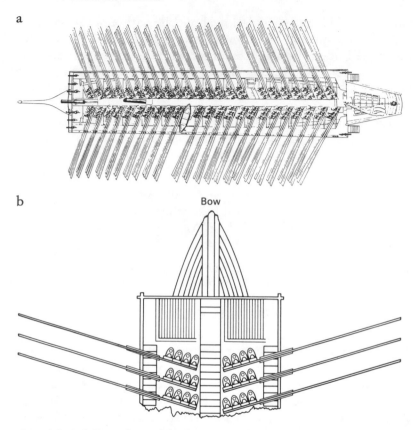

b   Bow

10a. Admiral Fincati's model of a sixteenth-century Venetian trireme *alla sensile*.
10b. The quadrireme *a scaloccio Real* which fought at Lepanto in 1571.

otherwise, that in triremes, for example, three men with three oares sate upon one banke [i.e. bench, the *alla sensile* system], some other that three men pulled at one oare [i.e. the *a scaloccio* system], directly against both the authority of ancient writers produced by themselves and contrary to the ancient portraytures remaining yet to be seene: so incredible a thing it seemed to beleeve that which in our galleyes nowadaye they never saw: whereas in truth Zosimus telleth us that very many yeares before his time they had discontinued to make any ships of the trireme type at all.

The ancient authority Savile is thinking of is probably Aristophanes, who spoke (*Frogs* 1074) of one oarsman in a trieres making wind and worse into the face of another (see below, p. 19); and one of the 'ancient portraytures' is probably the three-level ship on Trajan's column in Rome (fig. 4). Another may have been the relief of which the drawing in Cavaliero dal Pozzo's collection is all that survives (fig. 11; below, p. 141); a third possibly the Aquila relief (fig. 12; below, p. 145). It is as well that he did not take other examples than the trieres for his own explanation, but his main point is an important one, that people refused, in spite of the evidence, to believe in an oarsystem which was not actually practised in the galleys of their time.

Savile did not address himself to a formidable difficulty which had rightly worried a younger contemporary of Budé, Lazar de Baif. Appointed ambassador of the French king to the Venetian Republic, he wrote from Venice asking his friend Dinteville to send him some engravings, the majority from the relief on Trajan's column. In 1536, on his return to France, he wrote a monograph on ancient ships in which he included the engravings but adhered to the current theory that the ancient trieres was pulled on a one-level system. He accepted the two-level system in some ships presumably because

11. Drawing made in Rome between 1610 and 1635 for the Cavaliero dal Pozzo and now in the British Museum.

12. Fragment of a relief originating in Athens and now in the Museo Nazionale Abruzzo at L'Aquila.

this was a contemporary practice; but on the three-level ship on Trajan's column, which he discusses, he merely comments: 'I do not think that this is the trireme which the ancients used.' The opinion is understandable. The ship on the column has no deck, and triereis were undoubtedly decked in the fifth and fourth centuries BC. The human figures, greatly out of proportion, lend an air of implausibility. Nevertheless the ship unmistakably has three levels of oars. But Lazar de Baif's main objection is a new and sensible one, which has since his time played a big part in the discussion. If a trieres has three levels of oars, the word, containing the prefix *tri*, i.e. 'three', seems to *mean* a ship with three levels of oars; and if that is so, it seems to follow that the numeral in the series *tetrērēs, pentērēs* in Greek, *quadriremis, quinqueremis*, etc. in Latin indicates the number of levels of oars in these larger ships. And there is a very well attested *tesserakontērēs* built by Ptolemy Philopator,[6] which must then have had forty levels of oars. From this *reductio ad absurdum* the conclusion

6. Callixenus in Athenaeus 5.37, Plutarch, *Demetrius* 43.4. As Jurien de la Gravière (1878) observed (p. 769): 'La foi la plus robuste ici s'épouvante.'

has been generally drawn that a trieres could not, after all, have had three levels of oars.

In this early discussion one other contribution is notable. Barras de la Penne (1727), the captain of Louis XIV's galleys, and a man therefore of some considerable experience of oared ships, criticised accounts of the ancient ships such as Vegetius' by making the significant point that crews using oars of greatly differing lengths at different levels, such as would apparently be entailed in a three-level oarsystem, could not possibly synchronise their stroke; and with a large number of oarsmen synchronisation of stroke was vital. Admittedly, in *alla sensile* galleys the three men sitting on the series of single benches on each side of the ship would have pulled oars of different lengths; but since the difference would have been small in proportion to the total length of the oars and the men would have been sitting side by side, the difficulty of synchronisation would not have been very great.

This historical account teaches a clear lesson. Men from the fifth to the sixteenth century AD very naturally explained the ancients' galleys in terms of the ships they saw around them.

13. The Lenormant Relief in the Acropolis Museum at Athens (photo of the cast in the Museum of Classical Archaeology at Cambridge).

Discussion of the trieres' oarsystem received a new stimulus in 1859 by the publication of a marble relief (fig. 13), now known as the Lenormant relief, discovered on the Acropolis of Athens. It showed the middle part of the starboard side of an oared ship, and seemed likely from its date alone, about 400 BC, if by nothing else, to depict the standard warship of the time, the trieres (below, p. 139). A further fragment of this relief was subsequently found (fig. 14). In the second half of the last century, accordingly, many scholars and naval architects in Germany and France addressed themselves to solving the puzzle of how the trieres worked.

In *L'Illustration* of 23 March 1861 (and also in the *Illustrated Times* and the *Illustrated London News* a few weeks later) there is a picture of the Roman trireme built on the Seine for the emperor Napoleon III on the advice of Auguste Jal (eminent author of the *Glossaire nautique*) and to the designs of a distinguished naval architect, Dupuy de Lôme (fig. 15). Napoleon III was engaged in writing the life of Julius Caesar and instructed Jal to collaborate with Dupuy de Lôme in the building of a reconstruction of the sort of trireme that Caesar might have used, for display in the Exposition of 1867. Jal apparently relied on certain 'médailles' and on the Lenormant relief. The ship was built at Clichy in 1860–1 and launched in March 1861 in the presence of the emperor and his Minister of Marine. It appears to have been an embarrassing failure, and the reason is not hard to see.

According to the *Illustrated Times* it was 39.25 m long, 5.50 m broad, with the deck 3 m above the waterline. There are said to have been 130 oars at three levels (42, 44, 44), the upper two levels somehow seated on the deck and the lowest below it. From the pictures the ship seems to have been massively built, and fewer than 60 oarports on the port side are in fact visible. In a note on the reconstruction in his book on *La Flotte de Jules César* (1861) Jal says that the oars were of different lengths; the thranite oars (i.e., presumably, the longest) were 7.20 m. 'Nothing,' he says, 'is better established than the inequality in length of the three banks of oars: the "médailles" leave one in no doubt at all.' These 'médailles' have not been identified. It seems clear that although the breadth and height of the ship were about right, it was 2–3 m too long, far too heavily built, and greatly underpowered. The oars were also far too long, and being of different lengths and pulled at different levels would have been impossible for the 'matelots de Cherbourg' to synchronise.

14. Fragment of the monument of which fig. 13 is a part.

15. Photograph of an engraving showing the Roman trireme built for Napoleon III by Dupuy de Lóme and August Jal in 1860/1.

The Roman trireme's absence from the maritime parade at the Paris Exposition of 1867 was noted with regret by the press, and no mention of it appears in Napoleon III's *Histoire de Jules César* published the previous year. The ship is said to have been used in target practice and eventually sunk by torpedo.[7]

In spite of the embarrassment produced among scholars at the outcome of this venture, and the amusement of the general public, speculation continued. Graser (1864) based a reconstruction (fig. 16a) of the trieres' oarsystem on the lines of Aristophanes mentioned above, taken quite literally, but found that he had to decrease the space between one oarsman's seat and the next in each fore-and-aft file to less than the unitary length of two cubits (0.888 m), the *interscalmium* of which Vitruvius (1.2.4) speaks (below, p. 134). Cartault (1881) insisted on the observance of the two-cubit rule and modified Graser's arrangement accordingly. Lemaitre (1883; fig. 16b) protested against Graser's 'living wall' of oarsmen, and set his units of three oarsmen *en échelon* across the ship as well as fore-and-aft. All these systems were open to the fatal objection made first by Barras de la Penne, that it would be impossible for oarsmen sitting at different levels to pull in unison oars of greatly differing lengths.

In examining the Lenormant relief Cartault had noticed that the pair of longitudinal timbers through which the visible oarsmen were pulling their oars were in higher relief than the wales on the side of the ship below them, and suggested that the timbers in high relief were parts of an outrigger, like the *apostis* which in the Venetian galleys carried the tholepins, a sort of rectangular frame imposed on the gunwales. Assmann (1887) also suggested an outrigger, and identified it with the *parexeiresia* mentioned in Thucydides (4.12, 7.34). This suggestion also accounted for certain unexplained features of the relief as supports for the outrigger.[8] In 1895 Haack, a professional naval architect, published a reconstructed oarsystem which was later improved by another naval architect, Busley, in 1918. The result (fig. 16c), like the earlier design of Kopecky (1890: fig. 16d) and the more recent one of R. C. Anderson (1962; fig. 16e), incor-

7. I am much indebted to Mr J. S. P. Buckland for information on this sad tale. For the complete story see L. Th. Lehmann (1982).
8. Two brackets supporting the outrigger are identified in this reconstruction, which was followed in *GOS*, but the shorter 'bracket' now turns out to be the base of the deck stanchion resting on the upper wale.

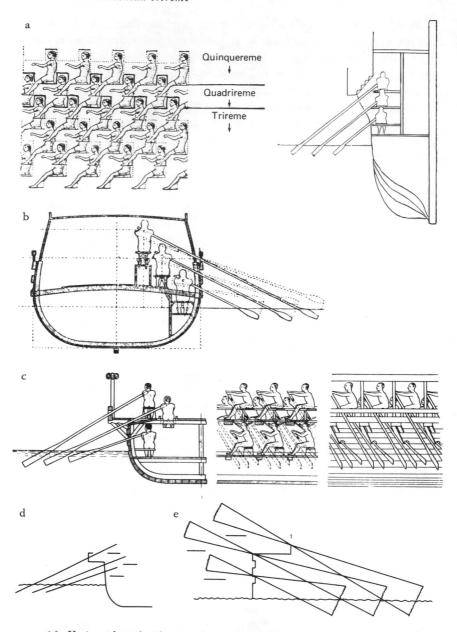

16. Various three-level oarsystems proposed for the trieres: (a) Graser (1864), (b) Lemaitre (1883), (c) Haack-Busley (1895, 1918), (d) Kopecky (1890), (e) Anderson (1962).

porates the outrigger and accounts very closely for the various details of the Lenormant relief, but like the earlier solutions fails in taking no account of Barras de la Penne's point. The oars in each unit of three oarsmen are consistently of different lengths.

In the mean time in Italy Admiral Fincati (1883) had reiterated the theory that the ancient trieres was pulled on the Venetian *alla sensile* system (fig. 10a), and Weber (1896) restated the theory that it was pulled on the *a scaloccio* system. The two theories, which had been put forward in the sixteenth century for reasons which are plainly inadequate and had been decisively rejected by Savile as inconsistent with the ancient evidence, were now given an undeserved new lease of life although the evidence now available made them even more untenable. In the first place a ship with 170 oarsmen (below, p. 111) arranged on the *alla sensile* system would necessarily have been much longer (48 m) than the 37 m allowed by the Zea ship-sheds (above, p. 4). In the second place, whereas the oars of *alla sensile* galleys were in the region of 12 m long (fig. 10a) to allow the gunwale to be a safe distance above the waterline, and were of three different lengths, the oars in a fourth-century trieres are shown by the naval inventories (below, p. 138) to have been about 4 m long. Again, the *a scaloccio* system is ruled out on many grounds, of which perhaps the most cogent is the passage in Thucydides (2.93.2: below, p. 136) in which each oarsman of a trieres is said to have 'carried his oar, his cushion and his oar-loop' from one side of the Isthmus to the other.

At this point W. W. Tarn (1905) entered the discussion. He severely criticised all the attempts that had hitherto been made to reconstruct a trieres of three levels of oars on the basis of the Lenormant relief, which in his view represented a ship with a single file of oars. Tarn's arguments were mainly concerned with the later types of oared warship. He had no difficulty in demonstrating the absurdity of regarding tetrereis, pentereis, etc. as ships of four, five and more levels of oars, and concluded like Lazar de Baif that the trieres could not have had three levels either.

Tarn's 'real' objection to the then current interpretation of the Lenormant relief, viz. that it represented a trieres with three levels of oars, was that such a ship would entail oars of different lengths. 'Such a ship', he claimed, 'is impossible: for if one thing be more certain than another, it is that oars of different lengths, where the difference bears more than a certain proportion to the length [i.e. the *alla sensile* oars excepted], cannot be rowed together, by one man to an oar, so as to be of any real use or turn out an efficient ship.' In this claim he was, of course, perfectly right. It was what Barras de la Penne had said many years before.

Following Tarn's arguments, Cook and Richardson published a reconstruction of the trieres (1905; fig. 17) with oars pulled on the *alla sensile* system – a ship which, as we have seen, could not have been accommodated in the Zea ship-sheds. Furthermore the oars were of three different lengths, 3.05 m, 3.65 m, and 4.11 m, which would hardly have satisfied Tarn's ruling and in any case were not in accordance with the lengths given in the naval inventories (above, p. 21 and below, p. 138). In Venice, of course, the oars of the *alla sensile* galleys were three times as long (fig. 10a), and thus allowed a reasonable height of gunwale above the waterline (freeboard); but Cook, using

17. The *alla sensile* oarsystem proposed for the trieres by A. B. Cook and Wigham Richardson (1905).

shorter oars, had to reduce the freeboard to a mere twelve inches. Such a ship, with a crew of 200, would be unseaworthy even by ancient standards. Notwithstanding these obvious objections and although the system employed was, in Savile's words, 'directly against both the authority of ancient writers . . . and contrary to the ancient portraytures remaining yet to be seene' it is still found attributed to the trieres in all standard works of reference in English. Liddell–Scott–Jones' *Greek–English Lexicon* (1939) is of two minds. The *alla sensile* system is attributed to the trieres, but one category of oarsmen, the thranites, are said to be highest, and another, the thalamians, are described as lowest.

It did however appear that the two practical objections to the three-level trieres might be met. The first objection, that if a trieres was a ship of three levels of oars, a *tetrērēs* (quadrireme) must have had four and a *pentērēs* (quinquereme) five and so on, was only valid if the name trieres *means* a ship with three levels of oars. She might, as seemed to be the case, *have* three levels of oars but be called after some other feature of which she had three. The name could alternatively derive from the fact that the ship had three files or columns of oarsmen ranging fore-and-aft on each side of the ship, in contrast to the Homeric pentecontor which had one, and the later two-level pentecontor which had two. Large numbers of files of oarsmen on each side of a ship might be clumsy; but they were not absurd, provided that there were not more than three levels, and this proviso could be met if the practice of putting more than one man to an oar had been adopted by the time these ships were built.

The second practical objection, that the oars of a three-level ship, being of different lengths at the different levels, would have been impossible to pull together in time, could also be met if the oars at the three levels could be arranged in such a way that in any one unit of three (one at the highest, one at the middle and one at the lowest level) the oars were all of the same length. This had manifestly not been the case in the published reconstructions of three-level triereis hitherto; and different lengths of oars at the three levels had been Tarn's 'real objection' to a three-level theory. It proved in fact possible to demonstrate in a working model (fig. 1), based on a projection of the Lenormant relief, that all three oars at different levels could be of the same length in any one unit. It was true that the fourth-century naval inventories recorded the spare oars of a trieres in two lengths (9 and 9½ cubits), but the difference is explained by Aristotle and Galen. Aristotle (*PA* 4.10, 687b18) says that in the human hand 'the end finger is short rightly and the middle finger long *as is the oar amidships*', and Galen (*UP* 1.24) specifically mentions the trieres in making the same point. The same thing is true of the oars in a naval whaler.

The removal of these two objections made it possible to look afresh at the evidence for a three-level trieres, and two vase-paintings (one a small fragment) were now available (pp. 148–51) to support the interpretation of the Lenormant relief as depicting such a ship. These arguments and conclusions appeared in articles in the *Mariner's Mirror* in 1941 and in the *Classical Quarterly* in 1947, and twenty-one years later *Greek Oared Ships* attempted to put together all the evidence available for ancient oared warships from the Bronze Age to the death of Alexander. A three-level trieres seems now to be generally accepted; and it is, at last, reasonable to undertake the further work leading to a satisfactory design. The imminence of an actual reconstruction serves to concentrate the mind wonderfully on evidence throwing light on the more important practical details.

In the next chapter we shall consider briefly how and why the trieres came to be developed, probably in the mid-seventh century BC, and how and why she came to be superseded as the standard warship of Mediterranean navies towards the end of the fourth century BC. Both processes throw light on the nature of the ship and of her employment.

2

*EVOLUTION AND SUPERSESSION OF
THE TRIERES*

Evolution

The trieres evolved to perform a specific role in warfare at sea. A brief review of the early history of oared warships in Greece will show what that specific role was, and give an idea of the nature and characteristics of the ship which was developed to perform it. When we turn to the account of the trieres' supersession during the course of the fourth century, the reasons for that supersession will illuminate that nature and those characteristics from a different angle as circumstances and change of tactical concept were forcing naval designers to abandon them.

The earliest use of the oared warship is described in the *Iliad*: the transport of men and their warlike gear to a scene of armed conflict on land. This seems to be the intended role of the long ships represented by the Naxos lead models of 2500 BC, the oared ships shown on the Syros 'frying pans' of a little later date,[1] the Late Minoan III ship of 1400–1200 BC, probably a one-level pentecontor (above, p. 8 n.3), on the Cretan larnax (fig. 18), and the Mycenaean ship on the pyxis from the Pylos Tragana tomb of 1400–1200 BC (fig. 19). Much more realistic examples of ships of the same type, with files of fifteen and twenty-five oarsmen on each side, are to be seen later on sixth-century Attic vases (e.g. figs. 20a and b).

The next stage in the evolution of the oared warship after the Mycenaean age is shown on the Aristonothos vase (fig. 21). Deriving as it does from the half-century at the end of which the trieres made its appearance, the painting is worth some attention. Two ships of markedly different types face one another, bow to bow, in conflict. The ship on the left can be recognised as a Greek oared warship of the type frequently shown on the Athenian Dipylon vases of the eighth century (figs. 22a and b) except that she has a deck, or at any

1. See Plate 1a and b in JSM (1980b).

18. Cretan larnax in the Heraklion Museum (LM III, *c.* 1400 BC).

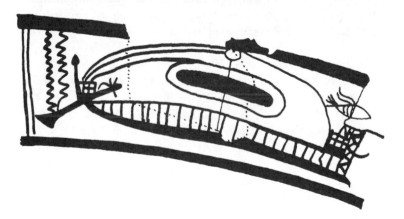

19. Scene from a Mycenaean pyxis from the Tragana tholos tomb, Messenia, 1200–1100 BC.

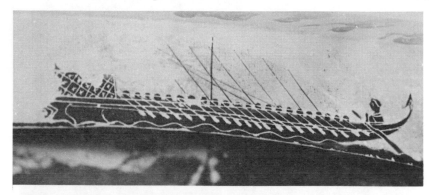

20a. Pentecontor from an Attic black-figure dinos, *c.* 520 BC.
20b. Triacontor from an Attic black-figure dinos by the Antimenes painter, *c.* 520 BC.

rate a raised fore-and-aft gangway, above the oarsmen.[2] Like the vessels of the Dipylon period in the Geometric style (see Glossary I(b)) she is asymmetrical: that is to say, while the stern curves sharply upwards the keel projects at the bow, making a forefoot or cutwater, a shape which is typically Greek, or, at least, Aegean. We do not know whether at this stage the forefoot was armoured and used as a ram. Earlier, when there is no evidence for fighting between ships at sea, the forefoot was present but was certainly not used for that purpose.[3] The second ship, on the right, probably Etruscan or

2. See *GOS* pp. 12–17.
3. Ships on vases of the Protometric and Geometric period have a forefoot, but are shown beached with fighting going on around them, never in confrontation at sea. See *GOS* plates 2d, 6a, b, d, and now F. H. van Doorninck Jr (1982), who nevertheless conjectures that they practised ramming.

21. Two oared warships of different types from a krater made by Aristonothos. Probably west Greek, 675–650 BC.

Carthaginian, has a bow-projection of a peculiar kind, a sort of beak applied rather high up to a hull which, without it, is of symmetrical shape. This downward-pointing beak seems designed to engage and hold the upper works of an enemy ship and, like the later Roman *corvus*, prevent disengagement while the boarding party did its work. However this may be, the painting depicts a fight at sea in which the armed men fighting from the ships are emphasised as the main offensive factor; the ram, if that is what it is, and the beak, are subsidiary. Nevertheless the Aristonothos vase ships, painted in the first half of the seventh century, show the direction which the development of the oared warship was taking. The trieres was soon to be developed, and forty years later occurred the 'first sea-fight' to which Thucydides refers (1.13.4). The characteristics which come to be associated with triereis in battle – power, speed and agility – are those demanded by ramming tactics, not by armed men fighting from ships. Ramming is therefore likely to have been a subsidiary tactic in the age which produced the Aristonothos vase, and the vase may well represent an action in which a ship equipped for ramming (i.e. with the forefoot bronze-sheathed) as well as for fighting from the deck is shown in conflict with a ship equipped for the latter only. If so it represents vividly an important stage in the development of the Mediterranean galley, and shows side-by-side the two modes of conflict which in turn dominated ancient naval warfare.

The first sea-fight to which there is more than a passing reference in the early historians is the battle described by Herodotus between a fleet of Phocaean pentecontors and a combined force of Etruscan and Carthaginian ships, in 535 BC, more than a century later than the

22a. Fragments of an Attic krater showing the forward part of an oared warship with hooked tholepins, 760–735 BC.

22b. Fragments of an Attic krater showing the greater part of an oared warship with hooked tholepins, 760–735 BC.

Aristonothos vase and the time of the trieres' emergence. In this battle the tactic of ramming was recorded for the first time. Herodotus (1.164.3) relates that the Phocaeans left their maritime city in Asia Minor (map 1) when it was threatened by the Persians in 540 BC, and embarked *en masse* in their pentecontors, taking with them their families and possessions. The pentecontors must have been capacious vessels with single files of 25 oarsmen a side, and a hold (*thalamos*) in which their possessions, at least, could have been stowed. This is the space 'under the thwarts' where in the *Odyssey* (13.20-2)[4] Alcinous, king of Phaeacia, put the bronze gifts which he sent with Odysseus on his homeward voyage, 'so that they should not get in the oarsmen's way'. The Phaeacian ship was a brand new pentecontor with a crew of 52: 25 oarsmen a side and 2 officers. For the Phocaeans' purpose the pentecontor, with plenty of stowage space, was suitable in a way that the trieres, as we shall see, was definitely not.

Sailing west to escape the Persian advance, the Phocaeans founded Alalia (map 1) in Corsica, but their presence was challenged by an alliance of two other, non-Greek, peoples, the Etruscans and Carthaginians. The Phocaeans with their 60 ships, presumably the pentecontors in which they had left Asia Minor, defeated the 120 ships of their enemies, but their casualties were heavy: 40 ships lost and the rest disabled 'with their rams twisted off' (1.166.2). The description implies that the rams were at an experimental stage, and the fact that the Phocaeans won in spite of a gross disparity in numbers further suggests that they were using the ram, albeit experimentally, and their enemies were not. This is the situation suggested by the encounter depicted on the Aristonothos vase, probably with the same ethnic components.

A further development in the oared warship is revealed by some evidence from as early as the eighth century BC. It may have contributed in due course to the perfection of the new tactic, although not originally evolved with that in mind. It seems that files or columns of 25 to 30 men a side in a long ship constituted the limit of

---

4. Cf. 9.98–9 where reluctant passengers are tied under the *zyga. Thalamos* is the normal Greek word for an inner chamber (e.g. bedroom or storeroom) and is used by the historian Timaeus (*FGrH* F 149) for the lower part of a trieres (unless *thalamious* is to be read for *thalamous*). The cognate *thalamē* has this meaning in later Greek (Lucian, *Nav.* 2).

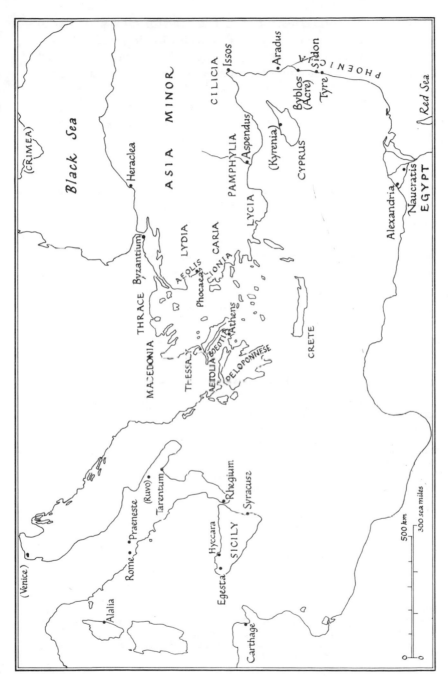

Map 1 The eastern Mediterranean.

practicability in wood construction. The need for ships which would transport more oarsmen to fight at their destination on land, or for ships with a higher ratio of oarsmen to length, was met by a remarkable and unique development which occurs from now on in Greek and Roman galleys, but nowhere else in the world until recently in Indonesia.[5] Oared ships began to be built in Greece and the Levant with two files of oarsmen a side, one file at a higher level than the other and the oarsmen in the upper file sitting in between (and, of course, above) the oarsmen at the lower level. In the eighth century both literature and vase-painting testify to this step, in both cases in relation to Boeotia. In Book II of the *Iliad* (509–10) it is recorded in the Catalogue of Ships that '120 young men went' in each of the Boeotian ships. The poet does not say that they all pulled an oar, but since Thucydides (1.10.4) goes out of his way to comment that they were at the same time both fighting men and oarsmen (*auteretai*) it seems likely that the poet had such a ship in mind and that Thucydides had reason to believe that it existed. If there were 60 men pulling oars on each side of a ship, they could only have been in two files, one at a higher level than the other. There is no suspicion of oars manned by more than one man before the fourth century.

5. Anderson (1962) p. 93 refers to biremes employed by Russia in 1795. These are likely to have used the *alla sensile* or, more probably, the *a scaloccio* oarsystems with two files of oarsmen at one level. C. Nooteboom (1949) gives photographs of Indonesian praus with oars pulled at two levels (see below, fig. 49). C.C. MacKnight (1980) refers to the prau which Pigafetta (ed. J. A. Robertson 1906 vol. 2 p. 101) saw in 1521 'with three rows of oars on each side (*avecq troys rengs d'avirons de chafcun coste*)', and claims that 'one of the best drawings of such a vessel comes from a view of the Dutch attack on Ceram in 1654' in F. C. Wieder (1925–37) vol. 5 pl. 119. But this drawing shows a vessel with catamaran-type outriggers on each side and two rows of paddlers sitting over the water on platforms between the gunwale and the immersed part of the outrigger. Pigafetta might conceivably have spoken very inaccurately of such a ship having (two) rows of oars on each side, but he is perhaps more probably describing either a galley rowed in the contemporary Mediterranean *alla sensile* fashion (the system having been imported into Indonesia by the Portuguese) or a locally developed three-level oared prau of which Nooteboom's two-level oared sailing prau may be a distant relation. More knowledge of the oar- and paddle-systems of Indonesian praus is much needed. MacKnight says that in the Indonesian archipelago long rather than round hulls were found when the transport of people and piracy were still significant functions. Conditions in Indonesia, both social and geographic, seem to have resembled fairly closely those of the early Aegean, and it would not therefore be surprising if long ships developed there in ways similar to those found in Greece. However, Indonesian long ships, with rising bow and stern, unlike the differently shaped Greek long ships, did not develop the ram, the feature which had such a marked influence on the evolution of the Greek warship.

Now a ship pulled by 60 men a side at two levels is what seems to be illustrated on an eighth-century Attic bowl found in Boeotian Thebes (fig. 23). Moreover, a two-level arrangement of oars is shown unmistakably on a relief from Sennacherib's palace depicting the evacuation of Tyre in 701 BC (fig. 24), and on sixth-century black-figure Attic vases (fig. 25). The development of the two-level oar-system can be recognised as, after the ram, a second effective and ingenious breakthrough in the evolution of the oared warship in Greece.

A development which doubled the number of men which could be accommodated in a ship of a given length opened two possibilities. Either the ship could remain at its maximum length and the number of men carried be doubled, or the number of men could remain the same and the length of the ship be halved. If the role of the oared warship was to carry as many fighting men as possible to the scene of combat, the former offered a clear advantage. If, on the other hand, the role of the ship was to manoeuvre so as to ram an opposing ship, the advantage of a doubled oarcrew is more doubtful. The increase in power probably would not compensate for the additional weight

23. Attic spouted bowl showing a warship with oars apparently at two levels, about 735–710 BC.

24. Relief from the palace of Sennacherib showing a two-level oared warship taking part in the evacuation of Tyre in 701 BC.

25. Attic black-figure amphora showing Dionysus in a warship with oars at two levels, about 510 BC.

of structure and men. To judge from the surviving pictures of two-level galleys from the sixth century, the new system seems to have been used to reduce the ship's length while keeping the same number of oarsmen (fig. 26). The fact that with the introduction of the two-level system no new names, e.g. *hekatontoros* (hundred-oared

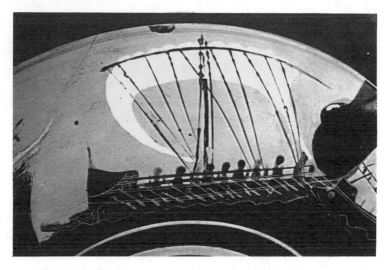

26. Detail of Attic black-figure cup showing one of two warships with oars at two levels, *c.* 510 BC.

ship), were invented but the names triacontor and pentecontor (thirty- and fifty-oared ship) continued to be used,[6] supports this impression. So it would seem that the objective of the naval architect was no longer the transport of the maximum number of men to the scene of action on land, but the power, speed and agility required by the new ramming tactics, and that the new system came to be employed in the way which would achieve this best, i.e. by keeping the manpower the same and decreasing the length. In speed and agility the two-level pentecontor would have been much superior to the one-level pentecontor, whose strength would be suspect unless the hull was much deeper than was needed merely to accommodate 25 oarsmen a side. The Phocaean pentecontors, as we saw, could carry a good deal more than the 50 oarsmen.

There is no doubt that the two-level system was used extensively, and it must be concluded that it did not entail different lengths of

6. The Greek word *diērēs*, meaning a ship with oars at two levels, does not occur until the second century AD in the grammarian Pollux. It is likely to have been manufactured as Greek for the Latin *biremis* which occurs in Horace and Livy (first century BC). The epithet *dikrotos* occurs in Euripides (*IT* 408) to describe a ship pulled by oars at two levels, and is employed by Xenophon (*HG* 2.1.28) to indicate that a trieres had only two files manned. Arrian (6.5.2) uses it of the two-level triacontors employed by Alexander on the Hydaspes in India.

oar. Experiment does in fact show that there is no difficulty at all in keeping the oars of each unit of two at different levels to the same length. The oarsmen and their tholepins in each unit can be regarded as placed on the circumference of concentric circles with the oar-blades at the centre. The upper oarsmen sit on the ship's thwarts (*zyga*) as the single file of oarsmen did in the Homeric pentecontor, pulling their oars either over the gunwale or through an upper row of oarports (fig. 27), while the lower oarsmen, sitting in what had been the hold (*thalamos*) of the ship, pulled their oars through a lower row of oarports. The oars throughout would have been of a length suitable to a man of average physique (below, p. 138).

Using the hold for an additional file of oarsmen did of course reduce the usefulness of the ship as a freight-carrier, and may be regarded as another step in the direction of a new concept of the warship as a specialised ramming weapon. The next step, the exact nature of which is not immediately apparent, was the invention of the trieres itself. The poet Hipponax, a native of Ephesus, who went into exile at Clazomenae in 542, a few years before the battle of Alalia, is the first writer to mention the trieres, and, in the same sentence, the ram (fr. 45 Diehl[3]). He urges the painter Mimnes 'not to go on painting a snake on the many-benched side of a trieres, so that it seems to be running away from the ram towards the helmsman'.[7]

Most of what is known about the trieres and its employment before the end of the fifth century derives from the Greek historians Herodotus and Thucydides. Both worked in the second half of the century. Herodotus was a native of Halicarnassus (mod. Bodrum) on the western seaboard of Asia Minor, a mixed Dorian-Greek and Carian city ruled at the time of the second Persian invasion of mainland

---

7. The crucial development to two levels was probably stimulated by the effectiveness of ramming as a means of incapacitating an opposing vessel and all those in her, compared with hand-to-hand fighting after boarding. If one ship could ram and hole another, it would by one swift stroke cause its victim to flood, lose stability, and be immobilised with its crew *hors de combat* – so much more efficiently and elegantly than could ever be possible by slogging it out with spear and sword. Furthermore, having disposed of one opponent, the ramming ship would immediately be free to manoeuvre towards attacking another. Thus ramming offered, at raised stakes, the opportunity of rapid victory in fleet actions to the most skilful and agile. In such actions large numbers of soldiers on board would encumber use of the ships' main weapon. It is probably no coincidence that the rise of the ram, a purely anti-ship weapon, and the agile two-level ship occurred at a time of expanding maritime trade and the accompanying need to exercise sea power in the eastern Mediterranean.

27. A scene showing the stern of the *Argo* engraved on a bronze casket in the Villa Giulia, Rome, end of the fourth century BC.

Greece by a Persian-backed monarch, a 'tyrant' in Greek parlance, the queen Artemisia. She commanded five triereis in Xerxes' invasion fleet, and Herodotus boasts that they had the highest reputation after the crack Sidonian squadron. He tells of her that Xerxes compared her with his other commanders at Salamis, saying 'My men have become women and my women men' (7.99.3, 8.88.3). Herodotus, then, grew up in an environment which was no stranger to the trieres and its skilled use in battle. Furthermore, in his extensive journeys in the eastern Mediterranean he is likely to have travelled in oared warships as well as in merchant ships. Thucydides, again, was no armchair historian. He was an Athenian who commanded a force of triereis in the Peloponnesian War, was exiled for his failure to prevent the capture of Amphipolis by Brasides in 424 BC, and thereafter devoted himself to writing a history of the war. As a man whose family had property in Thrace and who had also served as a naval commander, he fits very well the description which an anonymous writer at the beginning of the war ([Xen.] *Const. of*

Athenians 1.19) gives of Athenians and their retainers unconsciously acquiring the skill of pulling an oar by reason of overseas possessions and commands abroad: 'it is inevitable that a man who is often aboard ship should take an oar himself, and his retainers too, and learn the language of the sea'. So both historians, who are vital witnesses in our enquiry, speak of the trieres from personal experience; and although, as is usually the case with writers (other than epic poets) who deal with commonplace objects of their environment, what they say is not very explicit or detailed, their evidence on naval topics is to be treated with close attention.

Thucydides begins his history with an account of the growth of Greece and the emergence of sea power during the period of tranquillity and consolidation which followed the movement of peoples into and within Greece in the post-Mycenaean age. He notes (1.12.4–13.2) three features: increases in population, resulting in the main cities, in particular Athens and the cities of the Peloponnese, sending colonies overseas; increased wealth, which led to the displacement of aristocracies by popular 'tyrannies'; and most importantly increased power exercised at sea. 'The Corinthians are said first to have taken up ships in a way nearest to the modern, and triereis to have been built first at Corinth in Greece.'[8] The Egyptian pharaoh Necho (610–595 BC) is said by Herodotus (2.159.1) to have built triereis on the Nile for service in the Mediterranean, and in the Red Sea for service in the Indian ocean. This pharaoh, known as 'the philhellene',[9] had close ties with Greece, in particular with Corinth and Samos, and although he certainly employed Phoenicians in the exploration of Africa there is no good reason to prefer Phoenicia to Corinth as the originating source of Necho's fleets of triereis, even if there were, as is not improbable, triereis in service in the Phoenician cities at this time.[10] The most important point in Thucydides' state-

8. This statement has been taken by some (e.g. Lucien Basch (1969)) relying on the dubious testimony of Clement of Alexandria (*Strom.* 1.16.76) to mean, not that Corinth was the first city to build triereis, but that triereis were built first elsewhere, i.e. in Phoenicia. But see A. B. Lloyd (1972), (1975) and JSM (1979).
9. He was called 'the friend of the Greeks' in contrast to the normal attitude of Egyptian rulers to Greeks.
10. The question of the nature of the Phoenician triereis (see Basch 1969) is a difficult one, since until the second quarter of the fourth century BC there is a lack of representations of Phoenician ships that can be regarded as having three levels of oars, and at that date a three-level ship could as well be one of the ships of larger

a   b

28a. Octadrachm from Sidon, *c.* 380–374 BC.
28b. Stater from Arados, *c.* 350–332 BC.

ment is, however, that he clearly sees the trieres as introducing a new and modern kind of naval warfare. He continues: 'It appears that Ameinocles, the Corinthian shipwright, built four ships [i.e., in the context, triereis] for the Samians, and it is about three hundred years to the end of this war [i.e. the war between the Peloponnesians and the Athenians] when Ameinocles came to the Samians.' It seems likely[11] that owing to a faulty generation count this period is 50 years

denomination, e.g. a 'five' or a 'six', as a trieres. The impressions of cylinder seals on clay *bullae* depicting oared galleys and found in the treasury of the palace at Persepolis were made before the palace was burned in 330, but no more precise dating is possible. The coin series from the Phoenician cities of Arados, Byblos and Sidon show galleys after 450 (see figs. 28a and b), but only in the second quarter of the fourth century do they appear to be three-level ships, and at that date not necessarily triereis. Basch's reconstruction of the Phoenician trieres, without an outrigger and with the thranite oar nearly twice as long as the thalamian, would make practical men from Barras de la Penne to W. W. Tarn turn in their graves, and his 'five' with gangs of five men sitting and pulling one very long oar is most improbable as the type which became the standard warship in which the first Punic war was fought. There are no literary descriptions of Phoenician ships apart from the account in Herodotus (8.118.1–4: see pp. 131–2) of Xerxes' escape from shipwreck after Salamis, and the descriptions in the Greek historians of that battle, where the Persian ships included a Phoenician squadron. In both cases the capacity to carry large numbers of men on deck is indicated, but otherwise there is no suggestion of any difference from the ships of the Greek allies.

11. See Forrest (1969), A. B. Lloyd (1972), J. B. Salmon (1984) p. 218.

too long and that the date indicated is *c.* 650 rather than *c.* 704, and that 650 can be taken as the rough date of the invention of the trieres at Corinth. Thucydides proceeds to note that 'the earliest sea-fight too was fought by the Corinthians against their colony Corcyra (mod. Kerkyra, Corfu) 260 years before the end of the war'. This date, for the same reason, can now be taken to be *c.* 610. There seems to be a connection in Thucydides' mind between the first sea-fight and the invention of the trieres, not merely that Corinth was involved in both but that the latter led to the former, the trieres being the ship which symbolised the modern mode of fighting at sea.

The Bacchiad aristocracy at Corinth was succeeded by the popular 'tyranny' of Cypselus and his son Periander. The Bacchiadae appear to have taken refuge at Corcyra, although eventually members of the Cypselid dynasty ruled in Corcyra and in the other Corinthian colonies of the region. Since we can now place the invention of the trieres at the outset of the tyranny, when Corinth and Corcyra were enemies, it seems reasonable to see the invention as the outcome of naval rivalry between Corinth and her colony, and the first sea-battle as an engagement in which triereis were used by Cypselus or Periander in a fleet action which resulted in the establishment of Cypselid power in Corcyra.[12] It is likely that, forty years after their invention, Corcyra also employed triereis, and that what Thucydides has in mind when he speaks of the first sea-battle is the first engagement between fleets of triereis. The *réclame* of such an action would explain the adoption of the trieres, as the newest example of naval technology, by Necho in Egypt shortly afterwards.

The slow spread of the use of the trieres in the eastern Mediterranean can be linked to the slow growth of prosperity in the Archaic period (650–500 BC). The trieres was an expensive weapon which only the wealthiest states could afford. Thucydides makes just this point. Hipponax probably knew about it in the rich city of Ephesus. What Herodotus says (3.39–44) about Polycrates, who became tyrant of Samos in the latter years of the sixth century,[13] is illuminating. He

12. See Salmon (1984) pp. 221–2.
13. For the date of Polycrates see J. P. Barron (1964). If as Barron suggests and seems likely there was an earlier, very prosperous, Polycrates (572–40), who was responsible for the great public works, he would certainly have had a fleet of triereis, which would have ceased to exist when he collapsed under Persian pressure. The Polycrates II of whom Herodotus speaks would then have had to rebuild sea power from small beginnings.

initially had a fleet of 100 pentecontors[14] but later when he became more prosperous he went over to triereis and could send 40 of them, manned by his disaffected subjects, to support Cambyses' invasion of Egypt in 525. The trieres in Cambyses' fleet, which Herodotus mentions (3.13.1–2, 14.4–5), had a crew of 200.[15] Such a ship with three times as many crew as a pentecontor (with 50 oarsmen and 10–20 additional crew men and soldiers) would have been expensive to keep in commission, apart from the capital cost.

In 500 BC, in an attempt to extend their power across the Aegean, the Persians supplied the tyrant of Miletus with 200 triereis with which to subdue Naxos and the islands of the Cyclades. In his account of the campaign Herodotus tells the story (5.33.2) of the punishment of a trierarch named Scylax who failed to post a look-out on his trieres when beached. He was tied up with his head 'through the thalamian oarport'. It would seem that the thalamian oarport is specified, as distinct from the oarport in the higher part of the trieres, because there were at least two kinds of oarport in the ship and the thalamian sort, as being bigger, was suitable for this purpose[16] (below, p. 149).

A recent writer[17] has made the illuminating suggestion that the supply of 200 triereis to Miletus is an indication of Persian naval policy. The great increase in the naval potential of the Phoenician and Ionian states at this time is surprising, and seems unlikely to have come about if they had to rely on their own financial resources; but if Persia planned to create her own sea power with which to dominate the Aegean she may well have aimed to do it, as Rome did later in her naval war with Carthage, by financing construction of the ships wherever timber was available and paying her maritime allies to man them. There was always the danger of defection, as the Ionian revolt was soon to show, but it is to be noted that in the second Persian invasion of Greece, for which she mustered all her naval allies, she took the precaution of placing 30 of her own soldiers on board each of her allies' triereis.

14. J. A. Davison (1947) uses this account to date the introduction of the trieres in Greece, but see JSM (1979).
15. 2,000 men were punished, ten for each of the 200 men in the Mytilenian ship who had been murdered.
16. The thalamian oarport of a trieres is also mentioned in Aristophanes *Peace* 1232. The word in *Acharnians* 553 may refer either to the oarport or to the oar of the thalamian oarsman. See *GOS* p. 308 and note 2.
17. H. T. Wallinga (1984b).

In 499 BC when the Ionian cities and offshore islands revolted against Persia they had at their disposal large fleets of triereis, probably supplied by Persia, and among their early successes was the defeat off Cyprus of the Phoenician fleet, which remained loyal to Persia. But by 494 a new Phoenician fleet came north to participate in the siege of Miletus; it was joined by ships from Cilicia, Egypt and Cyprus. The Ionians mustered 353 ships to meet it, Chios sending 100 ships, Miletus 80, Lesbos 70 and Samos 60, with 43 from the lesser Greek cities of the Asiatic mainland. Herodotus (6.8.2) says that all these ships were triereis, and there is no good reason to doubt his word. It is interesting that Herodotus (5.99.1), speaking of the help which came to the Ionians from mainland Greece, says that 'the Athenians sent twenty ships bringing five triereis from Eretria with them'. The words suggest that the Athenian ships were not triereis. Athens, it appears, was still too poor, or was too much of a landed aristocracy to be willing, to aspire to sea-power.[18]

The overall command of the Ionian triereis was given to a certain Dionysius, who commanded the few ships sent by the expatriate Phocaeans. Herodotus (6.11.2–15.2) relates that he told his fellow seamen that if they were prepared to accept hardships now they would have work for the time being but would succeed in overcoming the enemy and winning freedom. 'But if you go on with your usual slackness and lack of discipline I shall not be at all surprised if you pay the king [of Persia] the penalty of rebellion.' There could be no clearer statement than this of the qualities which service in triereis demanded – hard work and good discipline. Herodotus goes on to describe the training sessions Dionysius gave the men:

He regularly took the ships to sea in line-ahead formation, so that he trained the oarsmen in making a breakthrough (*diekplous*) with the ships through each other's lines, and he turned out the soldiers on deck (*epibatai*) in full kit. Then for the rest of the day he kept the ships at their moorings, and gave the Ionians work to do all day.

After a week of this sort of thing the Ionians had had enough. When it came to the battle with the Phoenician fleet at Lade off Miletus,

---

18. Corinth is conspicuous by her absence. She had the ships, since a little later Athens borrowed 20 triereis from her for her war against Aegina, her own 50 ships not being up to fighting the Aeginetan fleet, which in the event was 70 ships strong. Thuc. 1.41.2, Hdt. 6.89, 92.1.

the Samian contingent of 60 ships began the action by advancing in line ahead (against the Phoenician ships in line abreast, with the intention of making the planned breakthrough), but with 11 exceptions all broke off the engagement, raising their sails and making for Samos,[19] followed by the Lesbian ships and most of the others. Only the 100 Chian ships, each with 40 picked citizen soldiers on deck (*epibatai*), stayed to fight, using the tactic of the breakthrough. They captured many enemy ships but lost most of their own, being very greatly outnumbered.

From this account of the training of the Ionian fleet and its ultimate defeat, a little can be learnt about the tactics of fighting the trieres at this time. In the first place sails were not used in battle, only oars. This is true of fighting at sea throughout antiquity. At a later period there is reference to sails actually being left behind when ships put out for battle. Here the ships that raise sail are breaking off the engagement, and the sails they raise may be the small rather than the main sails (below, p. 97). The breakthrough or *diekplous* is the fleet manoeuvre, by squadrons in line ahead, of pulling through the enemy's ships drawn up in the usual defensive fashion in line abreast (below, p. 53). A modern historian[20] speaking of the sixteenth-century Mediterranean galley emphasises its 'terrible vulnerability to attack from the side' which 'made the maintenance of a line abreast formation a matter of life or death'. The offensive tactic of the faster and more agile ships, at Lade as later in the century, was to break through the defensive line, approaching it in line-ahead formation and either outflanking it (the *periplous*) or punching a hole through which a line of ships could pass (the *diekplous*). This tactic depends primarily on the concept of the trieres as a ramming weapon. Some have seen the *diekplous* as a manoeuvre by individual ships, each trying to pass between two of the enemy ships drawn up in line abreast opposite. Such a manoeuvre by single ships is self-evidently suicidal, but ships in line ahead had a better chance of getting through, with some losses.

In the battle at Lade the various squadrons advancing on the enemy in line ahead used the manoeuvre which Dionysius had tried

19. The reason for this defection may have been political and connected with the absence of their allies the Corinthians.
20. Guilmartin (1974) p. 202.

to practise beforehand. The Samians broke off and sailed home, but the Chians employed the manoeuvre successfully. Nevertheless, the 40 picked soldiers which the Chians carried on deck show that the Chians were not totally committed to the ramming tactic, but regarded what Thucydides was to call 'the old-fashioned way of fighting at sea' (below, p. 64) as equally important. The two are not really compatible, since 40 fully armed men on deck would themselves have diminished the ship's speed and agility, and for reasons of stability required a more heavily built hull and a deck bulwark as well. To judge from practice in the second Persian invasion fleet in 480 the Persian fleet at Lade would also have carried 40 soldiers on deck.

By the standards of most later naval warfare in Greek waters, the battle off Miletus involved a large number of ships. The Ionian Greeks had 353 triereis. Herodotus says that the Persian fleet consisted of 600 ships, some of which may not have been triereis, since the Persian commanders when they learnt the size of the opposing fleet were afraid that they might not succeed in defeating them. Nevertheless, when a few years later Darius dispatched the first invasion fleet to mainland Greece it was composed of 600 triereis accompanied by cavalry transports.[21]

The naval resources of the Persian empire before the revolt of the Greek cities of Ionia were considerable, since Persia controlled besides the Ionian fleets the navies of Egypt, Phoenicia, Cilicia and Cyprus. After the suppression of the revolt, when not only the Asiatic Greeks but the islands also came into Persian hands, Persia's power at sea became even more formidable. Thucydides, in his account of the growth of navies in Greece, mentions only briefly the large eastern area of sea power (1.16): 'Darius, strong in the possession of the Phoenician fleet, enslaved the islands also.' First under Darius and then under his son Xerxes, these resources were now

---

21. G. L. Cawkwell (1968) pp. 1–5, thinks that this is a 'paper figure'. He puts weight on Herodotus' statement that at Salamis the two sides were about equal. This is roughly true in the sense that the allied ships only engaged two of the Persians' four squadrons (2 squadrons with 250 ships each at full strength). He also presses the point that 'after 479 we never hear of a Persian navy anywhere near as large as 600 ships, and all through the fourth century the largest number we hear of is 300'. But after 479 Persia lost the large Greek naval contingents from the coastal cities of Asia Minor and from the islands, and probably the non-Greek contingents from that area as well. In the fourth century the large Egyptian naval force was also denied her.

mobilised for the invasion of mainland Greece, as the natural follow-up to the invasion of the islands of the Aegean.

By the beginning of the fifth century the trieres was plainly recognised as the principal means of asserting political power in a region, the eastern Mediterranean, where the sea offered the natural method of communication between cities and nations. A warship at sea could either be a platform from which armed men engaged the armed men on a similarly constructed ship through missiles or hand-to-hand fighting; or she could be herself an offensive weapon by means of an armoured ram. These two concepts of the fighting ship were opposed and certainly made opposite demands on the naval architect, but for a time, possibly always, existed together. What may be termed the guided-missile concept required the designer to maximise speed and agility to the limit, while the fighting-platform concept required no more than that the ship should be brought under oar into firm and stable contact with the enemy ship. For the former purpose the armed men on deck would be the minimum necessary to repel boarders if withdrawal after ramming became accidentally impossible. For the latter purpose the largest possible number of men was desirable. Large deck manning implied a more solid upper structure, as well as a hull built for greater stability, than a small deck party would require, with the overall result of a slower and less manoeuvrable ship.

We shall be following the development of these concepts in some selected accounts of naval warfare in the fifth century, and shall attempt to gauge their implications for the fifth- and fourth-century Athenian trieres which we intend to reconstruct. We should not forget that the trieres also necessarily had to move out from her home port to the expected scene of conflict either under oar or under sail. This secondary function, as a warship moving from place to place, sometimes carrying extra fighting men for an action on land, also has implications for design which must be considered and given due weight.

Supersession

The desperate, but from time to time quite successful, efforts of Athens in the fourth century to maintain her power in the Aegean and the protection of her grain supply by the deployment of fleets of triereis will be touched upon in chapter 6. There was another area of naval activity in the fourth century – this was Sicily, where Dionysius of Syracuse was at pains to contain the growing maritime pressure of the great Phoenician colony in North Africa, Carthage. Carthaginian, like Athenian (and later Roman),interest in Sicily was prompted by the need for Sicilian grain to feed a large urban population. Carthage was a sea power, and Dionysius, with enthusiasm backed by ample resources, entered into naval competition with her, which resulted in the evolution of new types of oared warship, the 'four', *tetrērēs* in Greek, the 'five', *pentērēs* in Greek, and the 'six', which has no Latin and hence no English name, the Romans merely transliterating the Greek word *hexērēs*.

It appears that Aristotle attributed the invention of the 'four' to the Carthaginians (Pliny, *NH* 7.207 = Rose fr. 600). Diodorus credits Dionysius with the invention of the 'five',[22] and Aelian says that Dionysius' son, Dionysius II, invented the 'six' (*Poik. Hist.* 6.12). Although there was naval rivalry, there seem not to have been any large-scale naval engagements between Syracusan and Carthaginian fleets. 'Fours' and 'fives' seem accordingly not to have been built in large numbers. Dionysius went in a 'five' to a neighbouring city with a proposal of marriage, no doubt to impress his prospective in-laws, but the ships which he sent on three occasions to assist his allies the Peloponnesians were all triereis.

'Fives' turn up at Sidon in Phoenicia in 351. When Alexander, after defeating Darius on land at Issos (333), moved south to strike at the Phoenician cities, the main source of Persian sea power, which still dominated the eastern Mediterranean, the Cypriot kings who came over to his side had 'fives' as flagships; and there were 'fours' and 'fives' in the fleet of Tyre which he besieged.[23]

The fleet which Alexander built on the Indus and its tributaries consisted of small river boats, but when he returned from India to Babylon he found waiting for him two 'fives', three 'fours' and twelve triereis, which had been transported across the desert in pieces from Phoenicia (Arrian 7.19.3). It is difficult to guess what the role of the fleet was envisaged to be. There is a story that Alexander had plans, which his death brought to nothing, of building a vast fleet of 'ships

22. 14.41.3, 42.2, 44.7.
23. Diod. 16.44.6; Arrian 2.21.9, 22.2.

larger than triereis' with which to wage a naval war against Carthage.[24]

The news of Alexander's death in 323 aroused Athens to a burst of naval and military activity. The Assembly is said to have ordered the building and fitting out of 40 triereis and 200 'fours' (Diod. 18.10.2)[25] but it is unlikely that the programme was begun, certain that it was not completed. 'Fours' and 'fives' appear in the Athenian naval lists which survive for some of these years. There are 18 'fours' in addition to 392 triereis in 330–329, 7 'fives' and 50 'fours' in 325–324.[26] The bigger ships were becoming increasingly popular and Athens' ambitious plan to build 200 'fours' in 323 fits this pattern of development. But the final defeat of Athens' fleet at Amorgus in 322 put an end for good to her naval ambitions.

The fleets with which Alexander's successors fought for supremacy in the eastern Mediterranean were dominated by the larger vessels. For example, the first of these, the fleet of about 240 ships which Antigonus assembled in 315, was made up of 90 'fours', 10 'fives', 3 'nines', 10 'tens', and 30 open, i.e. unprotected, warships. The balance of about 97 ships was, by inference, made up of protected triereis (Diod. 19.62.8).

The trieres continued to be used as a warship, but the tactics and dispositions of fleets were now based on the larger ships. The reason for the supersession of the trieres as the ship of the line, and for the evolution first of the 'four', 'five' and 'six', and then after an interval of the ships of larger denominations, can only be the subject of guesswork until we know rather more precisely the answers to the sort of questions about them that we are now asking about the trieres. But it is possible to discern some pointers to the kind of answers which it may be possible to give. For example, the history and literature of the fourth century make it clear that it was becoming more and more difficult to recruit the skilled oarsmen on which the trieres relied. Further, it seems clear that the oarsystems of the ships of the higher denominations can only be explained satisfactorily on the assumption that more than one man sat to an oar, an

24. Diod. 18.4.4, cf. Arrian 7.1.2, Curtius 10.1.17–18.
25. The reading of Diodorus' manuscript, '200 tetrereis and forty triereis' has been arbitrarily amended to '200 triereis and forty tetrereis' and this is how the text is now read.
26. *IG* 2² 1627.24, 1629.801–11.

arrangement which was economical of skilled oarsmen since in each oar-gang only one skilled man was needed, as a modern historian remarked about a similar change in Renaissance galleys from single-manned to multiple-manned oars.[27] These constraints certainly contributed to, but are unlikely to have been the sole cause of, the change in tactical concepts which accompanied the supersession of the trieres. These new concepts seem to have arisen from the development of missiles thrown by ship-borne catapults and from an increase in the number of the military contingent, men in full armour, archers and javelin men, on board warships, and the importance placed on them. These developments called for larger ships which would be more stable and could carry protection for oarsmen and soldiers, and these larger ships were heavier and slower and lent themselves to none of the tactics on which the trieres had relied. The Macedonians and Romans, in whose interests these new fleets were operated, were content to see naval actions as opportunities for men in full armour to fight it out on deck. This was their forte and they saw to it that ships would be built to bring such fighting about. The new ships and the new tactics present the exact opposite of what the trieres was and what it had been built to do.

27. Guilmartin (1974) p. 101; 'Henceforth only one skilled oarsman, the man furthest inboard who feathered the oar and set the pace, was needed to each bench.'

3

THE SALAMIS CAMPAIGN

In tracing the evolution of the trieres and its subsequent supersession we have isolated certain characteristics and qualities which
the trieres possessed. We shall now turn to the ancient accounts of
actions in which triereis took part. These will reveal how these ships
were used in battle in the fifth century, and give some idea of the sort
of ships they were. Two actions, which took place in the course of
the second Persian invasion of mainland Greece, in 480, will be the
subject of the present chapter.

Artemisium

The Persian invasion force consisted of a large land army, which
crossed the Hellespont on a bridge of boats and made its way west
and then southwards, accompanied by a fleet of considerable size.
Herodotus (7 89 1–99 3) gives the number of triereis as 1,207, and
says that there were as well 3,000 smaller ships, triacontors,
pentecontors, oared supply ships (*kerkouroi*) and horse-transports.
He gives the following numbers for the various contingents of
triereis: Phoenicia, including Palestine Syria, 300; Egypt 200;
Cyprus 150; Cilicia 100; Pamphylia 30; Lycia 50; Dorian-Greek
cities 30; Caria 70; Ionian-Greek cities 100; 'the islands' 17; Aeolia
60; the Hellespont, excluding Abydus, which had the duty of guard-
ing the bridge, 100. The crews of nearly half of these could be described as Greek by origin or influence. The ships of the Phoenicians,
he says, were the fastest and of these the fastest were the Sidonian
ships. In a later passage (7.184.1–2) Herodotus puts the native crews
of all these ships at 200 men, which is likely to include, as the Athenian
crews of 200 did (below, p. 104), ten soldiers and four archers; and he
says that an additional 30 Persians, Medes and Sacae (the last of
whom were archers) went on the deck of each ship (i.e. were *epibatai*,
below, p. 132). The military complement of each ship would then

have numbered 44 and the additional troops would have made the Persian ships about 4 tonnes, or 8% heavier than those of the Athenians, at any rate, among the Greek allies. He describes (7.184.3) the 3,000 small oared ships, previously described as triacontors, pentecontors and *kerkouroi*, here loosely as pentecontors, and gives their crews as 80 each 'more or less' (i.e. 50 oarsmen and 30 petty officers, deck hands, and soldiers).

Keeping in close touch with the army on land, the invasion fleet moved through the newly built canal across the isthmus in the eastern prong of the Chalcidic trident, and then, after rounding the two western prongs, went north again to Therma (mod. Saloniki). From there the fleet, joined, Herodotus says (7.185.1), by a further 120 ships from Greek cities in the north Aegean, moved south in a long voyage down the harbourless coast of Magnesia (7.188ff.). On this stretch they met a great summer storm, and after huge losses, put by Herodotus at 400 ships, reached the harbour of Aphetae (mod. Platania Bay) opposite Artemisium on the northern tip of the long island of Euboea, where the ships of the Greek allies now lay (map 2).

The Greek land force sent to hold up the invading army at Tempe in Thessaly had been withdrawn before the Persians left the Hellespont; and the first skirmishes between Greeks and Persians took place on land when Leonidas and his Spartans unsuccessfully tried to hold up the Persians' advance at Thermopylae, and at sea when the Greeks engaged the Persian fleet now beached at Aphetae, and reduced by storm losses. These latter engagements, which were indecisive, have great interest as illustrating the tactical ideas and presuppositions of both sides.

The original Athenian force, probably dispatched to Artemisium the previous autumn (below, p.108), had numbered 100 ships, but by now this force had been increased to 127, some of the ships being manned partly by Plataeans. The Athenians had also provided 20 ships for Chalcis in Euboea, Athenian manpower not being sufficient to crew the 200 ships now built (below, p. 115). The rest of the allies sent 124 triereis and 9 pentecontors, the largest contingent, of 40 ships, coming from Corinth (8.1.1–2).[1] Although

1. Corinth had emerged as a sea power under Periander, who built a seaport at Lechaeum on the gulf of Corinth. Cenchreae was her port on the Saronic Gulf. He also constructed the haulway (*diolkos*) which enabled him to transfer his naval forces quickly from one side of the Isthmus to the other. See R. M. Cook (1979) p. 152 and note 11, also J. B. Salmon (1984) pp. 136–7 and notes 11 and 12.

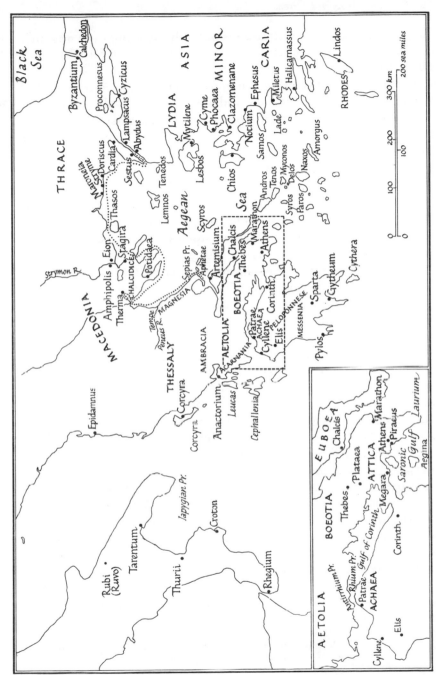

Map 2 The Aegean Sea.

Sparta contributed only 10 triereis her military reputation was such that the supreme command was given to her admiral (*nauarchos*) Eurybiades.

It is clear that between 499 when Athens had no triereis to send to the help of the Ionians at Lade and 480 when she had 200, more in fact than she was able to man at one time, Athens had made a serious attempt to become a maritime power. Herodotus (7.143–4) says that Themistocles persuaded the Athenians to spend a windfall from the silver mines at Laurium on building 200 triereis nominally for prosecuting her war with Aegina, her naval rival across the Saronic gulf, but probably also with the possibility of a second Persian invasion in mind. This information emphasises the great capital cost of a fleet of triereis. Herodotus speaks of Themistocles, after the engagements at Artemisium, taking 'the fastest of the ships' on a special mission (below, p. 95), and the Athenian ships are said later (8.42.2) to have been the fastest in the allied fleet. There seems to have been a tradition which Plutarch knew (*Cimon* 12.2) that the Athenian ships at Salamis were built by Themistocles 'for speed and agility in turning'. These qualities were, then, not just the result of the ships having been newly built but the outcome of deliberate design.

When the Greek allies saw the unexpected size of the Persian naval force at Aphetae, they were inclined, Herodotus says (8.4), to withdraw south by the inner channel. The Euboeans implored Eurybiades to stay till they could evacuate their households, but were unable to persuade him. By offering a large bribe, he alleges, they persuaded Themistocles, and he in turn persuaded Eurybiades and the Corinthians. Although greatly superior in numbers the Persian fleet did not at once come out to fight, but sent a force of 200 triereis southwards on a route east of Euboea to cut the allies' line of retreat through the inner channel. Their intention was to offer battle as soon as they heard that it was cut. The Greeks, however (8.9),[2] 'wishing to make trial of the Persian fleet's capability in fighting and in the 'breakthrough' (*diekplous*) came out late in that first day so that the action should not last long. They knew that in a protracted battle numbers would eventually tell. In response the Persian crews, or at

2. This action was, as Herodotus says, an exploratory skirmish, and it is unlikely that either the whole allied fleet put to sea or that the whole Persian fleet went out to meet them. The *kuklos* manoeuvre implies a small squadron rather than a whole fleet.

any rate some of them, embarked expecting an easy victory, 'seeing that the ships of the Greeks were few, while their own were many times more numerous, and faster', and encircled the Greek ships. This was the fleet manoeuvre known as the *periplous*, and was carried out by ships in line ahead (below, p. 81). At the first signal given the Greeks changed formation from line abreast, in which they could have been outflanked in the open water, and adopting the defensive tactic of slower ships, they

placed their ships with the bows facing outwards towards the Persian ships (now pulling round them) with their sterns aligned towards a central point. At the second signal they went over to the attack, although confined in a small space and with the enemy uncomfortably close. They captured [i.e. towed away after ramming[3]] thirty ships . . . and night came on the two sides as they fought an unequal battle.

The tactical aspects of this interesting and carefully planned exercise are reasonably clear. The Persian fleet, since the sending of the task force now about 600–700 strong, was still more than twice as numerous as the Greeks' 271 triereis (8.1.1–2). In spite of the reputation of the Athenian ships for speed, the Persian ships were also, apparently, in general faster (8.10.1). As such they accordingly took the initiative and a squadron attempted to get round the flank of the Greeks who would be drawn up in the normal line-abreast formation adopted by ships at the outset of an action after putting to sea in line ahead. The Greek squadron had a tactical reply to this move. They made a circle with bows outwards and sterns inwards. This formation was defensive in the sense that it prevented the faster enemy ships from getting behind their slower ships and attacking them in the beam or quarter where they were 'terribly vulnerable'.[4] but it also presented the enemy ships abeam to the Greek rams, so that if they went over to the offensive they would have the enemy ships open to attack. At the second signal, then, the circle exploded in all directions with considerable success, and the fall of night, as planned, prevented the Persians from securing ultimately the advantage which their greater numbers would have given them. The action

3. The disparity in numbers of fighting men on deck would be irrelevant to the issue in such circumstances.
4. See Guilmartin (1974) p. 202 quoted above.

shows not only a formidable grasp by the Greek commanders of the relevant tactical factors in the use of the trieres as a ramming weapon, but also, on the part of the crews, great skill and discipline in manoeuvre, and in both commanders and crew the nerve necessary to carry out a difficult movement with precision. Intelligent command was matched by the result of diligent and hard training.

The following night a second summer storm with thunder and heavy rain drove the task force of 200 ships on to the rocks of the eastern coast of Euboea and totally destroyed them. Next morning news of the destruction reached the allied fleet, and shortly afterwards further Athenian reinforcements of 53 ships arrived, the last of the 200 built with the money from Laurium. The allied fleet at Artemisium now numbered 324 triereis and 9 pentecontors, facing a Persian fleet reduced by the casualties of the previous day. A Greek squadron again came out late in the day against a Cilician squadron, and had some success (8.12–14).[5]

Next day the Persian fleet put to sea, adopting a sickle-shaped formation. At first the Greeks made no move, but as the enemy approached the beach at Artemisium they came out in full force, and took the initiative in attack. The Persian ships apparently fell into some confusion, but did not break their line, and the two fleets separated after some bitter fighting and heavy casualties on both sides. The general tactical picture shows a larger fleet in sickle-shaped formation, i.e. in line abreast but with the two wings threatening to envelop and move round the flanks of a smaller fleet. The rules required the Greek ships to adopt a line-abreast formation from the beach, and, as the slower ships, stay in it. Since to abide by the rules would have been fatal, and the ships, had they not put out, risked being destroyed or towed away by the enemy, the Greeks decided, in spite of being the slower fleet, to attack the enemy line, probably by squadrons in line ahead. The issue of the battle seems to have been indecisive, which is perhaps the best the Greeks could have hoped for under the circumstances (8.15–16). That evening the Greeks heard that the force heroically defending the pass at Thermopylae had been overrun, and took the decision to withdraw southwards, abandoning Euboea and Attica to the enemy.

5. Again the attack on the Cilician ships is clearly not made in full force.

Salamis

The last stage of the naval campaign was now reached. The Athenians, after some argument, succeeded in persuading their allies to regroup their ships on the landward beaches of the island of Salamis, instead of pulling them further back south of the wall which the Peloponnesians were building across the Isthmus. The fleet accordingly moved there from Artemisium and was reinforced by further ships which had assembled in the harbour of Troizen (mod. Poros) across the Saronic gulf southwards from Piraeus. In spite of losses the number of allied ships had now been made up to 378[6] (8.48), and Eurybiades remained in command.

The Greek fleet lay on an eastward-facing landward beach of the island of Salamis in what is now Paloukia bay[7] (map 3). The Persian land and sea forces had occupied Attica, the ships drawn up on the beaches in the various harbours. The Spartan commander was still in favour of completing the withdrawal to the Isthmus where the army had taken up position.

Before we turn to the battle itself a brief look at the number of ships involved on each side is necessary. Aeschylus puts the number of Greek ships at 300, 10 of which were especially fast, and the number of the Persian ships at 1,000, of which 207 were fast. It is just possible that he means that the fast ships were in addition to, rather than included in, the main totals, but scholars do not interpret the Greek text in that way.[8] The Persian total on this (unlikely) interpretation would be 1,207, which is the figure Herodotus gives for the Persian fleet at the review at Doriscus, and, with the reinforcement of 120 Greek ships, on their arrival at Sepias in Magnesia before the onset of the storms. He says that by the time of their arrival in Attica

---

6. See N. G. L. Hammond (1956) pp. 38ff., also *GOS* pp. 139–43, 150–3.
7. The main sources of information about the battle are: (1) the Athenian tragic poet Aeschylus, who wrote a play, the *Persians*, put on at Athens eight years after the battle, in which he probably fought himself and in which certainly a good part of his audience had fought; and (2) the historian Herodotus, who was a boy at the time of the battle and must have heard about it from participants on the Persian side, since he was a native of Halicarnassus (mod. Bodrum). He grew up to be a not uncritical admirer of Athens. (3) and (4): two later writers, Diodorus of the first century BC and Plutarch, who wrote at least a century and a half later than Diodorus, also provide some information which has value as representing a tradition independent of (1) and (2).
8. See Broadhead's commentary on *Persians* 342–3.

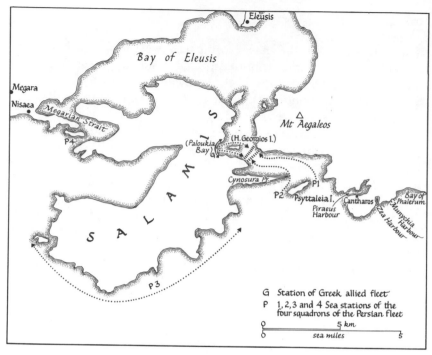

Map 3 The battle of Salamis.

reinforcements had made up the storm losses, which he puts at the incredible figure of 600. It seems likely that the initial failure to include the 207 fast ships in the total of 1,000 led to an exaggeration by that amount of the storm losses, and that the correct figure for the Persian fleet at Artemisium is about 600–700, and for Salamis about 1,000 (after further reinforcement). Both are plainly round numbers. This conclusion is confirmed by Aeschylus' division (*Persians* 366) of the Persian fleet into three squadrons and a detached force of 'others'. He speaks of one Persian as in command of a squadron of 250 ships (*Persians* 323–4). If the full strength of a squadron was 250, and the 'others' consisted of the 207 fast ships, the total is 957, very roughly 1,000. For the Greek fleet, Herodotus' final detailed figure of 380 is perhaps to be preferred to Aeschylus' round figure of 300.

The conclusion is that at Salamis there were between two and three Persian ships to one Greek. These were the formidable odds which Themistocles, taking advantage of the narrow waters of the straits, set himself to face. He faced also the more subtle task of bringing his allies, and his supreme commander, to fight. Later actions show that in fighting with triereis good tactics are more important than large numbers.

We may now return to the Greek fleet beached at Paloukia bay, opposite the now hostile Attic coast, but at least partly hidden from it by the island of H. Georgios (map 3).

Themistocles succeeded in solving one of his problems, and went some way towards solving another, by a simple intelligence operation. He sent his tutor Sicinnus, posing as a defector, to tell Xerxes that the Greeks were planning withdrawal to the Isthmus through the Megarian strait. Both Herodotus and Aeschylus give this story, which there is no reason to disbelieve. Xerxes' own sources of information may have corroborated the message since, indeed, it was not far from the truth. Xerxes acted on it and ordered his fleet to sea – according to Aeschylus, after sunset, according to Herodotus, after midnight – 'so that the Greeks might not be able to get away'. The Egyptian squadron was ordered to move round the seaward side of the island and seal the Megarian strait. This squadron, with further to go, might well have embarked at sunset. Of the other three squadrons, embarking possibly at midnight, one, probably the 207 fast ships, was detailed to patrol the seaward coast of Salamis in case the Greeks tried to abandon their ships and escape in small boats from that side of the island, while the other two patrolled the narrow straits on each side of the Persian-held island of Psyttaleia. Aristides, recalled from political exile by an amnesty, slipped through the patrolling ships and joined the Greek commanders at their council of war. He told them that, from what he had seen, they had no option but to stay and fight. Themistocles' first objective had been achieved; and by forcing the Persians to divide their forces he was approaching a solution to the problem of numbers.

As dawn broke on that late summer morning the two squadrons of ships sent to watch the eastern narrows moved up to reconnoitre the Greek position, probably without much expectation of an engagement, but thinking to find them gone or at least demoralised. As they nosed their way up the channels the Greek seamen, fresh after a night's rest, embarked in their 380 ships, and put to sea to face the two squadrons of the Persian fleet, each about 250 strong, the crews of which had been at the oar at least since midnight. Themistocles had thus achieved his third objective, to overcome the disadvantage of his slower ships (above, p. 53 and below, p. 60). His oarsmen were fresh, his opponents' oarsmen had been pulling, desultorily, for six hours at least. It must also be remembered that, as is likely, and as Diodorus (11.18.4) says, the Greek line, as it formed, spanned the narrowest part of the single channel which is about 1,200 m (1,310 yards) wide as it led up to the island now called H. Georgios. A trieres (overall beam 5.45 m) under oars (4.2 m each) occupied a beam space of a little less than 12 m (i.e. 5.45 m + ($\frac{3}{4}$ × 4.2 m × 2 = 6.3 m) = 11.75 m). If we allow 3 m between the tips of the oars of each trieres and 10 m between the end of the line at each end and the shore we find that only 80 triereis in line-abreast formation could move up the 1,200 m wide channel, and this is the formation which they must have adopted as soon as an engagement seemed imminent. It seems, then, that at least at the outset of the action the Persian superiority in numbers, already reduced by the division of their forces, was now to a great extent neutralised.

The reason why the Persians allowed this to happen seems to have been a fatal, if understandable, over-confidence, which led them to underestimate the Greeks' resilience. The Greek fleet was holed up in the Salamis channel. The Persians expected them to attempt withdrawal, as they had expected it at Artemisium. The withdrawal on that occasion had been successful because the task force sent to prevent it had been overwhelmed by a storm. The Persians hardly needed Sicinnus to tell them to repeat the manoeuvre. All that remained, it seemed, was to send the two squadrons at daybreak up the straits to complete the elimination of the Greek fleet. The last thing they must have expected was a confident naval confrontation. They had not learnt the lesson of the first skirmish at Artemisium.

There is a discrepancy between our two main authorities in the account of the battle that ensued. It must be remembered, however, that Aeschylus probably took part in the battle himself and was writing for many who had fought in it, while Herodotus' information must have been second-hand, and gathered from Persian sources. Herodotus says: 'The Greeks put to sea with all their ships, and as they came out the Persians attacked them.' The Greek line appeared to falter, but an Athenian ship drew first blood. In Aeschylus' more circumstantial account (*Persians* 386ff.) the Persian fleet, moving northwards up the channel, at first only heard the Greeks 'then quickly they were all plain to see'. The Greek ships, as they put to sea from the beach, were first obscured from the approaching Persian ships by the island of H. Georgios, and then came into view from behind it. Aeschylus continues: '. . . the right wing leading in orderly formation, then the whole fleet followed and after a clash they moved through behind the Persian ships and surrounded them'. It looks as if the faltering which was noticed by the Persians (and subsequently reported to Herodotus) as the Greeks moved up the channel in line abreast, was the well-practised manoeuvre of swinging from line abreast to line ahead, and that the Greeks with the right wing leading made a breakthrough on the Persian left and then rolled up the Persian lines attacking the ships in the beam or quarter. The manoeuvre was in fact a classical *diekplous* achieved by ships which were technically slower and should therefore have been on the defensive, but were able to adopt an attacking role because they were fresh and their opponents tired after a night at the oar. Nevertheless, a breakthrough of a line six deep was a notable achievement. The breakthrough at the right end of the Greek line is logical because Greek casualties in the breakthrough would thus have the advantage of the friendly Salaminian shore, always an important factor in battles fought with oared ships (pp. 62–3).[9] The Persian ships were, in Herodotus' eyes, the attackers because they were moving towards the Greek line, and for this reason, and also because in the dawn wind their ships with their deck bulwarks (pp. 156–7) became difficult to manage, were unable to adopt any of the classical answers to the breakthrough.

The Persian ships seem to have been thrown into confusion, and although in the succeeding mêlée there was some bitter fighting, and losses were suffered on the Greek side, the Persians never recovered, and their two squadrons were surrounded and destroyed. Xerxes realised that without command of the sea he would never conquer Greece, and decided to return to Asia, leaving his army, which withdrew northwards, to carry on the fight as best it could. The final and decisive defeat was on land at Plataea, but it was at Salamis with the skilled use of triereis that the invaders were halted and turned back, and Greek command of the sea established.

9. See A. W. Gomme (1953) p. 16.

In the narrow waters off Artemisium and in the straits between Attica and Salamis the Greek commanders adopted tactical movements, defensive and offensive, aimed at producing situations in which the ram could be used to advantage. Off Artemisium in the first skirmish and in the last battle the Persian commanders adopted tactics which were designed to achieve similar objectives. In the former the sudden Greek move from defence to attack caught the Persian ships unawares in an unfavourable position. In the latter again they were denied the success they might have expected from a *periplous* on both wings carried out by a more numerous fleet, when the Greeks attacked and a tactical stalemate ensued, 'with bitter fighting and heavy casualties on both sides'. In all these engagements the Greek ships exhibited that 'speed and turning ability' for which, Plutarch says (*Cimon* 12.2), Themistocles built the Athenian fleet.

It appears that the choice of offensive or defensive tactics in an engagement depended in the first place on a speed rating of the fleet as a whole. It appears also that a commander would know at the outset whether or not his ships were to be rated faster than his opponent's. There is no indication what the basis of this rating was, but we shall see (pp. 153–4) that it is likely to have been a matter of maintenance, and that a fleet that had recently been 'dried out' was automatically rated faster than one which had not. This overall 'maintenance rating' was apparently independent of another rating which a group of ships in a fleet might have had as 'fast' and which is likely to have been a matter of something different – specially light build or, possibly, recent construction. Again, it appears that the 'maintenance rating' and the choice of tactics which followed from it might be overridden on occasion by other factors. In the case of the last battle at Artemisium it was overridden by the necessity to escape from a tactically dangerous situation, the threat to the defensive line-abreast formation of a *periplous* on both wings. In the preceding skirmish it was overridden by the sudden presentation of a favourable opportunity to attack. In the case of the battle of Salamis the Greek commanders felt able to override the 'maintenance rating' because of another factor which they had contrived to bring into operation: the oarsmen of the fleet judged to be faster were tired, whereas the oarsmen of the fleet judged to be slow were fresh.

4

SYBOTA AND THE GULF OF CORINTH

In the fifty years between 480 and 432 Athens operated fleets in Egypt, Cyprus, and Asia Minor and achieved that greatness which Thucydides gives as the chief cause of the war which eventually broke out between her former allies and herself (1.118.2). The building of these fleets, their maintenance and operational procedures, their strategy and tactics, are all, for this period, a closed book for the modern student since we have no ancient account of them. The Salamis fleet had been financed by the silver mines' unexpected profit. The fleets now had to be built and maintained out of the tribute paid by the allies. Athens destroyed her naval rival Aegina, 'the stye in Athens' eye' as Pericles is said to have called her (Aristotle, *Rhet.* 1411a15–16); and she built the Long Walls from the upper city to her ports of Piraeus and Phalerum. Her helmsmen and other auxiliaries employed in triereis were now unrivalled in numbers and skill. So too was the most important cadre of all, trained and experienced oarsmen. Her shipwrights and naval architects had benefited from 50 years of trial and error, and brought to a degree of technical perfection the ship which had already at the beginning of Athens' career as a sea power become a sophisticated weapon built for a recognised tactical purpose. By 433 Athens had developed a formidable naval superiority over all other Greek states, in her exploitation of the offensive potentiality of the trieres and in the skill and seamanship demanded for its operation. This superiority is well demonstrated in an engagement in 433 between a Corinthian fleet and a fleet of her island colony Corcyra (mod. Kerkyra, Corfu), supported by Athenian squadrons. Thucydides emphasises the way in which Athens' use of the trieres differed from the 'old-fashioned' tactics of the Corinthians and Corcyraeans.

Sybota

The immediate causes of the outbreak of war between Athens and the Peloponnese was a dispute between Corinth and Corcyra over the allegiance of one of Corcyra's colonies. In the course of the dispute Corcyra, with a fleet of 120 triereis, defeated a Corinthian fleet of 75 ships with 2,000 hoplites on board (Thuc. 1.29).[1] For the next two years the Corinthians applied themselves to building ships and to recruiting 'oarsmen from the Peloponnese and from the rest of Greece by offering pay'. They offered pay, presumably, because the normal service of citizens could not produce enough oarsmen for the large fleet envisaged (1.31.1). For their part, the Corcyraeans sought an alliance with Athens, claiming that their navy was second only to the Athenian in size. Athens agreed to a defensive alliance, and sent ten ships with orders not to fight the Corinthians (with whom they were at peace) unless the Corinthians launched an attack by sea on Corcyra, or on one of her territories, and attempted a landing. The campaign which followed, involving on the one side 110 Corcyraean ships and first 10, then 20 more, Athenian ships, and on the other a fleet of 150 ships of the Corinthians and their allies, is described in considerable detail by Thucydides and is worth attention (1.45–54; see map 4).[2]

Moving north from their colony Leucas the Corinthian fleet encamped at Cheimerion (mod. Vemocastro) at a harbour near the mouth of the Paramythia stream. The Corcyraeans reacted by manning 110 ships and encamping on one of the two Sybota islands which, connected by a reef, make a natural, north-facing, harbour on the mainland side of the channel between the island of Corcyra and the mainland. In this position the Corcyraean fleet covered the southern approaches to the city of Corcyra which lies northwards on the eastern side of the island, but was separated by the channel from the fleet's forward base on the island at Leucimme (mod. Lefkimo). 'The ten Athenian ships were present as well.' Both fleets were supported by land forces. The Corcyraean land force was at Leucimme,

---

1. Like the later Corinthian fleet which fought the battle of Sybota this was an invasion force. With 42 troop-carriers and 33 fast triereis it would have carried 2,010 hoplites ($42 \times 40 + 33 \times 10$). 2,000 is a round number.
2. See N. G. L. Hammond (1945), who has elucidated the description from a close first-hand knowledge of the area.

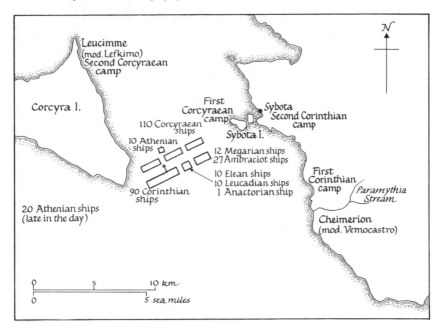

Map 4 The battle of Sybota.

the Corinthian consisted of non-Greeks on the mainland, the latter providing the reason for the Corcyraean ships bivouacking on the Sybota island instead of on the mainland opposite.

When the Corinthians were ready to make their assault on the island of Corcyra, they put to sea in darkness from Cheimerion, taking victuals for three days and with the ships cleared for action but apparently, as an invasion fleet, carrying extra troops.[3] They hoped, it seems, to slip past the Corcyraean fleet and cut it off from its base at Leucimme. However, as day broke they saw the Corcyraean ships already at sea and moving towards them. As soon as the two fleets saw each other they formed battle lines (i.e. line abreast) across the channel, with the Athenian ships in support of the right wing of the Corcyraeans, who were drawn up in three squadrons. On the

3. A fleet would normally (below, p. 95) expect to find food and water where they put ashore, but on this occasion, if they made the intended landing on Corcyra, they could not expect to get victuals immediately. Ships cleared for action left their main sails ashore, together with any other gear unnecessary for their immediate purpose (below, p. 97).

Corinthian side the Megarians (12 ships) and Ambraciots (27) formed the right wing (nearest the mainland). In the centre were the rest of the allies (Eleans 10, Leucadians 10, Anactorians 1) while the Corinthians (90) occupied the left wing with their fastest ships[4] facing the Athenians.

When the signals were run up on either side the two fleets engaged,

both having many hoplites on deck as well as many archers and javelin men, for the ships were still manned rather unscientifically in the old-fashioned manner . . . The fighting was hard, not so much in terms of matching skill with skill but because it resembled land-fighting more than anything else. For when the ships rammed each other they did not easily separate, because of the numbers and the press of the ships and because success in the battle was seen to depend more on the fighting men on deck [than on ramming]. They fought a pitched battle with the ships immobilised. Nor were there any examples of the breakthrough (*diekplous*), but they fought rather with courage and physical strength than with tactical skill.[5] As a result there was much clamour everywhere, and the fighting was confused. The Athenian ships stood by the Corcyraeans wherever they were hard-pressed, and overawed the enemy, but the Athenian generals did not start combat, bearing in mind the orders the Assembly had given them. The Corinthian right wing [39 ships] was in the worst trouble, for the Corcyraeans with twenty ships routed them, scattered them and chased them to the mainland.[6]

But on the left wing, where the Corinthians themselves were, they had much the best of it, as the Corcyraeans, whose numbers were fewer to begin with,

[could not send their right wing, of which the Corinthians were getting the better, any help from their left wing or centre, since they] had twenty ships [from the left wing] away in pursuit.

Seeing that the Corcyraeans were in difficulties the Athenians now began to help more openly, at first restraining themselves from actually ramming an enemy ship; but when the rout became obvious and the Corinthians pressed them hard, then everyone at this point took a hand in the action. There was no longer any holding back, but circumstances were such that the Corinthians and Athenians had inevitably to attack each other. After the

4. Literally 'with the ships that moved best in the water (*arista pleousai*)', i.e. those which had hulls in the best condition of maintenance and well-trained oarsmen. It may alternatively apply to those that were not troop-carriers (below, p. 153–4).
5. Thucydides is concerned to show the superiority of the Athenian ships in the modern mode of fighting.
6. Probably not all the way back to Cheimerion but to a nearer beach.

rout the Corinthians did not take in tow the ships they had swamped but pulled in among them and turned their attention to killing the men[7] rather than to taking them alive. And by mistake they killed their own men, not realising that their ships on the right wing had been worsted ... This sea-fight was the greatest, in terms of the number of ships involved, of any that had hitherto been fought by Greeks against Greeks.

Once the Corinthians had pursued the Corcyraeans to the shore they turned their attention to the wrecks [i.e. to towing them away] and to their own dead, and secured most of them and brought them to Sybota, a deserted harbour on the mainland of Thesprotia to which their land force of non-Greeks had moved up in support.

This harbour is of course the same as that beside which the Corcyraeans had bivouacked the night before, not on the mainland but on one of the two islands sheltering the harbour from the south. Once the Corinthian supporting land force had moved up to occupy the mainland side of it, the harbour was available for the Corinthians to use as a forward base. Harbour and islands seem both to have been named Sybota.

The two fleets with their supporting land forces were now facing each other across the channel separating the island of Corcyra from the mainland: the Corinthians at Sybota and the Corcyraeans at Leucimme.

When the Corinthians had completed this operation, they mustered their forces and moved out against the Corcyraeans. With the ships which [had been engaged but] were still seaworthy and with the others which had been with the Athenian ships [and were accordingly untouched] the Corcyraeans in their turn moved out to meet them, afraid that the Corinthians would attempt a landing in their territory. It was already late in the day and the paean had been raised for the attack, when the Corinthians suddenly backed water seeing twenty Athenian ships approaching. The Athenians had sent them in fear of what did in fact happen, that the Corcyraeans would be worsted and that their own ships would be too few to give them effective help. When the Corinthians caught sight of the approaching squadron they guessed that the ships were from Athens and thought that there were not only those they could see but more still, and began to withdraw. The Corcyraeans [who were facing east] did not see them since their approach [from the south-west] was less easily visible to them, and could not understand why the Corinthians were backing water, until some of them caught

7. The crews would have been holding on to their ships which though holed were still afloat.

sight of the ships and shouted out: 'There are ships coming up over there.'
Then they too withdrew as it was already getting dark, and the Corinthians
put about and broke off the action. So the two sides disengaged, and the battle
ended at nightfall.

As the Corcyraeans were pitching camp at Leukimme, the twenty ships
from Athens . . . after making their way through the corpses and the wrecks
pulled in to camp not long after they were sighted. In the darkness the
Corcyraeans at first were afraid that they might be enemy ships, but then
recognised them as Athenian and helped them to their moorings.

Next day the Athenian and Corcyraean ships came out from
Leucimme against the harbour of Sybota, and the Corinthians put
out to meet them, but there was no engagement as the Corinthians
were anxious to return to their home port.

Thucydides' detailed account of this campaign contains a number
of points of great interest concerning the trieres itself and about its
operational use.

The first point is a general one, and has a bearing on the nature of
the trieres as a fighting ship: the close reliance of the Corinthian
invasion fleet on a series of land bases, and a supporting land force,
in the comparatively short haul from Leucas to Corcyra (*c.* 78 sea
miles). From the Corinthian colony of Leucas the fleet moved first to
Cheimerion (*c.* 43½ sea miles) where a camp was pitched, the ships
moored and contact made with their non-Greek allies on the
mainland. In the battle the victorious Corcyraeans pursued the ships
of the Megarians and Ambraciots, who made for 'the mainland'
where the non-Greek allies could protect them, while the victorious
Corinthians pursued the Corcyraeans who, again, made for 'the
shore' of Corcyra where they could find protection from a land
force. Seeking the shore is the normal action of defeated, sometimes
even of merely outnumbered, oared ships, and plainly it is important
that the land should be friendly (see below, pp. 74-5).

It seems clear that the Corinthians intended to land on Corcyra.
This intention is confirmed not only by the Athenians' belief and the
Corcyraeans' fears, but by the number of hoplites (armed infantry
men), archers and javelin-men carried, and the victuals for three
days. The Corinthians could not count on finding food immediately,
which was what usually happened. Thucydides is not quite fair, at
any rate to the Corinthians, in talking about their 'old-fashioned'
way of fighting a sea-battle. Although the ships were in other re-

spects cleared for action, the circumstances of the mission demanded that they should carry as many troops as possible.

Actions are broken off at nightfall as much by reason of fatigue and hunger as anything else. On this occasion (and others: e.g. pp. 70–85) fleets set out in darkness before dawn to achieve surprise. There seems to have been no problem in navigating by night, provided that the sky was clear.

The two fleets are likely to have been approaching each other in line ahead by squadrons (below, p. 88). When they came in sight of each other, they formed line abreast. The Corcyraean ships were divided into three squadrons, each commanded by one of their three generals, presumably of about equal numbers, i.e. about 37 ships, while the 10 Athenian ships were in support of, probably behind, the Corcyraean squadron, on the right wing. The Corinthians' 90 ships, including their fastest, were placed on the left wing, with the intention, it appears, of making a breakthrough (*diekplous*) on that side and cutting off the Corcyraeans from their base at Leucimme (and Corcyra city, further north), and the Athenian ships were stationed opposite them to prevent that happening. The Corinthian centre was weak, with only 21 ships, while the right wing with 39 presumably matched the Corcyraeans' 37 ships. When Thucydides says that 20 Corcyraean ships routed the Corinthian right wing and pursued the ships to the mainland, he can hardly mean that the Corcyraean left wing consisted only of the 20 ships. As it turned out, the Corcyraean right wing was routed as the Corinthians intended; but, thanks to the Athenian ships standing by, there was no breakthrough and the Corinthians could only withdraw to Sybota and come out again in the evening, to be thwarted by the arrival of the second Athenian squadron.

The signals raised from the command ships must have been flags or pennants flown from the stern. Recognition by the crews was marked by the singing of the paean as the ships pulled in to the attack as at Salamis (*Persians* 393).

The 'old-fashioned' style of sea-fighting, in Thucydides' eyes, was a reliance on soldiers of various kinds on deck either repelling boarders or themselves boarding another ship. This style is in contrast to the modern way of fighting, exemplified in the engagements at Artemisium and Salamis, which consisted in the use of the trieres herself as an offensive weapon. The Athenians had by now become particularly proficient in this manoeuvre. There can be no doubt[8] that the Athenian ships, which only participated in the fighting when the rout of the Corcyraeans' right wing had become general and the hand-to-hand fighting was over, are not included in this description of the 'old-fashioned way'.

The operation of backing water, i.e. reversing the forward pulling stroke, is a regular manoeuvre under oar in battle and is frequently described. Backing off after the impact of ramming is essential, unless the 'old-fashioned way' of fighting is followed, when ships 'do not easily separate after ramming'. In ordinary navigation it is also the normal procedure when beaching stern first in mooring.[9] In this account it is distinguished from 'turning away' which is the practice in breaking off an action.

Thucydides' account of the action at Sybota both in its outcome and in the terms in which he describes the fighting underlines the superiority which the new tactics, and the design and training calculated to put them into effect, gave to even a small squadron. The Corcyraeans presumably knew nothing better than the 'old-fashioned way', but the Corinthians had it thrust upon them by circumstance. Even if cleared for action, laden with stores and extra troops they would have been severely handicapped in combat with fast Athenian ships cleared for action, but otherwise unencumbered.

Naupactus I

The naval battles fought at the outset of the war in and around the entrance to the Corinthian gulf underline further the tactical superiority which Athens had achieved – a superiority revealed at Sybota by the respect in which her ships were held and, by implication, in the terms used by Thucydides to describe the tactics her way of fighting superseded. Phormio, in command of a small squadron of ships at Naupactus facing much larger Peloponnesian fleets, demonstrates that superiority directly, both in success and adversity.

In the winter of 430 Phormio, sent by the Athenians round the Peloponnese with 20 ships, made Naupactus his base for a blockade

8. Jordan (1975) p. 187 concludes otherwise, but his conclusion does not follow from the text of Thucydides.
9. See *GOS* pp. 56, 311; 'The Mediterranean moor'.

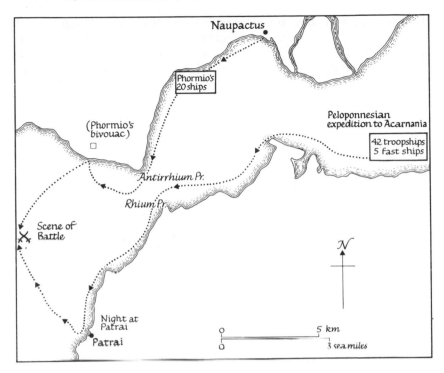

Map 5 The entrance to the gulf of Corinth: Phormio's first action.

of Corinth (map 5). Naupactus, an Athenian outpost just inside the gulf of Corinth on its northern shore, had been settled by exiled Messenians, inveterate enemies of Sparta (see note 11 below).

Meanwhile, the Corinthians and their neighbouring allies were planning to send a sea-borne expedition to Acarnania, an operation which would entail a naval movement past Phormio's squadron out of the gulf into the open sea. Acarnania was on the mainland, north of the entrance to the gulf. Realising that the expeditionary force moving past him on the southern shore of the gulf would at some point have to cross to the northern coast, Phormio did not attack them as they passed, preferring an engagement in open water, since his ships, though few, were fast while the Corinthian force consisted, with the exception of five ships, entirely of troopships. Thucydides now takes up the tale (2.83.3):

The Corinthians and their allies were not proceeding with their ships cleared for action but as an expeditionary force to Acarnania, little expecting that in face of their own fleet of forty-seven the Athenians would dare to go into action with twenty ships. They observed Phormio's squadron moving along [the northern shore] opposite them as they moved along the [southern] shore [to Patrae, mod. Patras], and when [next morning] they were making the crossing from Patrae in Achaea to the mainland opposite, they saw the Athenians advancing to attack and realised that they had not succeeded in putting to sea unnoticed in the darkness, but were forced to fight an action in the middle of the channel . . . The Peloponnesian ships formed as large a circle as they could, thus giving no opportunity for a breakthrough (*diekplous*), with their bows outwards and their sterns inwards, and the vessels that were accompanying them [smaller oared ships and merchantmen] were placed inside the circle as well as the five ships that were fastest, so that if the enemy did attack at any point they would have only a short distance to go to bring support. The Athenians with their ships in single file moved round the Peloponnesians in a circle and hemmed them into a small space, constantly encircling them at very close quarters, and making them look out for an immediate attack. Phormio had given orders to his captains not to attack until he gave the signal. He was expecting that the Peloponnesians would not keep formation, as infantry on land would, but that the ships would collide with each other and the smaller ships would be a cause of confusion; also that if the wind from the gulf [of Corinth] were to get up (that was what he was waiting for and what usually happened about sunrise) they would not remain steady for long. And he realised that the initiative was his to take when he wished, since his ships were the faster, and that that was the right moment for him to take it.

As the breeze freshened, the ships which were already in a constricted space were beginning to fall into confusion from the simultaneous effect of the wind and of the smaller vessels, and ship was jostling ship and poles were being used to keep them apart. And as the seamen [i.e. the deck-hands] were shouting and taking evasive action, and abusing each other, so that they were not listening out for the words of command or for the boatswains, and as the ill-trained oarsmen, being unable to recover their oars in the choppy water, made the ships unresponsive to the helm, at that precise moment Phormio gave the signal, and the Athenians, moving in to ram, first sank one of the flagships, and then went on with the intention of putting the rest of the ships out of action as they fell in their path. The result was that in the confusion none of the ships turned to fight, but they all fled to Patrae and Dyme in Achaea. The Athenians pursued and captured twelve ships, having put out of action at least one other in the engagement.

The first point to be made about this action is that in the initial stages it developed tactically on the same lines as the first skirmish at

Artemisium and for the same reasons. In each case, although on different grounds, one side was recognised to be faster and the other to be slower, with the result that the slower side, to avoid the breakthrough, adopted the circular formation, while the faster ships moved round the circle very close in line ahead with the intention of causing confusion. Off Patrae the Peloponnesians were slower because they were an expeditionary force on passage, while the Athenian ships were cleared for action and fast. At Artemisium the reason for the disparity in speed between the fleets was probably that the one had recently been 'dried out' and the other had not (below, p. 153). At Artemisium the slower side was also the smaller in number; the opposite was the case off Patrae, where Phormio's 20 fast ships attacked a slow Peloponnesian fleet of 47 ships, of which 5 only were fast and they were kept in reserve by a curious failure to understand the proper use of 'fast' ships in battle.

By letting the enemy move out through the entrance of the gulf to Patrae, and then catching them during their early morning dash across to the mainland coast (a move they had to make if they were to carry out their mission to Acarnania), Phormio ensured that the battle, when it came, would be in open water where his own faster ships would have the room to manoeuvre. The circular formation had been exploited offensively at Artemisium by the Greeks, and it exploded successfully. On the present occasion the Peloponnesian commanders certainly read the situation right. They went by the book in adopting the correct defensive formation but were prevented from using it offensively by Phormio's superior knowledge of local weather conditions and by the inexperience of their own oarsmen. Like all good commanders Phormio had a firm grasp of the strategic features of the situation, the enemy's obligation to cross the open sea and the relative characteristics of his own and the enemy's ships, and was thus able to choose the tactical situation most favourable to himself. His knowledge of local conditions and his ability to forecast the tactical choice which the enemy would take enabled him to harass their ships and to make his attack at the right moment. The gross disparity in numbers was thus overcome. In the next engagement the circumstances were different. Phormio's local command of the sea was to be directly challenged.

Naupactus II

After its defeat, the Peloponnesian fleet gave up its objective and
withdrew south to Cyllene on the west coast of the Peloponnese,
mustering further ships. The Spartans in response sent three more
commanders, including the talented and daring Brasidas. Phormio
asked for reinforcements and was sent 20 ships, but on their way
round the Peloponnese they were diverted southwards to Crete, and
were delayed there. The Peloponnesian fleet of 77 ships, in due course,
moved north to Rhium on the southern side of the entrance to the
Gulf, but this time they came not as an expeditionary force loaded
with gear and additional troops and accompanied by support vessels,
but as a fleet cleared for action and intent on destroying Phormio's
smaller force. Phormio, still with only 20 ships, could only keep
watch on them from Antirrhium on the northern side of the narrow
entrance (2.86.5; see map 6).

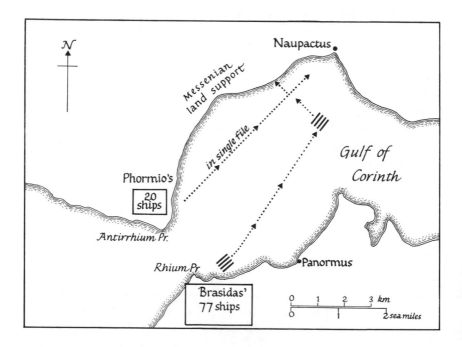

Map 6 The entrance to the gulf of Corinth: Phormio's second action.

And for six or seven days they lay moored opposite each other, practising and preparing for battle, resolved on the one side [the Athenian] not to move into the narrows, thinking that the enemy there had the advantage.

Thucydides presents (2.87) Brasidas encouraging his men by claiming that their lack of skill was compensated by greater daring and numbers; also that whereas in the previous action the Peloponnesian fleet was not prepared for battle, in the coming action they would be seeking it. Phormio is shown explaining the tactical situation:

I shall not stage the contest in the Gulf if I can help it, nor will I move into it. I see plainly enough that a confined space is a disadvantage to a few ships, even if they are used with skill and are faster, against many ships inexpertly used. The fact is that one cannot properly move against a ship to ram it, if one cannot get the enemy in one's sights from some way off, and if one cannot retire if need be in a difficult situation. There are no opportunities for carrying out a breakthrough or a sharp turn, which are the manoeuvres of a faster moving fleet, but [in a confined space] it would be necessary to turn the sea-fight into a land-fight, and in those circumstances the larger fleet wins.

Phormio's orders to his men were:

to stay near the [beached] ships in good order, to act on the words of command with alacrity, particularly since there is little room between the fleets for embarkation and attack [and so it was important to get off the beach and into a defensive formation quickly][10] and in the battle to regard disciplined movement and silence as the most important things. These are necessities in most warlike operations and not least in fighting at sea. And you must repel the onslaughts of the enemy in a manner worthy of your former actions.

Themistocles, in the allied council of war on the eve of Salamis used an argument that is in one respect the opposite of the argument which Phormio used here (see p. 152). Themistocles thought it safer to fight an enemy fleet faster and more than three times more numerous than his own in the narrow waters between Salamis and Attica rather than in the open waters of the Saronic Gulf adjacent to the Isthmus. He was afraid that in the open water the ships of the Greeks would be surrounded by the faster and more numerous

10. This is just what the Corcyraean fleet failed to do in 428 (below, p. 77) and the Athenian fleet failed to do at Notium and Aegospotami (above, p.9 n. 4). It was essential for a fleet putting to sea from a beach to get into formation very briskly, since a ship on its own was very vulnerable.

Persian fleet, which contained the expertly operated Phoenician and Ionian squadrons. Phormio's ships, unlike the Greek ships in 480, were faster and they were also more expertly operated than their opponents. They had already shown that in open water they could literally make rings round the more numerous enemy ships and throw them into confusion, and hoped to do so again.

In the event, Phormio, like the Peloponnesian commanders in the previous battle, found that his freedom of action was limited by his responsibilities, since, just as they on the previous occasion were an invasion force under orders to proceed to Acarnania, he now had to defend Naupactus. Accordingly, when at dawn the enemy moved, in columns of four parallel files of ships, along the southern shore of the Gulf in an easterly direction, Phormio had no option but to keep pace with them, moving with his 20 ships in line ahead, single file, along the northern shore. The Peloponnesian right wing, to which the fastest ships had been assigned, was leading (2.90–92.3),

so that if Phormio concluded that their objective was Naupactus and moved in that direction to counter it, the Athenian ships would not succeed in escaping attack by moving ahead of the Peloponnesian wing (at the head of the column) but that these ships (being fast) should head them off . . . As the Peloponnesians expected, Phormio, worrying about the undefended position (of Naupactus) when he saw the Peloponnesians coming out, in response hurriedly and reluctantly ordered embarkation, and moved (eastwards) along the coast, while his supporting land force of Messenians[11] made a similar move in turn. The Peloponnesian commanders saw the Athenians moving along in single file ['to the wing'] and already within the gulf and not far off the land. That was what they had been waiting for, and at a signal they turned abruptly and swung from line ahead to line abreast, each ship making for the enemy as fast as possible, and intended to cut off all the enemy ships. Some eleven of them, however, which were at the head of the file, slipped past the Peloponnesian [right] wing and its turning sweep, and succeeded in getting through to free water. The rest they caught and drove in flight towards the land and made useless, killing those Athenians who did not succeed in making their escape by swimming. Some of those [nine] ships they took in tow and were pulling them away empty, except for one which they had already captured complete with its crew, but the Messenians, coming up in support, went into the sea in full armour, boarded some ships and

---

11. These Messenians, exiled from their land by Sparta, had been encouraged by Athens to settle at Naupactus and were now on hand to supply the necessary supporting land force for the Athenian squadron (see Salmon 1984 p. 281).

recovered them by climbing on to the decks and fighting, although they were already under tow.[12]

This second action in the gulf gives another detailed, and rather different, picture of triereis manoeuvring in battle. The usual formation of line abreast was adopted by neither fleet at the outset; both moved off 'to the wing', staying in line ahead. The Peloponnesians with 77 ships appear to have adopted a column of four files (of 20, 19, 19, 19), since in this way they could cover the Athenian file of 20 ships, but being four deep would be that much more formidable. When the Peloponnesian column reached what they considered a favourable point they took the initiative and each ship executed a sharp turn to the left so as to present a front of four ships deep, line abreast. In this formation, which made a breakthrough virtually impossible, they bore down at full speed on the single Athenian file 'inside the gulf and not far off the land' with the intention of forcing them ashore if they could not ram them first. They caught nine of them. The action of the Messenian land force, in recovering some as they were actually being towed away with a prize crew on board, illustrates the role so often played by supporting land troops in a sea-battle fought close to the shore.

However, the engagement was not yet over. Phormio had had nearly half his ships put out of action. The crews that escaped and the hulls that were recovered could play no further part that day, but the 11 ships which had succeeded in slipping past the enemy net were making for Naupactus with all speed, pursued by 20 fast Peloponnesian ships. All, with one, possibly deliberate, exception, reached the harbour, and had time to turn and range themselves 'by the temple of Apollo' in line abreast with their bows facing seawards, ready for defence if the enemy moved in against them (2.91.1). When the Peloponnesian ships came up, the crews were singing the paean for the final attack.[13] One Leucadian ship, far ahead of the others, was

---

12. These Athenian ships, cut off by the enemy sweep, did what such ships normally did and ran for a friendly shore, but some had been rammed before they could get there since some at least of the crews are said to have escaped by swimming. Others got near enough to the shore for the Messenians to wade into the sea and board them, engaging the enemy on deck as they were actually being towed away.

13. For the paean see above, pp. 65 and 67. Silence is enjoined on other occasions. 'Clamour' is the mark of an ill-disciplined crew.

chasing the laggard Athenian ship. It so happened that a merchantman was anchored off shore in deep water, as merchantmen normally were, and the Athenian ship, reaching it first and swinging round it in a tight circle, rammed the Leucadian ship and holed it.[14]

This unexpected strike confused the Peloponnesians; success had caused their formation to become ragged, so, with the intention of waiting for more of their ships to come up, some of the ships dug in their oars and stopped in their tracks, putting themselves at a disadvantage in view of the short distance between them and the enemy, who were in a posture to attack. Others through unfamiliarity with the place ran their ships aground. When the Athenians saw what was happening, they regained their confidence, and at a single command went over to the attack with a shout.[15] Because of all the mistakes they had already made, and their state of disorder, the Peloponnesians resisted for only a short time, and then turned and made for Panormus, the place from which they had set out. The Athenians in pursuit captured six of the nearest ships and recovered their own, which the enemy had put out of action near the shore and first taken in tow.

This remarkable account, whose truth there is no reason to doubt, underlines the qualities which made the Athenians so formidable in the practice of warfare at sea: refusal at the outset to accept the logic of numbers and of a tactically unfavourable situation, refusal to accept defeat when nearly half their ships were out of action, a magnificent and glorious opportunism and an ability to react quickly and decisively to a sudden change of fortune. Knowing the superior agility and ramming ability of their ships, the Athenians were really fighting with a different sort of weapon from their enemies, who did not know how to use fast ships when they had them. Provided that Athenian commanders had the ability to keep or recover favourable tactical circumstances, superior numbers were of little avail to a less skilful enemy. It was a brilliant, if rather brittle, form of warfare brought by the Athenians to a pitch where tactical professionalism had become decisive.

Thucydides does not tell us the name of the ship's captain whose tight turn was so effective, but he does give the name of the captain of the Leucadian ship he rammed, Timocrates the Spartan, who killed himself as his ship began to fill with water.

14. We are told later that the ship filled with water.
15. See n. 13 above. There was no time for a paean.

Corcyra

The tactical use of the trieres is again illustrated by another engagement in western waters two years later. On this occasion Thucydides does not give the Athenian commander's name. In 427 the Athenians sent a small force of twelve ships to give support once again to a Corcyraean fleet against the Peloponnesians (Thuc. 3.77–8). The 60 Corcyraean ships outnumbered the 57 sent against them, but by going into action off the beach in a careless way they got into difficulty. The Athenians, afraid of being enveloped by the large numbers of the enemy drawn up in line abreast, launched an attack on the enemy's wing and put a ship out of action. The enemy, themselves now afraid of a breakthrough, formed a circle in the approved manner, and the Athenian ships moved round them and tried to throw them into disorder, as they had done off Patrae. But the Peloponnesians, apprehensive of a repetition of that battle, threw against the Athenians the ships that had been successfully fighting the Corcyraeans, causing the Athenians to make a gradual withdrawal, backing water, towards the harbour of the city, 'so that while they were doing so, the Corcyraean ships should as far as possible escape first, since they were retiring slowly and the enemy was facing them. The battle on these lines went on until sunset.'

The tactical movements in this engagement, so far as concerns the 12 Athenian ships and the part of the Peloponnesian fleet not in action with the Corcyraean ships, followed normal lines. A small force of fast ships facing a larger force of slower ships in line abreast formed line ahead and attacked a wing to make a breakthrough. The breakthrough succeeded and the larger force formed a circle to prevent attack from the rear; the faster ships then moved round them trying to put them into disorder. So far, this was according to the book, but on this occasion there was a second squadron of ships which had been successfully engaged elsewhere and now intervened, forcing the twelve ships to withdraw, greatly outnumbered. This they did, backing water and with their bows to the enemy to cover the Corcyraeans' escape 'as far as possible'. One can only admire the Athenians as they passed through their tactical movements, from line ahead to close encirclement, and from that to line abreast, as they backed water slowly towards the harbour, all the time presenting the Peloponnesian ships with the threat of attack. This is a cool professionalism that reflects intelligent command, tight discipline and hard training. Thucydides certainly intended us to notice and admire these qualities. He had, of course, commanded Athenian ships himself.

5

CYNOSSEMA, CYZICUS AND ARGINUSAE

Thucydides gives a detailed account of the dispatch and fortunes of the great Sicilian expedition which Athens mounted in 415. It contains a good deal of information about the trieres and its crew which will be introduced into later chapters, but it has little to offer about the tactical deployment of the ship and its performance in action. In Sicily Athenian proficiency in these two fields, by the nature of the operation, was not called upon until the peak of the fleet's effectiveness, both in manpower and in ships, was long passed. Furthermore there was no large-scale sea-battle until the military requirements of the siege of Syracuse had placed the ships in an impossible position, and the Syracusans with Corinthian help had devised modifications to their ships to take advantage of it. Given the diplomatic and military aims of the adventure, to bring Sicily firmly into the Athenian sphere of influence, not even a Phormio could have plucked a naval victory from an operation marked by a series of diplomatic reverses and military defeats, following the defection of one of her generals, the death of another and the sickness of a third.

The Athenian disaster in Sicily was followed by a war at sea in the north-eastern Aegean, sometimes called the Ionian war, in which Athens struggled to keep open her remaining supply lines with the Black Sea. We find a description of this war first in Thucydides and then, when Thucydides' history comes to an end, in Xenophon, also an Athenian, and Diodorus of Sicily. Xenophon was born shortly after 450 BC and his career, like Thucydides', made him familiar with the trieres and its operation. His account provides the only detailed record of the movement, at top speed, of a fleet of triereis during a long day, and also includes descriptions of three naval engagements, each of which illustrates some new aspect of the deployment of triereis. Diodorus wrote in the first century BC but his account of one of these battles makes more sense than Xenophon's. He is thought to rely on the fourth-century historian Ephorus. As a whole, the history of this war emphasises the degree to which the security of Athens came ultimately to depend on her naval control of a distant theatre of operations, the Hellespont, and the adjoining coasts and islands, as providing the necessary forward bases.

The disaster in Sicily incited Athens' enemies to prepare a naval force to cross the Aegean and to challenge her domination of the seaboard of Asia Minor. For her part Athens devoted her ever resilient energies to the replacement of the ships she had lost. The Peloponnesian fleet was now encouraged, and rather intermittently paid, by Tissaphernes, the Persian governor of the southern coastal region of Asia Minor. It used Miletus as its main base, while the Athenians used Samos. Both sides manoeuvred, but neither was willing to risk an engagement which might be decisive (Thuc. 8.78–80). At Aspendus in Pamphylia Tissaphernes retained a Phoenician fleet of 147 ships, but hesitated to bring them north and commit them to the Peloponnesian side. Persian policy was to keep the Greeks fighting among themselves (Thuc. 8.87.4).

Cynossema

In the summer of 411, on the invitation of Pharnabazus, the governor of the northern coastal region, who promised to subsidise the Peloponnesian fleet if it were brought north into his province, the Spartan commander Mindarus moved from Miletus towards the Hellespont with 73 ships. He was following up a successful incursion into the Thracian Chersonese made earlier in the summer by 16 of his ships. They were now back at the Peloponnesian forward base of Abydus and were being watched by a similar small force of Athenian ships lying northwards about 1½ miles (2.7 km) across the straits at Sestus.[1] Mindarus' move was a direct challenge to the Athenian general Thrasyllus at Samos, who responded by moving north with 55 ships, intending to get to the Hellespont before him. The Athenian fleet was joined by more ships and the general Thrasybulus.

1. Sestus had been established by the Athenian general Strombichides in 411 as a fort to control the Hellespont (Thuc. 8.62.3). Aristotle (*Rhet.* 3.10, 1411a14) quotes the Athenian Peitholaus' description of Sestus as 'the meal table of Piraeus'. As de Sainte-Croix says (1972: p. 48) Sestus was 'the king-pin of their defence of the whole Hellespont' at this time. The Spartans had their base on the other (south) side of the strait at Abydus.

Mindarus was delayed by bad weather and moved as far as Chios, where the Athenians planned to keep him. But while they were attempting to put down a revolt at Eresus, on the western coast of Lesbos, Mindarus put out from Chios, telling no one where he was going, and slipped through the channel between Lesbos and the mainland on a remarkably fast passage to Rhoeteum just inside the straits (see below, p. 97).

The Athenians at Sestus, learning of Mindarus' arrival and afraid of being trapped inside the straits, eluded the enemy ships at Abydus, but ran into Mindarus' fleet coming up the straits from Rhoeteum at dawn. The Athenians lost 4 ships, but 14 escaped to Imbros. Mindarus now had 86 ships and tried to take Elaeus on the southern tip of the Thracian Chersonese. He failed and returned to Abydus. By now the Athenians in Lesbos had news of Mindarus' arrival in the Hellespont. They gave up the siege of Eresus and in a day's voyage (of 60 sea miles: 110 km) reached Elaeus, where they beached their ships, and after bringing in the squadron from Imbros made preparations for an engagement with Mindarus.

The action (Thuc. 8.104) began when the 76 Athenian ships which were moving north-east from Elaeus in column in the direction of Sestus, approached Cynossema and the 86 Peloponnesian ships, including a Syracusan squadron, came out from Abydus, also certainly in column, along the coast in the opposite direction (south) to meet them (map 7). As the two columns turned into line abreast to face each other, Mindarus with his fastest ships was on his own left wing (which had been leading the column) facing Thrasybulus' squadron on the Athenian right (which had been bringing up the Athenian rear). The Syracusans were on Mindarus' right wing facing Thrasyllus' squadron (which had been leading the Athenian column). Mindarus' plan was, with his fast ships, to move round the Athenian right wing and prevent Thrasybulus getting out of the straits, while driving the Athenian centre onto the land, which was close at that point. The Athenian tactical response was to extend their line on the right beyond the promontory of Cynossema. They succeeded in avoiding encirclement, but at the expense of thinning their centre, which was driven ashore. However, the two wings of the Athenian line each carried out an encirclement of the opposing wings and routed them, a remarkable achievement at the end of a pull of more than 20 kilometres (11 sea miles). They then turned inwards against

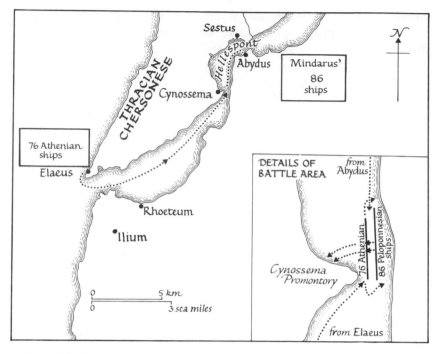

Map 7 The battle of Cynossema.

the successful but now disorderly centre of the Peloponnesian fleet, which they succeeded in routing in turn. The Athenians, with their double *periplous*, scored a clear tactical victory, although the enemy ships were able to take refuge on the friendly southern shore, and only 21 were lost. The Athenians lost 15. The chief gain was to Athenian morale. After the Sicilian disaster they had been afraid of the Peloponnesian fleet with its Syracusan allies: 'now they stopped thinking that their enemies were any longer worthy of consideration in naval matters'.

Alcibiades, the Athenian general who had defected *en route* to Sicily, was now reasserting allegiance to Athens and regaining favour with the navy of Samos. He returned there from the south at the moment of this victory, and reported that he had prevented Tissaphernes sending the Phoenician fleet north to help the Peloponnesians. For the time, at any rate, the threat to Athens' lifeline to the Hellespont seemed to have been averted.

Thucydides' history breaks off after the battle of Cynossema, and the story of the naval war in the north-eastern Aegean is taken up by Xenophon and Diodorus. Xenophon's history opens at the beginning of winter (411) with the arrival at the Hellespont of the Athenian general Thymochares 'with a few ships'. An engagement followed in which the Peloponnesians had the advantage. Then the Rhodian commander Dorieus arrived at daybreak with 14 ships, having used darkness to cover his approach. His ships were spotted by an Athenian look-out, and 20 ships put out against him. Dorieus promptly beached his ships and fought from the shore. He was outnumbered and if, as seems likely, he had been moving under oar during the night his oarsmen would have been tired. At that moment Mindarus happened to be 'making a sacrifice to Athena at Ilium' (Troy) overlooking the sea, and made haste to launch his fleet from Abydus and bring in Dorieus' ships. The Athenians responded and there was a day-long battle in which Alcibiades, arriving from Samos with 18 ships, played a decisive role. The Athenians took 30 ships and recaptured some of their own. The fleets then withdrew to their local forward bases at Abydus and Sestus for the winter. Thrasyllus went back to Athens to report and ask for more men and ships, while the rest of the Athenian fleet sailed in various directions to collect money, leaving 40 ships as garrison in Sestus.

Cyzicus

For the events which followed in the early part of 410, leading up to and including the battle of Cyzicus (Map 8), we have two main sources – a scrappy account in Xenophon (1.1.11–23) so much condensed as not to make sense at times, and a very detailed account in Diodorus (13.49.2–51), which is thought to derive from Ephorus.[2] Diodorus therefore deserves attention. In both historians the Athenian ships at Sestus, threatened by Mindarus with 60 ships at Abydus, withdrew outside the Straits to Cardia on the other side of the Thracian Chersonese. Then, in Diodorus, Theramenes, Thrasybulus and Alcibiades were summoned, and when they arrived 'the generals were eager for a decisive battle'. Mindarus meanwhile had moved to

---

2. See Andrewes (1982) pp. 15ff., to whom I am indebted for the elucidation of the various accounts of the battle.

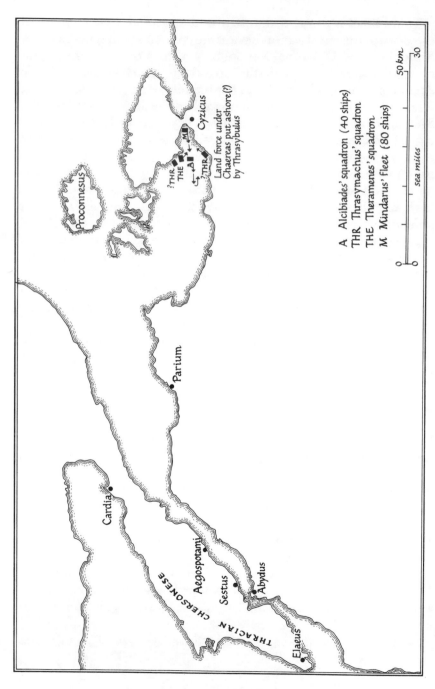

Map 8 The battle of Cyzicus.

A   Alcibiades' squadron (40 ships)
THR Thrasymachus' squadron
THE Theramenes' squadron
M   Mindarus' fleet (80 ships)

Land force under
Chaereas put ashore (?)
by Thrasybulus

Cyzicus

Proconnesus

Parium

Cardia

Aegospotami

Sestus

Abydus

Elaeus

THRACIAN CHERSONESE

sea miles

50 km

30

0

Cyzicus, besieged and stormed it. The Athenian generals, determined to recapture Cyzicus, re-entered the Straits, arriving first at
Elaeus. Then they made an early start and, passing the Spartan base
of Abydus in the dark so that the size of their now reinforced fleet
should not be detected, reached Proconnesus (mod. Marmora)
where they spent the night (Elaeus–Proconnesus about 138 km = 75
sea miles). Xenophon, less plausibly, says that the 86 ships of the
Athenians mustered at Parium, Alcibiades going on ahead and the
other generals following, and from there they moved by night under
oar and arrived at Proconnesus (only about 25 sea miles: 46 km) at
about the time of the midday meal. Both accounts stress the precautions taken to ensure that Mindarus should not know the
strength of the Athenian fleet. Xenophon sees Alcibiades as the
leading spirit, pressing ahead to Parium and giving instructions to
the other ships to follow him 'with their main sails left behind', i.e.
cleared for action, and impounding all shipping on arrival at Proconnesus. In Diodorus the moves are less dramatic, but, suggesting
deliberation and planning, are more believable. The same is true of
the two accounts of the battle which followed.

Xenophon has the Athenian fleet putting to sea in a rainstorm and
finding, when it cleared, that Mindarus' 60 ships were in sight carrying out manoeuvres away from the (western) harbour of Cyzicus and
already cut off from it by the Athenian ships. 'But the Peloponnesians, when they saw that the Athenian triereis were in far greater
numbers than before and were near the harbour fled to the shore;
and mooring their ships together they fought their enemies as they
pulled down upon them. Alcibiades, however, with twenty ships
effected a *periplous* and landed on the shore.' Xenophon's account, as
has been pointed out, does not make sense. If Alcibiades was already
between Mindarus and the harbour, why does he have to effect a
periplous to get to the shore? Diodorus' account removes some of the
difficulties, while reducing the dramatic role of Alcibiades.

In the first place, Diodorus makes plain at the outset that the
Athenian operation was an amphibious one aimed at the recapture
of Cyzicus. The generals' first step was to land troops from the ships
under Chaereas on Cyzicene territory with orders to march on the
city. Then they divided the ships into three squadrons under
Theramenes, Thrasybulus and Alcibiades. 'Now Alcibiades with his
own squadron went on far ahead of the others with the intention of

drawing the Spartans out to a battle, while Theramenes and Thrasybulus devised an ingenious plan to encircle the enemy and cut them off from retreat to the city when once they had been seen moving out.' Plutarch, in his *Life of Alcibiades* (28.6), puts the number of Alcibiades' ships at 40; but the numbers in the other squadrons are not given. Diodorus continues:

Mindarus seeing only Alcibiades' ships approaching and not being aware of the presence of the others scented an easy victory and boldly came out from the city with eighty ships. When he drew near Alcibiades' squadron, the Athenians, as planned, pretended to withdraw, and the Peloponnesians cheerfully pursued them with all speed, sensing victory. But when Alcibiades had drawn them a good distance away from the city he raised the signal and at that moment his ships suddenly swung round in unison to face their pursuers, and Theramenes and Thrasybulus moved on the city and cut off the Spartans' retreat.

It has recently been suggested[3] that the two squadrons of Theramenes and Thrasybulus moving unseen southwards from Proconnesus must have waited behind a promontory just north of the western harbour of Cyzicus, which would have concealed them from Mindarus' ships as they emerged from the western harbour. Hotly pursued by Alcibiades, Mindarus was forced to do what oared ships usually did under such circumstances, and run for the land, and to seek the protection of Pharnabazus' land force of mercenaries. A land-battle then ensued, Thrasybulus putting ashore 'the rest of the troops on his ships', and urging Theramenes to make contact with the force marching on the city under Chaereas. It looks as if Thrasybulus' ships had been troop-carriers which had earlier put ashore their extra armed men in preparation for the sea-battle, and were now putting ashore the regular hoplite *epibatai*. It is possible therefore that Thrasybulus' ships had put ashore Chaereas' troops earlier and had remained off the southern shore, eventually moving behind Mindarus' ships from the south, as Theramenes' ships did so from the north. The fighting on land was long and obstinate. Mindarus was killed and the city of Cyzicus retaken. All the Spartan ships, with the exception of the Syracusan squadron, which was burnt by the crews, were towed away to Proconnesus. It was a famous victory, and Xenophon records the message sent back to

3. By Andrewes (1982) pp. 20–1.

Sparta and intercepted by the Athenians: 'The ships are gone, Mindarus is dead. The men are starving. We don't know what to do.'

In Xenophon the operation for the recapture of Cyzicus appears to have been a hasty, unplanned attack in which an impetuous Alcibiades succeeded single-handed in destroying Mindarus' fleet, thanks to a fortunate rainstorm, some quick opportunism, and a mysterious *periplous*. The land-battle is played down. In Diodorus the operation is clearly amphibious, carefully planned and deliberately carried out. The choice of Elaeus rather than Sestus as the starting-point, the night voyage to Proconnesus past Abydus, where they might have been observed, are both to be noted. On the following day there is the landing of troops on the coast west of the city, not near enough to be observed but within marching distance of the place where land action was to be expected later in the day. Finally there is the ambush behind the promontory planned to effect a *periplous*, possibly a double *periplous*, of Mindarus' fleet and cut off its retreat. The whole naval operation seems to have been worked out to lead up to the land-battle by which a friendly shore was, temporarily at any rate, converted into hostile territory and which consequently resulted in the total destruction of Mindarus' fleet and the recapture of Cyzicus. The importance of command of the shore, which we have seen at Sybota and in one of Phormio's actions in the gulf of Corinth, is here very strongly reinforced. The naval engagement, once rescued from Xenophon's distortions, provides another example of warfare with the trieres as practised by the Athenians: the quick 180° turn of Alcibiades' ships, and the *periplous* carried out by the remainder, are good illustrations of the tactics they employed.

Arginusae

In the following year (409) Lysander, Sparta's new naval commander in the eastern Aegean, was able to build up and refit a naval force of 70 ships at Ephesus, including 25 ships which the Syracusans built at Antandrus in the gulf of Adramyttium to replace those lost at Cyzicus, while the Athenian fleet operated from Samos. After an unsuccessful action at Notium, for which Alcibiades was held responsible by the Athenians although he was not present, Alcibiades was replaced by Phormio's son Conon. When Lysander's year as nauarch came to an end[4] he was succeeded by Callicratidas in command of a fleet now numbering 140. Conon, with 70 ships, was caught at sea by Callicratidas and forced to fight at the entrance to the harbour of Mytilene, losing 30 ships, although the crews were saved. Callicratidas held the entrance to the harbour and brought up troops on the land side. Conon got word to Athens, and the Assembly reacted vigorously to the news of his plight. They voted a relief force of 110 ships, putting aboard all who were of military age, slaves and free men alike, and within 30 days all were manned and had put to sea. The new fleet moved to Samos, where it was joined by 10 Samian ships and 30 more from other allies as well as any Athenian ships that happened to be in the area. The total eventually came to more than 150. Callicratidas did not hear of the relief force until it was already at Samos, and leaving Eteonicus with 50 ships to contain Conon at Mytilene, put to sea with 120 ships, reaching Cape Malea in time for the midday meal. On the same day the Athenian crews were eating their midday meal on the Arginusae islands across the strait from Mytilene (Map 9).

Callicratidas spent the night bivouacked on the south-eastern promontory of Lesbos, from where he could see the fires of the Athenian camp 8 sea miles (14.7 km), or little more than an hour's pulling, across the water. He attempted to put to sea at midnight, but a rainstorm prevented him. At day-break his men embarked and pulled across the channel, 'the ships all in single file ready for the *diekplous* and *periplous* because they were the faster fleet'. The phrase 'in single file' cannot be taken to mean that the whole fleet was in a single file: 120 ships in single file would have been strung out over at least three miles of water. Callicratidas' ships, like the Athenian as we shall see, were probably divided into squadrons of 10–15 ships, and each of these would have advanced across the water in single file, the normal formation for ships 'ready for a breakthrough or encirclement'. Callicratidas was on 'the right wing' – that is to say, the squadron which he led was in the proper place for a fleet commander, on the right wing.

In the early morning light, when Callicratidas' fleet was seen

4. Having held the office once in 408/7. Instead he was appointed to the subordinate office of *epistoleus* (secretary) but with the power of *nauarchos*.

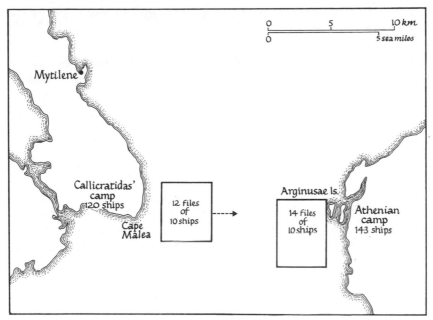

Map 9 The battle of Arginusae.

approaching, the Athenian fleet put out to meet him (*HG* 1.6.29).[5]
'The Athenians put out to sea in response with the left wing', i.e. the
left wing put to sea first. Xenophon gives the Athenian battle
stations in detail. They are of some interest as displaying another
(tactical) answer to the breakthrough and encirclement.

Aristocrates led on the left wing with fifteen ships, then Diomedon with
another fifteen. Pericles was stationed in support of [i.e. behind] Aristocrates,
and Erasinides in support of Diomedon [each presumably also with squadrons of fifteen ships]. Beside Diomedon were ten Samian ships in single file;
their commander was a Samian called Hippeus. Next were the ten ships of
the [Athenian officials called] taxiarchs, these also in single file. Behind [i.e.
in support of] these were three ships of the [other Athenian officials called]
nauarchs, and certain other allied vessels. Protomachus formed the right
wing with fifteen ships, and beside him [i.e. to his left] was Thrasyllus with a
further fifteen. Lysias was in support of Protomachus and Aristagoras of
Thrasyllus [both again presumably with fifteen ships]. This was their for-

5. For this battle see JSM (1974).

mation, so that they should not offer an opportunity for the *diekplous* since their ships were the slower.

About the tactical situation Xenophon could not be more explicit. Callicratidas' fleet, advancing with its squadrons in single file, was, as the faster, 'ready for the breakthrough and encirclement', ready in fact to challenge the Athenians at their own game. The reason why the Athenian ships were the slower on this occasion is not given, but the fact seems to have been recognised by both sides. The Athenians accordingly adopted a defensive posture, not on this occasion the circle (possibly because of the size of their fleet and its closeness to the shore), but instead a formation of squadrons in depth. The Samian ships (10) and the 'ships of the taxiarchs' (10) which formed the centre are said to be in single file. They seem in this respect to be in contrast to the four squadrons on either wing, which were then in more than one file. Similarly, when Callicratidas' squadrons are described as being 'all in single file' they are in contrast to the Athenian squadrons, of which only two are in single file. Squadrons of 15 ships may be in three files of five or five files of three; three files of five ships are likely, since the two squadrons so ordered, one in support of and behind the other, would present a formation the total depth of which would be 10 ships, matching in depth the two squadrons of 10 ships each in single file. The diagram (fig. 29) sets out the formation of the two fleets before the engagement began.

The two fleets fought for a long time, 'their ships first in a mass and then scattered, but when Callicratidas, as his ship rammed another, fell into the sea and disappeared', the Athenian right wing got the better of the Spartan left, and the Peloponnesians fled to Chios and Phocaea while the Athenians moved back to the Arginusae islands. On the Athenian side the losses were 25 ships, with their crews as well, except in a few cases, while the Spartans lost 9 of their own 10 ships and more than 60 ships of their allies. The Athenian fleet split up: 47 ships under Theramenes and Thrasybulus, both now serving as trierarchs, were detailed to go to pick up the crews of the lost ships, who were still clinging to the floating wrecks, while the rest were to relieve Conon at Mytilene. Bad weather kept both forces inactive and the crews could not be saved. The dispatch boat gave the Spartan commander at Mytilene the news of the defeat. He concealed the truth, but raised the siege and withdrew to Chios. Those

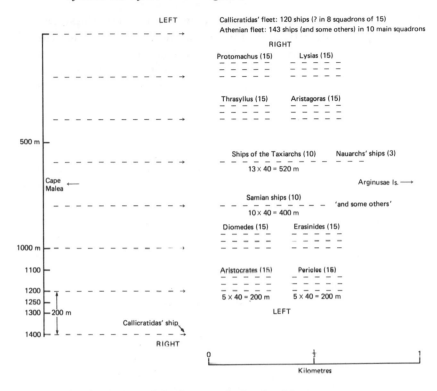

29. The disposition of the fleets at the battle of Arginusae.

of the generals that returned to Athens were charged in the Assembly with failure to rescue the crews of the lost ships and were put to death, in spite of Socrates' protests at the illegality of the trial.

The three engagements in the region of the Hellespont during the later stages of the Ionian war, which we have looked at in some detail, have considerable tactical interest. They underline the qualities of ships and seamen which gave success in all three cases to the Athenians.

The sickle-shaped formation adopted by the Persian fleet in the main engagement off Artemisium suggests an attempt, not in the event successful, to move round both flanks of a shorter enemy line of ships drawn up abreast. At Cynossema the 76 Athenian ships moving into the straits in column on the north side were met by

Mindarus' larger fleet of 86 ships moving in column on the south side in the opposite direction. As the two fleets drew level they turned and faced each other in line abreast. Taking tactical advantage of his longer line Mindarus sent his fast ships to make a *periplous* of the Athenian right wing, which had been in the rear of the column, while attacking the centre and driving it ashore. In reply the Athenians, temporarily abandoning their centre, did the unexpected and brought off a *periplous* on *both* wings, routed their opponents and then came to the rescue of their centre. Tactical skill and high performance brought them success. At Cyzicus the tactical picture was a deliberate set piece, carefully planned; but again it required high performance from ships and men.

Arginusae is of great interest because Xenophon for once gives a clear account of the dispositions and tactics on both sides. Here the Athenians, unusually, had the larger number of ships, and the Spartan ships were rated faster. The reason probably was that the Athenians were fielding a scratch fleet as regards both oarsmen and ships. They are to be seen adopting a heavily defensive posture, and sticking to it. The faster Spartan ships attacked by squadrons in single file 'ready for the breakthrough and the *periplous*' in spite of the enemy's superiority in numbers. As we have seen many times, superiority in performance was regarded as counterbalancing inferiority in numbers. For their part the Athenians adopted an interesting answer to the threat of a breakthrough, which is perhaps foreshadowed by Brasidas' formation in the second of Phormio's actions in the Gulf.

We have been able to watch the trieres in a succession of engagements during the fifth century, and to gain a clear picture of what was demanded of her designer in construction and of what was demanded of her crew in action. Good acceleration and good turning capacity were required to enable her to take the position from which she could hit her opponent most effectively. Certain conditions of hull and loading, as well as of maintenance, qualified the trieres for the rating 'fast', and the fast triereis were clearly those best able to achieve their tactical objectives in battle: in attack the breakthrough and *periplous*, quick turns, ramming and withdrawal; in defence a quick start from a stationary defensive line or circle to take advantage of targets suddenly offered. Performance of this high quality in a ship with a crew of 200 required fitness, training and discipline in the men, and in the ship the maximum lightness of build and a high standard of maintenance. These engagements also bring out clearly a rather unexpected point: the close reliance of the oared warship on support from the land and the consequent importance of the friendly shore. This point is perhaps not so unexpected if we take into account the way in which individual triereis, and trieres fleets, normally moved from place to place. This will be the subject of the next chapter.

6

NAVAL MOVEMENTS

Performance in battle was the main function of the trieres, but it was not the only one. She was the means by which Athens exerted her influence throughout the eastern Mediterranean. Fleets had to move from home port to overseas base, and from there to the areas of conflict. Sometimes triereis carried only the minimum of fighting men on board; sometimes a fleet consisted of a few triereis so manned, with the rest carrying 30 extra troops each for deployment on land, sometimes all the ships were such troop-carriers. For example (Thuc. 2.23.2), when the Spartans invaded Attica at the beginning of the Peloponnesian war in 431, Athens replied by sending a force of 100 triereis round the Peloponnese 'and on them 1,000 hoplites and 400 archers', i.e. the normal complement of armed men carried (below, p. 110). This force reached the western seaboard of the Peloponnese and Cephallenia, where it joined 50 Corcyraean ships in raids on Spartan territory. Two years later another expedition (Thuc. 2.56.2) of 100 ships was sent against the Peloponnese accompanied by 50 ships from Lesbos and Chios. On this occasion the Athenian ships carried 4,000 Athenian hoplites. Experience had presumably shown that naval confrontation was not be expected, so that the ships employed could all be troopships carrying the extra 30 men on deck. That operations on land were contemplated is shown by the inclusion in the force of 300 cavalry carried in special horse-transports.[1]

The long voyage from Piraeus round the Peloponnese to Cephallenia raises certain questions. In a speech at this time, when plague and the Spartan incursions into Attica were weakening Athenian morale, Thucydides (2.62.2) shows Pericles reminding his

---

1. See below, p. 157. Thirty horses could be carried in each horse-transport which, Thucydides says, were first on this occasion triereis suitably modified. It appears that these transports were pulled by 60 oarsmen (*IG* 2² 1628.154f.). They were probably *thranitai*.

countrymen of the power which their naval superiority gave them:

> You think that you rule only your allies,[2] but I say that of the two elements that are manifestly for our use, land and water, you are the complete masters of one in its entirety, both as you now go about it, and if in the future you should wish to go about it more widely; and no one, be it the king of Persia or any other nation in the world at present, will interfere with your movement on it with your present naval armament.

These are proud words, and Athens' resources at the time in men and ships would seem to justify them, but to understand fully what is involved in this claim, and the sense in which it may be true, we must examine, in as much detail as is possible, the logistics of the movement of triereis on active service.

When Herodotus speaks of the Greek fleet's move southward after the battles of Artemisium he says (8.22) that Themistocles took a number of the fastest ships and put in at the beaches between Aphetae and Attica where the Persian ships were likely to go ashore for drinking water. There he carved messages on the rocks urging the Ionian Greeks serving in the fleet to desert to the Greek allies, or at any rate to fight half-heartedly. The story is based on a fact, that triereis did not normally carry supplies of drinking water, even for the short run from Aphetae to Attica, but could be counted on to go ashore for it.

Piraeus to Mytilene

Going ashore for meals and bivouacking for the night was regular practice with the crews of triereis on long voyages. This is implied by the account in Thucydides (3.49) of the famous non-stop voyage (of about 184½ sea miles, 340 km) under oar from Piraeus to Mytilene in Lesbos (map 10). On the suppression of the revolt of Lesbos in 427 and the fall of Mytilene the Athenian Assembly took the decision to put to death all the men captured, and sent a trieres to tell Paches, the Athenian commander, to carry out the sentence; but on the following day they thought better of it, and

2. The members of the Delian League, formed after the repulse of the Persian invasion for the liberation of the Greeks of Asia Minor and the islands, were technically Athens' 'allies', but she now openly claimed to rule them.

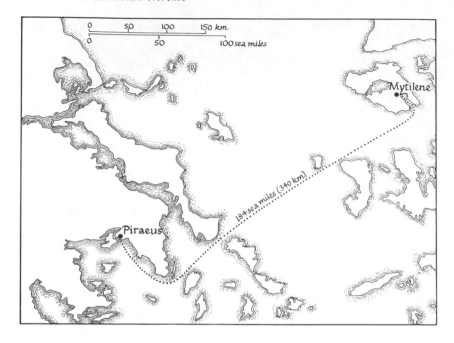

Map 10 Piraeus to Mytilene.

sent at once a second trieres as quickly as possible, in case, if the first trieres got there first, they might find the city destroyed. It had a start of about a day and a night. The Mytilenian representatives at Athens gave wine and barley bread for the ship and promised great rewards if it arrived first. The crew [of the second ship] made such haste that they [did not stop for meals but] pulled and ate at the same time, barley bread mixed with wine and olive oil, and [they did not bivouack for the night but] some slept and others pulled, turn and turn about. By good luck they had no contrary winds, and while the other ship did not make haste on such a disagreeable errand, the other hurried in the way described. The first ship did in fact arrive first by enough time to allow Paches to read the decree and start taking steps to carry it out, but the second ship put in after it and was in time to prevent the actual executions.

The story makes it quite plain that the normal practice was to take meals and sleep on land, and not to pull in shifts but all together all the time, and that to take food and drink and to sleep on board, and to pull in shifts, was a practice only justified by these special circumstances.

Chios to the Hellespont

Mindarus' dash from Chios to the Hellespont before the battle of Cynossema is a voyage described in detail by Thucydides (8.101). After leaving Chios (map 11),

they made land first in Phocaean territory at the harbour of Carterea [39 sea miles: 72 km] and took their midday meal there. Then they moved along the Cymaean coast and took their evening meal at Arginusae on the mainland opposite Mytilene [26 sea miles: 48 km]. The whole day's voyage was 65 sea miles. From there [next day] when it was still quite dark they moved along the coast and arrived at Harmatus on the mainland opposite Methymna [68 sea miles: 126.5 km], and when they had hastily taken their midday meal they proceeded along the coast to Lectum and Larisa and Hamaxitus and the places in that region, and arrived at Rhoeteum in the Hellespont before midnight [56 sea miles: 103 km]. The total distance covered in this second long day was 124 sea miles or 229 km. Some of the ships beached at Sigeum and other places nearby.

As they bivouacked and prepared their evening meal in the darkness, their camp-fires were seen by Athenian look-outs posted from Sestus.

Piraeus to Corcyra

(1) Iphicrates' voyage

If such constant reliance on the land was, as it appears to be, a feature of the voyages of fleets of triereis, as it was of their battles, the question arises how an Athenian fleet of 100 ships in 431 could move round the Peloponnese without any friendly territory to make them welcome on the many stops they would have made on the way. The account of Iphicrates' voyage to Corcyra in 372 (Xen. *HG* 6.2.27–30) gives a good indication of how such a voyage was conducted. It is described by Xenophon as an example of good leadership.

He proceeded with his journey and at the same time made all necessary preparations for action, at the outset leaving his main sails behind as if he was expecting an engagement. In addition, even if there was a following wind he used his small [boat] sails little, but progressed by oar [instead, presumably, of using main sails and boat sails when the wind was favourable]. Thus he both improved the fitness of his men and achieved a higher speed for his ships. Often, also, when he was on the point of giving his men the order to get their evening meal, he would take them out to sea in line ahead

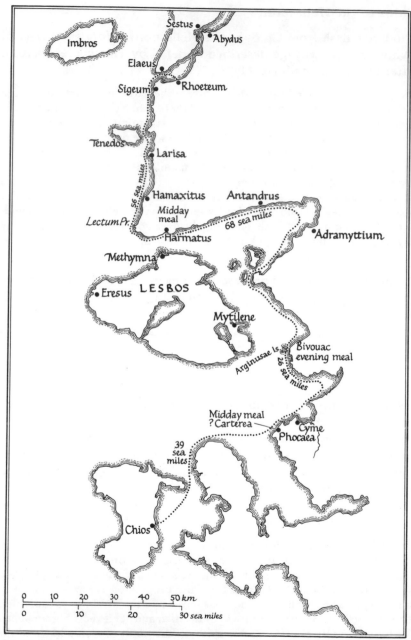

Map 11 Chios to the Hellespont.

in these regions, and turning them about and forming line abreast [the routine manoeuvre] he made them race to the shore for a prize. When they were taking their midday meal he used to set a guard on land and putting up masts in the ships he had a look-out set from them. [These would seem obvious precautions since they were in enemy territory.]

He often put to sea after the evening meal, and, if pulling was necessary, he rested the men in turn. In passage by day he proceeded, according to the signal given, sometimes in line ahead, sometimes in line abreast, so that the crews combined making progress with reaching waters dominated, as they expected, by the enemy, only after practising and learning everything that related to fighting at sea. And although they usually took their midday and evening meals in enemy territory, yet by doing only what was necessary he got to sea before enemy forces arrived, and made a quick get-away.

It looks as if the coast of the Peloponnese was thinly enough populated for it to be possible for an enemy fleet to go ashore for water, meals and bivouacking provided that precautions were taken.

What Thucydides and Xenophon do not tell us is how such fleets were victualled. Since no markets would have been open to them on the voyage round the Peloponnese, the triereis would have had either to take victuals on board or to make a rendezvous with supply ships. The former is the more probable. The Corinthian invasion fleet in 433 had taken victuals for three days when the ships left Cheimerion (above, p. 63).

(2) The Sicilian expedition

The Athenian need for bases on the Peloponnesian coast is shown by Demosthenes' occupation of Pylos, which Thucydides represents as the fortunate outcome of an Athenian fleet becoming stormbound there in 418 (4.3–4), and by his later construction of a fort, abandoned the following year, on the Peloponnesian coast opposite Cythera when *en route* for Syracuse with the relief force in 414 (Thuc. 7.26.2, and 8.4).

At any rate, however the victualling was effected in 431 on what was soon to become a routine voyage for Athenian fleets, Thucydides gives no hint about it in relating the first stage of the voyage of the fleet of triereis in the Sicilian expedition of 415. He says that the supply ships and other triereis assembled at Corcyra. It seems likely then that the main fleet of triereis carried their victuals on board for the four or five days the voyage from Piraeus to Corcyra would have taken. They would of course have gone ashore for water, for the preparation of meals and for bivouacking at night. Where they could do this safely would have been by now well known to Athenian commanders.

Corcyra to Rhegium

Thucydides interrupts his narrative of the preparations for the Sicilian expedition (map 12) with an account (6.33–4) of a debate at Syracuse about the prospects of invasion, in which the Syracusan statesman Hermocrates is shown putting forward a plan to deter the invading force before it reached Italy. He suggested the dispatch of a

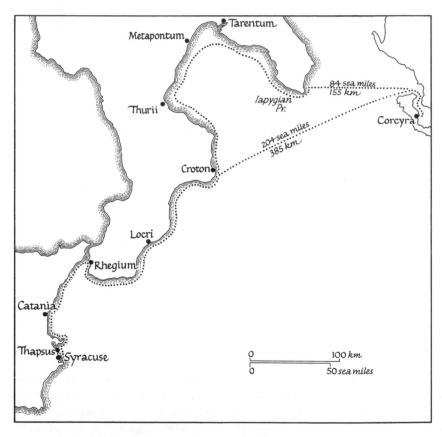

Map 12 Corcyra to Rhegium.

Syracusan naval force with two months' victuals (necessarily carried in supply ships) to Tarentum. 'The open sea', he said,

is wide for them [i.e. the Athenians] to cross all together. It would be hard for them to keep formation [i.e. in column] in the long crossing [of 84 sea miles]; and so moving slowly and arriving in small groups, they would be easy to attack. If on the other hand they were to invade with the fast ships in a closer formation cleared for action, then if they use their oars [for the crossing] we should be making our attack on them when they are tired after the crossing. Alternatively, if they took the decision not to cross under oar but under sail, we could withdraw to Tarentum; and they, after making the crossing with a small amount of victuals as men going into battle, would be at a loss for food in an uninhabited area. Either they would stop where they were and be besieged, or, after attempting to move along the coast they would distance themselves from the rest of the expedition [at Corcyra] and their morale would be low since they would have no sure knowledge about the position of the cities [of the region] whether they would take them in or not.

Hermocrates' conclusion was that, faced with these alternatives, the Athenian force would not even set out from Corcyra.

The strategic analysis which Thucydides puts into Hermocrates' mouth is penetrating and throws a clear light on the limitations of the trieres as an all-purpose warship. The distance from Corcyra to the heel of Italy is about 155 km or 84 sea miles, not much more than half the distance which could be covered by a trieres comfortably under oar 'in a long day' (see n. 4 below) but the oarsmen would be in no shape for a battle on arrival. The fleet, it must be remembered, consisted of three main elements, the fast ships, the troopships and other oared vessels (smaller than triereis) with the merchantmen, which in a crossing under oar they would have taken in tow. Whether the fleet moved under oar or under sail, the crossing would be slow and the ships would inevitably split up into small groups, any of which would be an easy prey for a squadron of fast triereis operating out of the nearby base of Tarentum. The alternative was for the 60 fast ships to make the crossing by themselves, cleared for action, with the intention of destroying the opposing fast squadron and clearing the way for a safe crossing by the rest of the fleet. But after a day at the oar the oarsmen of the fast triereis would arrive tired and be faced by Syracusan ships with fresh crews. If the Athenian fast ships waited for a favourable wind and crossed under sail, the

Syracusans could refuse battle, and the Athenian ships, without supplies, would have nowhere to go for victuals since the supply ships would have been left behind. If they bivouacked the Syracusans could besiege them; if they pressed on they would become further and further separated from the rest of the fleet (and their supplies), and would have no prospect of receiving hospitality from any city. The logic was good, but the Syracusans were not so convinced of the urgency as to adopt his plan.

The first thing which it is interesting to observe is that the direct route of 204 sea miles from Corcyra to Croton is clearly beyond the capacity of a trieres. Even the shorter route to the Iapygian promontory is a 'long crossing' for such a ship.

The analysis is clear evidence that a fast trieres cleared for action carried only the minimum of victuals, i.e. for one day. If not cleared for battle (and thus not in a position to achieve the highest performance of which it was capable) it might carry provisions for a longer period, but the normal source of victualling for triereis on the move was either a supply ship or a market in a friendly city. The crew had, as we shall see, a victualling allowance for the purchase of food. In this analysis of the capability of a trieres under oar, the fatigue factor is also emphasised.

The Athenian fleet, after the routine voyage of about 390 sea miles round the Peloponnese, duly met the rest of the allies and the support vessels at Corcyra. The fleet was divided into three squadrons sailing separately 'so that they might not sailing together make difficulties in procuring water and harbours and provisions'. This is a revealing sentence. Three triereis were then sent on ahead to find out which cities in southern Italy and Sicily would make them welcome (6.42–4).

All the ships began together to cross the Ionian sea to Italy; and when they reached the Iapygian promontory [the heel of Italy] or Tarentum, or where each happened to make a landfall, they made their way along the Italian coast, the cities refusing them admittance to market or town, but allowing them water and beaching facilities, Tarentum and Locri not admitting them even to these, until they came to Rhegium [the toe of Italy]. And they now mustered their forces there, and since the Rhegines did not admit them to the town, they constructed a camp in the precinct of Artemis, where the Rhegines provided a market for them, and they hauled their ships out of water there and rested.

The distance from Corcyra to Rhegium is about 375 sea miles or 680 km.

The speed of triereis

The speed of a trieres on the move from place to place deserves some consideration. When conditions were favourable sails were certainly used since sails were carried, but passage under oar was regarded as faster.[3] The most specific statement about the speed of a trieres under oar is given by Xenophon, who states that the passage from Byzantium to Heraclea on the southern coast of the Black Sea, a distance of about 129 sea miles (236 km), was 'a long day's voyage[4] for a trieres under oar' (map 13). Since, as we have seen (above, p. 97), a fleet in a hurry would put out before dawn and arrive after dark, a 'long day' can be taken as 16 to 18 hours. With a break for the midday meal of one to two hours, depending on the degree of haste, the two periods of pulling may have been 8½ to 7 hours long. On Xenophon's Byzantium–Heraclea run of 129 sea miles there is no indication of haste. With a 17-hour 'long day' and a 2-hour break the average speed works out at 8.6 knots. If the working day was longer or the break shorter, or both, the speed would have been correspondingly less. It appears[5] that although there is a westward current in the Bosporus strait there is a current eastwards under normal conditions along the southern coast of the Black Sea. This factor may therefore be discounted.

Mention has already been made (above, pp. 95–6) of the famous non-stop voyage from Piraeus to Mytilene in 427, preceded by the more leisurely voyage of the ship which set out the day before. The precise time each ship took is not given by Thucydides, and there is therefore no accurate basis for calculating the speed of either ship.

3. Xenophon (above, p. 97) says that Iphicrates in his voyage round the Peloponnese achieved a higher speed for his ships by proceeding under oar. In *The Greek Trireme* (1984) one of the 'historical requirements for the reconstruction of the trieres' is said to be: '(9) to carry sail for oars to be used in passage only in sufficient or contrary winds'. It seems that we should now add: 'or when the ship was in a hurry'.
4. Xen. *Anab.* 6.4.2. It is interesting to note that in one manuscript the reading was 'a very long day'. The scribe may have been a Byzantine who knew what he was talking about.
5. This information emerged in the *Times* correspondence mentioned above, p. xvi.

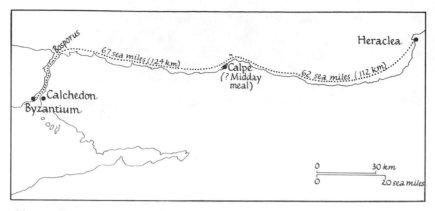

Map 13 Byzantium to Heraclea.

The distance between the two places is about 184½ sea miles (340 km) by the most direct route (map 10). We may guess that the first ship set out at about midday on the day the Assembly (which began its meetings in the early morning), no doubt after some discussion, passed the decree. She arrived at about midday on the third day, spending 24 hours at sea and two nights and one midday break on land. On this calculation she made a speed of about 7.7 knots when at sea. The second ship might have taken 24 hours in all, the oarsmen under pressure pulling their oars in shifts at the same average speed as the first ship. Compared with the trieres in Xenophon's voyage, the first ship, under no pressure, was certainly on the slow side, while the second ship did well to keep up the same speed as the first ship for twenty-four hours.

Mention has also been made (pp. 85–7) of Mindarus' dash from Chios to Rhoeteum before the battle of Cynossema. This is the most detailed account we possess of a naval movement by a fleet of triereis (map 11). Thucydides gives the details because he had the means of knowing them, and because it was a remarkably fast passage of about 190 sea miles in two days, one of them a very long one. Since the fleet was in a hurry it certainly moved under oar. The second day's pulling, of about 124 sea miles (229 km), starting well before dawn, say 5.30 a.m. and ending 'before midnight', say 11.30 p.m., was a 'long day' of 18 hours in which perhaps as little as one hour can be allowed for a 'hastily taken' midday meal. With two continuous periods of 9 hours' pulling and an overall distance of 124 sea miles the average speed works out at 6.9 knots. If the midday break was longer or if the day started later or finished earlier, both of which are perhaps likely, the average speed would have been higher (e.g. 7.3 in 17 hours' and 7.7 in 16 hours' pulling), but it should be remembered that this is a movement of a whole fleet, where the speed is the pace of the slowest, and not of a single ship, as the other voyages were.

The first stage of the voyage of the Athenian fleet on the Sicilian expedition (map 2), the 390 sea miles from Piraeus to Corcyra, appears to have been taken by triereis alone, unaccompanied by supply ships, and is likely to have been made under oar, since that was faster, and the ships would have needed to keep together off enemy territory. On the assumption of a speed of seven knots and a sixteen-hour day, including a midday break of two hours, a day's passage would have been just under 100 miles and the total time taken four days. The next stage, on which the triereis were joined by supply ships, of 376 sea miles from Corcyra to Rhegium (map 12), would have been taken much more slowly. In the first stage the crews would have been able to exist on the victuals they took with them; in the second, after the 84 sea mile crossing in the open sea to the heel of Italy when the triereis again would have taken their own victuals, the triereis would have had to wait for the supply ships making their way under sail or oar to victual them for the rest of the voyage. On this stretch the speed of the expedition would have been that of the slowest, i.e. about 5 knots. If that is taken as the average speed for the whole of the second stage to Rhegium, the second part of the voyage would have taken 5–6 days. Allowing then 3 or 4 days for the muster of the fleet at Corcyra, the whole voyage from Piraeus to Rhegium, for each of the three divisions of the fleet sailing at intervals one after the other, may have been completed in 14 days, given favourable winds. Unfavourable conditions, of which there is in fact no mention, could have delayed the fleet at any point, but particularly when it was accompanied by supply ships on the second stage.

It is interesting to compare, in point of speed, the account in Xenophon (*HG* 2.1.30) of another fast voyage, probably not by a trieres. After Aegospotami Lysander sent news of his victory to Sparta by a Milesian 'pirate'. His ship may have been a pentecontor or a hemiolia.[6] He arrived 'on the third day'. Since he must have started fairly late on the first day, he appears to have covered the distance, of about 390 sea miles from Aegospotami to Gytheum, in less than 48 hours at an average speed of just over eight knots. It must be assumed that the ship was pulled continuously, since even if only one stop was made the speed would have been impossibly high.

It looks as if eight knots was a possible average speed for an oared warship in a hurry, but that the normal speed was less. There is no recorded example of a voyage in which sail and oar were used together.

6. See JSM (1980a) where it is suggested that, since the word *hemiolios* means 1½, the hemiolia was a ship with three files of oars ranging fore and aft throughout the ship at one level, i.e. 1½ files on each side. Half the oars would be pulled by one oarsman and the other half by two.

7
THE MEN

In chapters 3–6 we have observed the trieres through the eyes of contemporary writers as she took part in actions and moved from place to place on passage, and we have formed an idea of the nature of her performance under these conditions. The next step is to focus more closely on the ship herself, to see her, as it were, from the inside. First, in the present chapter, we shall identify the different sorts of men who went to sea in her and worked the fleets of triereis in the fifth and fourth centuries. Then in the following chapter we shall concentrate on the structure of the ship as it is to be seen in contemporary literature and deduced from the relevant archaeological material.

Overall number of crew

The number of men who formed the crew of a trieres is given in several historical passages spanning our period. In Herodotus (3.13.1–2), the Mytilenian ship with a crew of 200 which took part in Cambyses' invasion of Egypt (525 BC) can hardly be other than a trieres, since no other type of ship in service at the time could have had a crew of nearly that size. Later Herodotus gives (7.184.1) the number of men in the native crews of the 1,207 ships of the Persian invasion force in 480 as 241,000 and says that he calculated on the basis of 200 in each ship. The 30 extra Persian troops were in addition to the native crews. It seems to have been the same on the Greek side. When Cleinias joined the Greek fleet at Artemisium he was said (8.17)[1] to have brought his own ship and a crew of 200, and

1. H. T. Wallinga (1982) says p. 465: 'it would be rash to consider Kleinias' crew as typical' and argues that triereis were normally undermanned. I do not find his detailed arguments convincing, and in general it seems unlikely that the Greeks should go to the trouble of devising a complicated oared ship in which the maximum number of men was packed into the minimum space and then regularly leave it undermanned. Cleinias' ship was not of course one of those which were the subject of the Decree of Themistocles'.

later in the fifth century (Thuc. 6.8, 8.29.2) the pay of a ship's company is calculated on the basis of a crew of the same number. In the next century the maintenance allowance of the crew of a fast trieres is worked out by Demosthenes (4.28) on a similar basis. It is, incidentally, interesting to notice that the pay of all members of the crew was the same, in spite of the difference of status which we shall observe (below, p. 110) between some members and others. The conclusion is safe that throughout the period of which we are speaking a full-strength trieres, not carrying extra troops, had a crew of 200 men besides the trierarch.

The 'Decree of Themistocles'

Of all the documents of Greek history which have been preserved the most vivid, and the most interesting, by reason of the occasion as well as of the particularity of the information it gives, is 'the Decree of Themistocles'. Inverted commas are necessary because the inscription we have is thought to record not the actual decree but a literary version of it current in the fourth century.[2] It records the measures taken by the Athenian Assembly in 481 to meet the threatened Persian invasion. These measures, which were put forward by Themistocles, include the mobilisation of the fleet and contain information which is likely to be reliable about the manning of the trieres in the fifth century and is certainly a reliable guide to the manning of the trieres in the fourth century. The document may be used here as a framework for treating the commander and the various components of a trieres' crew.

After provision for the evacuation of Attica, the following instructions are given to the *strategoi*, the annually elected officers whom we usually call 'generals' but who commanded the armed forces of the city of Athens both by sea and land:

Trierarchs (sea-captains) (lines 18–23)
The generals are to appoint as from the following day two hundred suitably qualified trierarchs, one for each ship, and to assign the ships to them by lot. The qualifications are the possession of land and a house in Attica, children born in wedlock, age not over fifty.

2. Meiggs–Lewis: no. 23. I use the text of N. G. L. Hammond (1982) pp. 84, 85, 86 and 88, which is Meiggs–Lewis' 'but without their restorations'. For it as a literary version see Hammond's note 33 p. 83.

At a later date service as a trierarch was a public duty, lasting a year and laid on citizens of a high property rating, although, as we shall see (p. 121), a patriotic citizen could volunteer for the office. The trierarch was issued with a ship, probably, as here, by lot. He could draw the gear, for which he was personally responsible, from the public store, or he could provide his own. Pay and an allowance for victuals was in theory provided by the city through the fleet commander, but, as we shall see (pp. 120–7), the trierarch was responsible for keeping his ship at sea and felt obliged to meet these expenses from his own pocket, if the money was not forthcoming from the commander (below, p. 123). What the responsibility of the trierarch was in 480 is uncertain. Cleinias was able to provide a ship and pay the crew from his own resources, but he came from one of the richest families in Athens and the case is mentioned because it was exceptional. The allocation of ships to trierarchs by lot seems to have continued, since in the naval inventories of the last half of the fourth century ships are specified as having been allocated by lot to a trierarch or not so allocated.

There follows a section dealing with the crew in three divisions. A similar division of a trieres' crew into three occurs in a fourth-century speech written for an Athenian audience and concerned with naval matters ([Dem.] 50: below, pp. 120–7). The categories are (1) hoplites carried on deck (*epibatai*), (2) auxiliaries (*hyperesia*), and (3) oarsmen (*nautai, pleroma* and, once, *trierarchema*).

Deck soldiers (epibatai) and archers (toxotai) (lines 23–6)
The generals are to call up the *epibatai*, ten for each ship, aged between twenty and thirty, and four archers.

Nothing is said about their allocation to ships, for the reason that they are both reckoned for this purpose as part of the *hypēresia,*[3] and as such are covered by the following sentence dealing with the allocation of the *hypēresia* as a whole to their ships by lot. That the *epibatai* were soldiers, carried on deck and nowhere else in the ship, is shown elsewhere and in particular by a story in Herodotus (8.118–19: pp. 131–2), the point of which is that certain Persian notables, specifically called *epibatai*, were being carried on deck. The *epibatai*, who were, unlike the Persian notables, soldiers, had only a secon-

---

3. See JSM (1984a) p. 50. Also Neil Robertson (1982).

dary function in battle, since the ram was the main offensive weapon, and would fight at sea only if, after ramming, the ship was for some reason unable to back off. We hear of them fighting on land.[4] It is possible that their principal function was disciplinary (i.e. to support the authority of the trierarch) since Aristotle (*Politics* VII.5.7, 1327b) speaks of them as 'controlling the ship'. It is difficult to see the extra Persian soldiers on the ships of the Persian invasion fleet having any other purpose than to enforce discipline and prevent desertion. They were not like the extra troops on the later troop-carriers, who had to be taken by sea to the scene of intended action, since the Persian fleet was accompanied by a large army moving by land.

The ten *epibatai* had the highest status in the ship after the trierarch. They are mentioned second in the decree, and this is the position they occupy in the crew-lists in inscriptions from the beginning of the fourth century.[5] They join the trierarchs in pouring libations at the ceremonial departure of the Sicilian expedition (Thuc. 6.32.1). When in 426 the general Demosthenes lost 120 of his 300 *epibatai* from 30 triereis employed as a land force in Aetolia, Thucydides comments (3.94–8): 'so great a number of men all of the same age perished there, the best men in truth whom the city of Athens lost in this war', which suggests that the *epibatai* were in physique an élite force.

The four archers are distinct from the ten *epibatai*, i.e. they were not carried on deck. Since an inscription of *c*. 412–411[6] gives them a descriptive adjective *paredroi*, 'sitting beside', it may be that they were posted in the stern beside the trierarch and helmsman and acted as their bodyguard in an action. The latter would certainly have been vulnerable and would have needed protection, being too busy to defend himself. Four seems to have continued to be the regulation number in the fifth century (e.g. Thuc. 2.23.2), although the crew-lists in the fourth century often give only two or three. One (*IG* 2² 1951, 82ff.) records 11 *epibatai* and 3 *toxotai*. The 400 non-Cretan archers listed as part of the Sicilian expedition (Thuc. 6.43) were presumably serving in the usual details of four on each of the 100 Athenian triereis.

---

4. E.g. in Demosthenes' expedition to Aetolia mentioned below.
5. *IG* 2² 1951.79–82.   6. *IG* 1² 950.137.

Hypēresiai (lines 26–7)

The generals are to assign by lot also [i.e. as well as the trierarchs] the *hypēresiai* to the ships at such time as they allocated the trierarchs by lot (to the ships).

Examination of the use of the word '*hypēresia*' in naval contexts in the fifth and fourth centuries[7] leads to the conclusion that it stands for a group of men on board a trieres who are regarded as assistants to the trierarch. This group in the fourth century sometimes includes the *epibatai*, and always includes the archers. Here the two are mentioned separately; but since nothing is said about their allocation by lot to the ships, it seems that they are included for this purpose with the rest of the *hypēresia*. The *hypēresia* is always distinct from the oarsmen (*nautai*). For example, in the description of the preparation of the Sicilian expedition Thucydides makes the distinction twice in succeeding sentences (6.31.3):

The fleet was elaborately fitted out at great expense to the trierarchs and to the city. The public treasury gave a drachma a day to each oarsman and provided empty hulls, sixty fast and forty troop-carriers and the strongest *hypēresia* for [each of] these. In addition the trierarchs gave bonuses to the *thranitai* among the oarsmen (*nautai*) and to the *hypēresiai*.

We have seen that the regular *epibatai* on a trieres numbered ten, and the archers usually four. The total number of oarsmen is nowhere given, but the naval inventories (below, p. 137) give the number of oars, apart from spares, as 170. Since there is a passage in Thucydides (2.93.2) which shows conclusively that each oarsman in a trieres pulled his own oar, the total number of oarsmen must also be 170. It follows that the number of men in the *hypēresia* was 200 less 170, i.e. 30: 16 in addition to the 10 *epibatai* and 4 archers. Five of these are identified in the work of an anonymous author writing about 430 BC ([Xen.] *Const. of Athenians* 1.2) in Athens. Speaking of the men 'who give the city its power', in addition to the ordinary citizens, the *dēmos*, who pull the oars, he mentions by name the helmsman (*kubernētēs*), the boatswain (*keleustēs*), the purser (*pentēkontarchos*), the bow officer (*prōrates*) and the shipwright (*naupēgos*). An inscription[8] adds a sixth, the pipeman (*aulētēs*).

7. See JSM (1984) p. 50.   8. *IG* 2[2] 1951.94–105.

The helmsman was, naturally, an important person, equivalent to the master in a modern ship and ranking sometimes with the trierarch and *epibatai*. He was in complete charge of navigation under oar and sail, assisted principally by the bow officer (fig. 30). In Plato (*Alc.* I.125C) the art of helmsmanship is said to be to give orders to the boatswain, whose business it was to manage the oarsmen and get the best out of them. A passage in Xenophon (*Oecon.* 21.3) illustrates the boatswain's job vividly:

On a trieres when the ship is at sea and the oarsmen have to make a day's voyage under oar, some boatswains can say and do the sort of thing that stimulates the men to work with a good heart, but some are so tactless that it takes them twice the time to complete the same voyage. In the first case the boatswain and oarsmen come ashore sweating and congratulating each other, in the other they come in cold, hating their foreman and hated by him.

A sixth-century vase-painting of a 20-oared ship under oar gives a good picture of the boatswain (as well as the bow officer) looking astern to the helmsman for orders (fig. 31).

The name *pentēkontarchos* looks like a traditional one and gives no clue to his duties. To judge from the duties attributed to him in the speech *Against Polycles* (below, p. 124) he seems to have been a sort of captain's secretary or purser, ranking next to the helmsman and put in charge of purchases and expenditure. The function of a shipwright in a large wooden ship on active service needs no elaboration. There is a reference to the pipeman in Euripides (*Electra* 432) where the chorus sing of the dolphins who love the pipe plunging in time with its music. His position in the ship may be indicated by another passage of Euripides (*Hypsipyle* 61–7) where Orpheus the musician of the Argonauts plays his lute at the foot of the mast. The *aulētēs* seems likely to have set the rhythm for the oar-beat on a long pull, increasing or decreasing the rate of striking as the helmsman required.

There remain ten members of the *hypēresia* to be accounted for. Men would have been needed to work the ship under sail. There were two sails, the main sail amidships and the 'boat' sail forward (pp. 176–9), and there seems to be a reference to two parties, one under the orders of the helmsman and the other under the orders of the bow officer. Xenophon (*Anab.* 5.8.20) describes how 'in a storm with

30. Attic black-figure cup signed by Nicosthenes showing two oared warships with helmsman and bow officer, *c.* 530–510 BC.

31. Attic black-figure hydria showing an oared warship with helmsman, boatswain and bow officer, 570–550 BC.

a high sea running, because of a mere nod the bow officer gets angry with those in the bows and the helmsman gets angry with those in the stern'. Since helmsman and bow officer are on the stern and bow platforms respectively, the parties must also be based there. The existence of such bow and stern parties is confirmed in a later source,[9] probably relating to a tetreres in the Rhodian navy. They number five in each case. The sails of a tetreres are not likely to have required

9. See JSM (1984a) p. 56 note 21.

more men to work them than the sails of a trieres. We can then safely identify the remaining ten men of the *hypēresia* as belonging to such gangs. When not needed to work the sails they could be employed as spare oarsmen, to take the tiller or bail the ship. These were the men on the Peloponnesian ships in Phormio's first action in the gulf of Corinth who used poles to keep the ships from colliding with each other 'and shouted and abused each other' (see above, p. 70).

In his speech to the Athenian Assembly in 432 Pericles identifies (Thuc. 1.143.1) an important source of Athens' strength: 'the helmsmen we have in the fleet are Athenian citizens, and the *hypēresiai* also, whom we employ are in greater number and of better quality than the *hypēresiai* of all the rest of Greece'. When her navy was destroyed in 404 she exported these skilled personnel to Phormio's son Conon in Asia Minor, and in the fourth century we find them going as mercenaries to Syracuse and the Bosporan kingdom.[10]

[Oarsmen (nautai)] (lines 27–38)
The generals are to write up on the white boards also [i.e. as well as writing up there the trierarchs and *hypēresiai* whom they have allocated by lot to the ships] the [oarsmen][11] by ship: the Athenians from the deme registers and the foreigners from the lists of the polemarchs. They are to write them up, distributing the men in companies (*taxeis*) to the number of two hundred (companies) in divisions of a hundred in number and to write at the head of each company (*taxis*) the name of the trieres and of the trierarch and of [each member of] the *hypēresia*, so that they [i.e. the oarsmen whose names are thus posted] may know onto which trieres each company [of oarsmen] is to embark. When all the companies [of oarsmen] are made up and assigned to the triereis by lot, the Council and the generals are to man all the two hundred ships, making sacrifices ... And when the ships are manned the generals are to send help to Artemisium in Euboea with one division of a hundred ships, and with the (other) hundred ships they are to take stations around Salamis and the rest of Attica, and mount guard.

The orders to the generals in respect of the oarsmen are clear enough. Two hundred oarcrews (*taxeis*) are to be formed and are to be allocated by lot to the two hundred ships like the trierarchs and *hypēresiai* previously mentioned. The number of oarsmen in each *taxis* is not mentioned since it is constant (determined by the oar-

---

10. *IG* 2² 212: 346 B.C.
11. There is a gap in the inscription here which can neatly accommodate *tous nautas* (the oarsmen, acc.). In this context the supplement is virtually certain, as is *taxei* (dat.) in the gap of five letters five lines below.

system of a trieres) and would be a matter of common knowledge. The ships are in two divisions, each 100 strong and with a separate mission, one to go north to the tip of Euboea to meet Persian ships coming down from the north and the other to mount guard in home waters against any Persian squadron coming, as the first Persian invasion had come, across the Aegean.

The oarsmen fall into two categories, Athenian citizens and foreigners. It must be assumed that the Plataeans and Chalcidians who helped to man the 200 Athenian ships (Hdt. 8.1.1–2) fell into the latter category. Athens' decision to develop a large fleet of triereis in the few years before 481 must have involved a deliberate and irreversible switch of her manpower to the navy, and even then she was unable to man all the ships herself. It must also have involved a considerable training programme in oarsmanship. It seems clear that the oarsmen in the trieres fleets of the fifth and fourth centuries were very much a specialist cadre. Only in exceptional circumstances was an oarsman used as a fighting man on land. In 428 Athenian naval resources were fully stretched, with 200 triereis at sea in home waters, another force raiding the Peloponnese and some ships also probably in northern waters, as well as 40 ships sent to Lesbos to avert a threatened revolt. It is therefore no wonder that when reinforcements had to be sent to Lesbos they included 1,000 hoplites who also served as oarsmen. Thucydides here (3.18.4) uses the word *auteretai*, which he had used before only of the Greeks at Troy. In Homeric conditions such a thing was normal, but it was highly abnormal in the fifth century.[12] Again, later in the same year, in the final assault on the Spartans trapped on the island of Sphacteria the Athenians used some of their oarsmen as light-armed troops (all except the *thalamioi*)[13] (4.32.2), and in 409 the Athenian general Thrasyllus setting out from Athens for the Ionian war equipped 5,000 of his 8,500 oarsmen with light weapons. These are the exceptions which prove the rule, that oarsmen were specialists, too valuable to be risked in battle.

The skill of pulling an oar in a trieres was a matter of hard training

---

12. At 6.91.4 Alcibiades suggests to the Spartans that they should adopt the same emergency practice in sending help to Syracuse.
13 *Thalamios* is correct for the oarsman (*not thalamites*, a word which only appears in a scholium on Aristophanes, *Frogs* 1074, but constantly turns up as 'thalamite' in modern contexts (below p. 139 n.8).

and constant practice. Before the outbreak of the war with Athens Thucydides (1.80.4) makes the Spartan king Archidamus admit to his countrymen that they were inferior to the Athenians at sea, and that 'if we train and make preparations to meet the Athenians at sea, that will take time', while Pericles is represented (1.142.6–9) as making this comment to the Athenians:

As for the Peloponnesians gaining knowledge of seamanship, that will not come easily to them. If you, who have practised since the Persian wars, have still not brought your skill to perfection, how can men achieve anything who are farmers . . .? The fact is that sea power is a matter of skill, like everything else, and it is not possible to get practice in the odd moment when the chance occurs, but it is a full-time occupation, leaving no moment for other things.

What happened with unskilled oarsmen is shown in Phormio's first engagement in the gulf of Corinth. When the water got rough they were unable to recover their oars after the stroke (2.84.3). The historians often remind us that the oarsman's skill was only maintained by constant practice. For example, in the winter of 426 when the Athenians for once had only a few ships in commission – a small force in Sicily and 20 ships moving round the Peloponnese on their way to Naupactus – they manned 40 ships to send to Sicily, 'partly', Thucydides says, 'because they would thus, they thought, bring the war in Sicily to an end more quickly, and partly because they needed to exercise their naval forces' (3.115.4). When Mindarus was preparing his fleet for battle with the Athenians in the Hellespont in 411, Diodorus (13.39.3) says that he spent five days 'carrying out manoeuvres and training his men'. And Xenophon's account (*HG* 6.2.27–30) of Iphicrates' voyage from Piraeus to Corcyra in 374 emphasises its aspect as a training exercise. It was probably the lack of skilled oarsmen in the second and third quarters of the fourth century which led to the adoption by the aspirants to sea power of ships with a less demanding oarsystem, carrying out tactics which also demanded less of the oarsmen whom they had managed to recruit.

Pericles' assertion of Athenian skill in seamanship at the oar and at the helm is confirmed by the anonymous author (1.19) already quoted (above, pp. 111–12):

The Athenians, because of their overseas possessions and the public offices they hold abroad, learn to use the oar as second nature, both themselves and their attendants. In fact when a man is often at sea he must of necessity take an oar himself and likewise his slave, and learn the language of the sea. The majority are able to pull an oar when first they set foot aboard a warship, having had the preliminary training man and boy up to that moment.

This passage gives a glimpse of the background to Athenian naval expertise. The picture is 50 years later than Themistocles' mobilisation decree, and even now, Pericles reminds his hearers, Athenian skill has not yet been brought to perfection. In 481 she was at the beginning of her naval programme, but had already taken decisive steps.

So much, then, for the citizens whom the generals were instructed to call up for naval service. Who were the foreigners who were also to be called up – those 'on the lists of the polemarchs'? The polemarchs were state officials who are known later to have had some legal functions in connection with the resident aliens. In the speech from which quotation has been made above Pericles in 432 claimed that were the foreign oarsmen in the Athenian fleet to be lured away to the fleets of her enemies by higher pay the Athenians themselves and their resident aliens could fill their places on the oar-benches. It seems, therefore, that the foreigners on the lists of the polemarchs are probably resident aliens for the most part, but also the Plataeans and Chalcidians who were manning Athenian ships. The foreigners whom the Spartans might lure away with higher pay in 432 are a different category, which did not exist in 481. Pericles continued: 'when it came to the point none of the foreigners whom we employ would accept exile from his country and on top of that service on the side [i.e. the Spartan] with a smaller prospect of winning the battle, all for the sake of a few days' higher pay'. From such words it is plain that these foreigners in the fleet are men from the cities of the Athenian empire on whom she could enforce the penalty of exile if they defected.

An interesting insight into the composition of Athenian oarcrews is given by a passage in the letter of Nicias reporting from the Athenian camp before Syracuse to the Athenian Assembly in 414 (Thuc.7.13). He gives the reasons why his oarcrews are not now up to strength: enemy cavalry raids on foragers, desertion of retainers, repatriation of pressed mercenaries, defection or desertion of volunteer mercenaries (who had been attracted to Athenian service by the high rates of pay), and lastly the fact that some oarsmen had persuaded the trierarchs to accept as substitutes for themselves slaves captured at Hyccara (earlier in the year on the north coast of Sicily) and had thus impaired the fleet's efficiency. We have already seen an indication that attendants had an opportunity to learn to pull an oar like their masters, when travelling abroad, and were sometimes called upon to do so. The retainers who are here said to have deserted were probably such servants, and in both cases they seem likely to have been slaves. It is not their lack of skill but their desertion which Nicias notes as damaging. The Hyccaran slaves on the other hand lacked the necessary skill, and it appears that their being accepted as substitutes for their masters rested on the decision of the trierarch. Slave oarsmen were unusual in Athenian ships at this time, but they are sometimes to be found and they were not always lacking in skill. When the Athenians were hard pressed to relieve Conon at Mytilene in 406, they promised freedom to the slaves who served in the ships they sent.[14] Such an incident clearly indicates that their service in the fleet was unusual. Isocrates exaggerates for the sake of an epigram when he writes in 355 (8.48.2): 'Then [when we had an empire], if we manned triereis, we sent foreigners and slaves aboard to serve as oarsmen but citizens to serve under arms [i.e. as *epibatai*, of superior status]. Now we use foreigners as hoplites [i.e. *epibatai*] and compel our citizens to pull an oar.' Slave oarsmen were, however, used in large numbers by the Corcyraeans at Sybota, since out of 1,050 prisoners taken by the Corinthians in the battle 800 were slaves (Thuc. 1.55.1), and we hear later of slave oarsmen on Chian ships (Thuc. 8.15.2). There were certainly no slaves among the oarsmen called up under the Decree of Themistocles.

Pay

The decree makes no mention of the pay for naval service and nothing is known about it at this date. It is probable that the crews served without payment, as part of the duty required of citizens and resident aliens of Athens, but crews serving away from home are likely to have received maintenance. Later there was both pay and a main-

14 *IG* 2² 1951.117, Xen. *HG* 1.6.24.

tenance allowance. At the beginning of the Peloponnesian War, as we have seen, Athens' enemies could talk of luring away her oarsmen by promise of high rates of pay. And the Egestaeans in Sicily encouraged Athens' intervention in the island by sending a month's pay for the ships, which can be worked out as one drachma a day for each of the 200 men on each ship, the same for the whole ship's company irrespective of status. This appears to have been a high rate, since in the account of the expedition Thucydides says (6.31.3) that 'it was equipped at great expense by the trierarchs and by the city, the treasury paying a drachma a day for each oarsman . . . as well as supplying *hypēresiai* of the very best, while the trierarchs for their part gave an additional bonus to the *thranitai* among the oarsmen in addition to the pay from the treasury'.

How the city 'supplied *hypēresiai* of the very best' is obscure, but there is evidence later[15] that the city had some sort of control over skilled naval personnel, since *hypēresiai* recruited for service abroad by the Bosporan kings in 346 are 'granted' to them by decree of the Athenian Council. In view of what is said immediately afterwards about bonuses given by the trierarchs to the *thranitai*, Thucydides would certainly have mentioned it if 'supplying' *hypēresiai* had involved bonuses. It seems likely, then, that the city paid a flat rate of pay to all the ship's company and that if any bonuses were paid in the interests of the ship's efficiency they came out of the trierarch's pocket. Lysias says (21.10) that for the whole period of his trierarchy (before 405) he employed the foremost Greek helmsman Phantias, 'persuading him with money'. And we shall see how much 'persuasion with money' was incumbent upon an Athenian trierarch in the middle of the next century if he was to maintain an efficient ship (below, pp. 120–7).

Only half the rate of a drachma a day was actually payable to Athenian crews while on active service; the rest became due when the ship was paid off in Piraeus. Thucydides (8.45.2) tells how Alcibiades in exile in 412/11 advised the Persian governor Tissaphernes, who was then the paymaster of a Spartan fleet operating on the coast of Asia Minor, to 'cut down the pay of the Spartan seamen so that instead of an Attic drachma a day only 3 obols (½ dr.) were given', i.e. he advised him to adopt the Athenian system of giving

15 See JSM (1984a) p. 54.

half-pay to seamen abroad. The reasons Alcibiades gives are likely to
be the reasons behind the Athenian system. He told Tissaphernes to
tell the Spartan commanders that

the Athenians, who had had experience of naval matters a longer time than
they, gave only three obols to their men not so much for lack of money as
with the intention of keeping their oarsmen from becoming well-off and
above themselves. [If given full pay] some were likely to become unfit by
spending their money on things which made them sick, others would desert
because they had no balance of pay, as a kind of hostage, to look
forward to.

Athenian trierarchs, who had to recruit oarsmen abroad to replace
deserters, had, of course, to offer full pay ([Dem.] 50.18). A similar
system designed to discourage desertion was in force in the British
navy from the seventeenth to the nineteenth century.

In addition to pay there was also, as we have mentioned, a maintenance allowance. Crews seem to have been responsible for buying
or otherwise acquiring their own victuals. There was no organised
provisioning. In Nicias' letter (above, pp. 117–18) one of the reasons
given for the shortage of oarsmen was that some had been cut off by
the enemy cavalry while foraging; and the weakness of the Athenian
position at Aegospotami (Xen. *HG* 2.1.27) lay in its distance from
the places where the men could acquire victuals. They regularly scattered up and down the Chersonese when they came ashore at midday, and that was their undoing. The amount of the maintenance
allowance in the fourth century seems to have been two obols a day
(Dem. 4.28) for seamen and soldiers, and one drachma for cavalry,
who had to feed their horses as well as themselves.

The banker trierarch

Employing the framework of the 'Decree of Themistocles' of 481 we
have been able to identify the various members of the ship's company of an Athenian trieres in the fifth and fourth centuries, and by
the use of later information largely supplied by contemporary Greek
historians have been able to add some flesh to the bare bones of that
identification. This provides us with the necessary knowledge of
how many men must be accommodated in our replica and of where
in the ship were the working stations of the members of the *hypēresia*.

The nature of the oarsystem and the consequent position of the oarsmen will be discussed in the next chapter. We may conclude this chapter with a look at a second document, which gives a unique insight into the human side of naval service in the age of the trieres. It is a speech written in the middle of the fourth century for (possibly by) the banker Apollodorus ([Dem.] 50). His family had recently been granted Athenian citizenship and he had volunteered for the trierarchy with a touching enthusiasm. His ship was ordered to sea in 362 and was part of a squadron sent to the NE Aegean to build on the recent successes there of Conon's son Timotheus commanding a fleet of the Second Athenian League. The speech gives a revealing glimpse of what it was like to be a trierarch in a League fleet in those years, and adds a touch of grass-roots realism to contrast with the optimistic claims for Athenian sea power voiced by Demosthenes and other politicians at this time.

Apollodorus is suing Polycles, the man appointed to succeed him in command of the ship after his year of service, for the extra expenses he has incurred because Polycles was not ready to take over the ship until five months and six days had elapsed after the due date. He describes (4) the occasion for the dispatch of his ship. 'On the twenty-fourth day of Metageitnion [August/September] in the archonship of Molon when an Assembly had been held and many great matters had been reported to you, you voted that the trierarchs should launch their ships. I was one of the trierarchs. I need not go into details of the emergency which occurred for the city at that time.' But of course he does: the grain supply from the Black Sea was under threat. 'You voted that the trierarchs should launch their ships and bring them round to the mole,[16] that the councillors and the heads of the demes should make demesmen's lists and returns of seamen, that the ships should be dispatched without delay and aid sent to our allies in the various theatres of war.'

The size of the squadron dispatched is not given, but the task it had to perform is clear, to expel Alexander, tyrant of Pherae, from the island of Tenos (a League member), to seize the opportunity of interfering in the affairs of the kingdom of Thrace, and to protect the grain ships sailing from the Black Sea from interception by

16 The *choma* in Munychia, an artificial mole or hard from where the officially appointed *apostoleis* dispatched expeditions (*IG* 2² 1629.178ff.).

Byzantium, Calchedon and Cyzicus,[17] which though technically still members of the League were on the point of secession. The aim of the interference in Thrace was the recovery of the Thracian Chersonese, which was always regarded as a vital Athenian interest in view of its position dominating the Hellespont. Apollodorus' ship seems to have been part of the force sent to the NE Aegean, but he gives no clues to what he did in the actual period of his trierarchy, since the burden of his speech is to recount the duties he had to perform, and the expenses he had to incur, in the excess period of five months and six days.

We may return to his description (7) of the dispatch of the expedition. 'When the oarsmen listed by the demesmen did not appear, apart from a few who were no good, I dismissed them, and by mortgaging my property and borrowing money I was the first to man my ship, hiring the best oarsmen I could procure, giving large bonuses and advance payments to all of them.' The normal method of manning a ship with oarsmen seems to have broken down, so that recourse was had to the open market. Oarsmen were normally paid in full only on return to their home port, as we have just seen. 'Furthermore I furnished the ship with equipment entirely of my own, taking nothing from the public stores,[18] and the gear was the finest and most magnificent in appearance of all the trierarchs' gear in the fleet. As to auxiliaries (*hyperesia*), I hired the best that could be had' (above, p. 111). In addition to the trierarchal expenses Apollodorus says that he also paid the advance taxes which were levied to cover the cost of a naval expedition. This advance payment of tax was itself regarded as a duty, like trierarchal service, to which men of means were liable, and as a serving trierarch he could have claimed exemption from it.

In two other speeches from this period, one, *On the Trierarchic Crown*, by Demosthenes (51) and the other, *Against Euergus* (47) by an anonymous author, similar claims are made. It appears from all these

17 For Alexander of Pherae see Cargill (1981) pp. 87, 169. G. de Sainte-Croix (1972) App. 8, p. 314 says that states had a tacitly recognised right to take action of this sort if they were short of grain.

18 See *GOS* pp. 188–9 and the inscription in n. 16 above. The ten annually appointed overseers of the dockyards were responsible for issuing gear from the public store to those trierarchs who applied for it, and for recovering it after use. Others like Apollodorus preferred their own.

speeches that the trierarch's first duty was the launching of the ship to which he had been allotted; the second the manning of it with oarsmen; the third the provision of gear (oars, masts, sails, ropes, etc.) which he could either draw from the public store on loan or provide on his own account; the fourth the enrolment of the *hypēresia* (helmsman, bow officer, boatswain, etc.); finally to bring the ship round 'to the mole' for inspection by the officials who were appointed for the dispatch of the expedition (*apostoleis*), and then to give the ship her trials.

In theory the oarsmen of Apollodorus' ship should have been men on the demesmen's list called up for service, but since the men who came forward in this way were neither sufficient in number nor up to Apollodorus' standard, with the enthusiasm and pride of the new Athenian citizen as well as the resources of a banker, he hired the best crew he could get. This action turned out a mistake, as he says later (15–16):

The fact was that in so far as I had manned the ship with good oarsmen in my keenness for a good reputation, so the rate of desertion in my ship was the highest in the fleet. In the case of the other trierarchs the oarsmen who served from the list stayed with them, looking forward to their safe return home, whereas mine, full of confidence in themselves because they were good at pulling an oar, went off at the places where they were likely to be re-engaged at the highest rate of pay.

It appears that the responsibility for providing victualling money for the oarsmen (and no doubt for the rest of the crew as well), whether men from the demesmen's list or hired by the trierarch, lay with the general in command, but he did not always, or was not in a position to, provide it, and in the circumstances it was up to the trierarch to give it 'since if they didn't eat, they couldn't pull an oar' (53–4).[19]

Apollodorus also had to hire the *hypēresia* for his ship, although in theory they, again, should have been performing military service. They seem here to include the ten hoplites (*epibatai*), although later

19 The Athenian commander of the League fleet of usually Athenian ships had to draw on contributions (*syntaxeis*) of the League members in the region where he was operating on their behalf and for their protection. The contributions were fixed by the Council of the League. At this period when pressure was being exerted from outside for many members to defect it is understandable that contributions were not readily forthcoming.

in the speech the latter are mentioned as distinct from the rest of the *hypēresia* (above, pp. 109–10).

In view of all this enthusiastic provision it is not surprising that Apollodorus' ship was selected by the general as his flagship and was employed on various special missions because of her speed. Nor is it surprising that his appointed successor was slow in taking over the ship, which, while an outstanding performer, was so much more expensive to keep at sea than the usual run of triereis.

All that Apollodorus says about his trierarchal year is the following (11):

> It is common knowledge that there are two things which finish a trieres, first if the trierarch does not see that his men are paid, and second if the ship returns to Piraeus during commission, because there is a high rate of desertion and the oarsmen who do not desert refuse to re-embark unless the trierarch offers them more money to meet their family expenses. Both these disasters happened to me . . . I received no pay from the generals for eight months and I sailed home with ambassadors because my ship was the fastest, and then back again when I was given the task by the people of taking the general Menon to the Hellespont in place of Autocles who had been voted out of office.

He had to hire replacements for the deserters with big bonuses and advance payments, and to give those who stayed with him 'something to leave behind for the maintenance of their families'.

Apollodorus is more informative about the duties he had to perform after the expiry of his trierarchal year (map 14). His ship was part of a force under the general Timomachus operating in the Straits. It was here that he suffered the high rate of desertion of which he complains. He received orders to go to the Crimea and bring back the grain fleet from there in convoy (17), since word had come that the Byzantines and Calchedonians who commanded the Bosporus strait 'were again taking the grain ships into harbour and compelling them to discharge their cargoes'. The general produced no money for pay, but Apollodorus was able to use his credit as a banker to raise funds at Sestus from two Athenians, and he sent his purser (see above, p. 112), Euctemon, off to Lampsacus with money 'and letters to the foreign correspondents of my father' telling him to hire the best oarsmen he could. On Euctemon's return he had orders to put to sea, but Euctemon fell ill and Apollodorus had to take on another purser. When Apollodorus returned to Sestus after

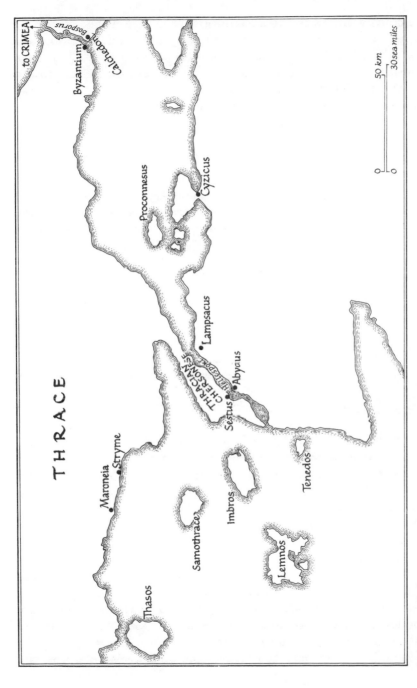

Map 14 Apollodorus' extra duty.

the convoy duty with the autumn grain fleet from the Crimea, he hoped to be able to sail home, but (22–3) 'when a delegation came from the people of Maroneia asking for an escort for their grain ships' Timomachus ordered the trierarchs to take the ships in tow to Maroneia 'a long voyage [74 to 78 sea miles] in the open sea'. Maroneia was presumably entitled to ask for this service as a member of the League. From Maroneia the squadron moved to Thasos. Then, Timomachus came and with the help of the Thasians convoyed grain and mercenaries to Stryme on the Thracian coast 'planning to seize the place himself'. However,

the people of Maroneia opposed us . . . and the men were exhausted after their long voyage and towing ships from Thasos to Stryme [43 sea miles]. Besides, the weather being stormy and the coast without harbours and offering no opportunities to go ashore for the evening meal, since it was hostile, with foreign mercenaries and neighbouring non-Greeks encamped round the city walls, we had to ride at anchor all night at sea, unfed and without sleep, on the alert lest the Maroneian triereis should attack us. What was more, it happened that at night in this season of the year [late autumn] there was rain and thunder, and a great wind got up. You can imagine the result, the state of despondency into which the men fell and how much desertion again took place after this experience. The original oarsmen [i.e. those recruited at Piraeus] had been through many hardships and had got little for it, all in fact that I was able to spare for each man, in addition to what they had already had from me, by borrowing, since the general was not even giving them what was sufficient for their daily needs [i.e. the minimum victualling allowance].

The hostility of the people of Maroneia to Timomachus' planned raid is a striking example of the 'freedom and autonomy' of the members of Athens' new model League. It is striking too that although Maroneia had triereis of her own, she made the League fleet tow the grain ships from the Hellespont for her.

Finally, after using Apollodorus' ship on various errands, Timomachus decided to send the ships off home, and put a deputy on Apollodorus' ship as commander of the squadron with instructions to pay the men the victualling allowance daily. He did not do so, and at Tenedos (a consistently loyal League city), after meeting his successor and failing to get him to take over the ship, Apollodorus had once more to use his banking connections to borrow money to get the ship home.

Enough perhaps has been told of the woes of Apollodorus, the rich, newly-made, Athenian citizen whose rather naive enthusiasm both his commander and his successor seem to have exploited shamefully. His speech, supplemented by the two other relevant speeches from the same period, tells us a good deal about the naval life of the time, the procedure for the dispatch of an expedition, the responsibilities of the trierarch, the various categories of the ship's company, details of naval pay and victualling, and the vicissitudes of service in a ship of the fleet of the Second Athenian League. The point of view is unique.

8

∘∘∘

THE SHIPS I

In this chapter and the next we shall discuss the ancient evidence for
the main structural features of the trieres, and a chapter on materials
will follow. When these discussions are completed it will be time to
call in the naval architect to design a ship which will be capable of the
performance required of the ancient trieres, accommodating the
members of the crew in their respective positions and satisfying
the evidence for the structure. The making of the replica from
equivalent materials and by the ancient methods will then be
outlined.

First two general points must be made. One of the reasons why no
remains of a trieres have been found on the sea-bed, while remains of
contemporary merchantmen do occur (fig. 5), is that the trieres had
a positive buoyancy, and did not sink when flooded.[1] The transitive
verb *kataduein*, which we find in accounts of sea-battles and which is
usually translated 'sink', does not mean 'sink' in the accepted sense
of the word in modern contexts – i.e. 'send to the bottom'. Passages
in the Greek historians show that the word means, rather, 'swamp',
since when ships were put out of action by ramming in deep water
and their crews either swam away or were drowned or killed by the
enemy, the wrecks themselves were towed off or drifted away. At
Artemisium the Greek allies thus 'capture' 30 ships (above, p. 53).
This fact emerges from a number of naval engagements and particularly clearly from the account of the action at Sybota in 433
(above, p. 65). Some of the wrecks are said to have been towed away,
and when the second Athenian squadron appeared in the evening
just as battle was about to be joined for the second time that day, the

---

1. J. G. Landels (1980) pp.148–9. The fact is confirmed by JFC's calculations: he
   draws attention to an observation, in connection with the Sybota action, made by
   A. F. B. Creuze (1841): 'The vessels spoken of as sunk were evidently merely
   stove in and waterlogged.' In Xenophon (*HG* 1.7.32) a general escapes on a ship
   which had been 'sunk' (*katadutheisēs*).

ships had to make their way 'through corpses and wrecks' which wind or current were taking up the Corcyra strait (above, p. 66). The trieres, then, was light enough to float when holed, and either was not ballasted at all, which is the most likely, or if ballasted the ballast was not sufficient to overcome her buoyancy. Other evidence for her lightness comes from the fact that in spite of her size the trieres could be hauled across the Isthmus of Corinth (above, p. 50 n.1).

The second general point concerns the nature of the archaeological evidence. In the absence of any actual remains of a trieres we have to make do with representations – some reliefs, one or two vase-paintings, a vase in the shape of a ship's bow, and some coins. All of these show Greek oared warships of the age of the trieres, but none of them is labelled as such. The only labelled picture of an ancient warship is the graffito of a Roman quadrireme found at Alba Fucentia in Italy (fig. 32). The single piece of hard archaeological evidence for the trieres which we possess consists of the remains of the Zea ship-sheds in Piraeus, which are known to have been built to house triereis (fig. 9), and thus allow us to calculate the maximum dimensions these ships could have had. We are driven to infer the method

32. Graffito from Alba Fucentia showing a warship labelled *navis tetreris longa* ('four' long ship), first century BC – first century AD.

of hull-construction (fairly safely, in fact) from the remains of contemporary merchantmen, e.g. the Kyrenia ship (fig. 5). Merchant
ships did sink, and their cargoes protected some at least of the hull
timbers from decay and the ship-worm. A large warship's ram has
recently been found on the sea-bed at Athlit near Haifa, with some
hull timbers adhering to it which show the same method of construction as the Kyrenia ship (see below, p. 168 and fig. 33).

Accommodation of trierarch and *hypēresia*

In the previous chapter we identified the various members of the
crew and established the general position in the ship of the non-
oarsmen. The helmsman and his protective archers occupied the
stern platform at deck level, and the helmsman's deck party were at
any rate based there. The trierarch and the pentecontarch are also
likely to have been in the stern. On deck were the ten *epibatai*, and in
the bows the bow officer and his party on the bow platform at deck
level. The boatswain (*keleustēs*) and the pipeman (*aulētēs*) were certainly below deck with the oarsmen. The ship's carpenter (*naupēgos*)
might have been anywhere, probably below deck where he would
have had a place to keep his tools. There is some evidence for a small
cabin for the trierarch underneath the stern platform aft of the

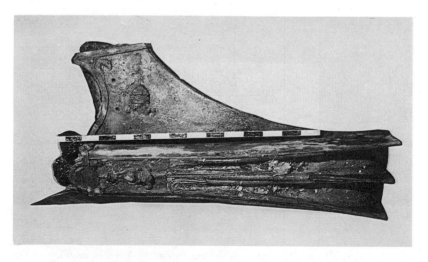

33. The Athlit ram before the removal of the timber.

oarsmen. The full-scale representation of the stern of an oared warship cut in the rock beside the steps leading up to the acropolis at Lindos shows a trace of such a cabin (fig. 34). When Alcibiades returned to Athens after exile in 407 in command of a trieres (Xen. *HG* 1.4.18) 'he did not immediately disembark but went up on deck to see if any of his friends were there to welcome him'. If he 'went up', he must have had accommodation below the level of the deck. Such accommodation is perhaps implied by the story in Herodotus (8.118.1–4) of an incident when Xerxes was returning home after Salamis in a Phoenician ship which he had boarded at Eion in Thrace for the voyage to the Hellespont. The ship could hardly have been other than a trieres.

And as he was on his way a high Strymonian wind caught him. He was rather severely tossed about, the ship being overloaded, with the deck packed by a large number of Persians in his entourage. The king panicked, and shouted to the helmsman asking what chance they had of making port. The man replied: 'Master, no chance at all, unless we get rid of all these men on deck (*epibatai*)', and Xerxes is said to have declared: 'Men of Persia, it is now up to

34. The relief carved beside the stone steps leading up to the Acropolis at Lindos, *c*. 200 BC.

each one of you to show his care for the king, it seems that my life depends on you.' At that the Persians made obeisance and jumped into the sea, and the ship, thus lightened, made its way to Asia in safety . . . This is the story of Xerxes' return, but [Herodotus adds] I don't believe a word of it. For if the helmsman had really made this reply, the king would quite obviously have ordered the people on deck to go below, since they were not only Persians but very important Persians at that; and since the oarsmen were Phoenicians he would have thrown a number of them into the sea to make room below for the Persians.

This story has been told at length not simply to make the point that if Xerxes shouted to the helmsman he cannot have been sitting beside him in the poop but must have been in accommodation below. The reason for the digression is that it contains a number of other points. The first is that it proves conclusively that the word *epibatēs* means someone carried on deck, here the Persian notables, in the normal crew armed men. The second is that, while there may have been a small cabin for the trierarch and an important passenger, there was no room elsewhere below decks for anyone else. The story further shows most dramatically that the weight of many men on deck dangerously reduced the ship's stability and hence its sail-carrying capacity and ability to maintain steerage way in a storm. In such weather the ship could hardly have been proceeding under oar.

Accommodation of the oarsmen

The main problem facing the reconstructor of the trieres concerns the accommodation of the 170 oarsmen in a hull of the required length. In the single-level oared long ship as described by Homer the oarsmen sat on thwarts (*zyga*) and kept their stores under them, and, in the sixth century, pentecontors carried large loads in addition to the oarsmen. Some of the oarsmen in a trieres are called *thalamioi*, and since *thalamos* is a word for the ship's hold it is reasonable to draw the conclusion that when oared ships began to be pulled by oarsmen at two levels the oarsmen at the lower level were called *thalamioi* because they occupied the space which had previously been the hold below the oarsmen who sat on the *zyga*. These latter oarsmen seem to have pulled their oars, naturally enough in view of their position low down in the hull, through oarports, which are mentioned in con-nection with a trieres by Herodotus (5.33.2-3: above, p. 41) and by Aristophanes (*Peace* 1232). Thranites appear as an important class of oarsmen in Aristophanes (*Acharnians* 162-3) and Thucydides (6.31.3), but there are no clues in literature to their position in the ship, and the name itself is not very helpful (see below, p. 141 for a possible derivation).

There is a passage in Xenophon's treatise on household economy (*Oecon.* 8.8) which is generally relevant to the oarsmen's accom-modation. He uses the example of the trieres to drive home the lesson that in the home speedy movement and good order are important: 'Why is the trieres, fully manned, such a terror to the enemy and a joy to her friends except by reason of her speed through the water? And do not those on board avoid getting in each other's way only if they take their seats in order, swing forward in order, go aboard and go ashore in order?' In Xenophon's eyes the trieres' chief virtue was speed. Theophrastus (*Enquiry* 5.7.4) writing about timber in the fourth century confirms that lightness was a prime consider-ation when he says that silver fir was used in the trieres' construction for this reason. To Aeschylus (*Persians* 336, 408–9, 415) in the pre-vious century the tactical function of the trieres is to ram. These three aspects together support the historical picture of naval action with triereis 'in the modern manner'. Speedy, agile movements of lightweight craft were planned to take advantage of 'the galley's terrible vulnerability to attack from the side', and defensive tactics were devised to avoid these manoeuvres. The pursuit of speed and agility through lightness of construction resulted in an oar-machine[2] packed tightly below deck with oarsmen and with little room for anything else. Strict discipline had to be observed to avoid physical clashes, and in handling, we recall, a boatswain was needed who had the knack of getting men to work cheerfully together. The reconstructor must expect to create a physical environment which matches these demands.

So much in general; now for some of the details. The remains of

2. Aristotle (*Rhet.* 1411a24) says that Cephisodotus (possibly the Rhodian sculptor) called triereis 'complicated mills'. One fourth-century trieres is called by the name Kouphotate ('Lightest'), *IG* 2^2 1629.1.

the Zea ship-sheds have already been mentioned. Enough of the foundations have been preserved to allow measurement of the slipways[3] (figs. 9 and 35). They have a maximum dry length of 37 m (121 ft 5 in.) and a clear width between the columns (which separated one ship-shed from another) of 6 m (19 ft 6 in.). The gradient is 1 in 10.[4] The ships themselves are likely to have been a little shorter and a little narrower than these dimensions.

They were manhandled by not less than [one hundred and] forty men up the slipway and by not less than [one hundred and] twenty men down.[5] These men would have room to stand beneath any outrigger so that room would not have to be provided for them on each side of the ship. The dimensions are very relevant to the oarsystem, inasmuch as the oarsmen must be accommodated in a ship of this length and breadth. They do in fact rule out the *alla sensile* system of the fifteenth and sixteenth centuries in the Mediterranean (see p. 21).

As regards the oarsystem, we may consider in the first place whether any clue is given by the name 'trieres' itself. The word seems to mean 'three-rowing'. Aeschylus uses a revealing alternative, *triskalmos*, i.e. a ship with three tholepins. The trieres, then, could be regarded as having three tholepins (*skalmoi*), not of course in the whole ship but in some obvious unit, where other ships had a different number.[6] This obvious unit is the one given by Vitruvius (1.2.4), a Roman architect who worked in the principate of Augustus, as the *interscalmium*, the unit of length in an oared ship between one tholepin and the next in a fore-and-aft file of oarsmen. Although the word *interscalmium* is itself half Greek, he adds an illuminating Greek equivalent, a word which has been corrupted in the manuscripts to *diphēciaca* but can be recognised as *dipēchiakē* (or, as the scholiast suggested, *dipēchuia*) meaning (in both cases) 'of two cubits', i.e. 0.888 m, a reasonable 'room' for an oarsman to occupy in a fore-and-aft file. Such a unit of length in an oared ship would contain one tholepin in a simple pentecontor, two in a two-level pentecontor,

---

3. See the chapter by D. J. Blackman in *GOS* pp. 181–92. The Zea ship-sheds were excavated and published by Dragatzes (1886) pp. 63–8 and pls. 2–3.
4. This is the same gradient as the Phoenician ship-sheds recently excavated at L'Ilot de l'Amirauté (communication to JFC).
5. *IG* 1³ 153. Lewis's supplements in brackets.
6. See JSM, *CQ* 41(1947) 122ff; Aeschylus, *Persians* 678, 1074.

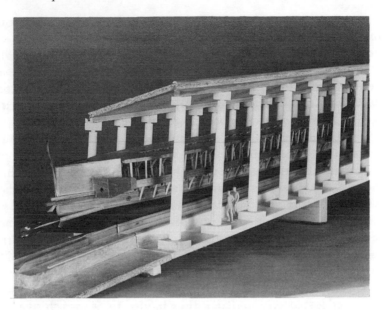

35a. A model of a reconstructed ship-shed housing the model trieres shown in fig. 2.

35b. Reconstructed scene at the top of a slipway inside a ship-shed.

and in a trieres could have three. This appears to have been the way in which Aeschylus regarded the trieres. Alternatively the word 'trieres' could have described a ship which had three files of oarsmen ranging fore-and-aft on each side of the ship in contrast to the simple pentecontor which one such file and the two-level pentecontor with two. The Romans tended to classify their oared ships in this way, as having so many files (*ordines*) on each side.

If the trieres had three tholepins to each two cubit unit in the same way as the pentecontor had one or two, it is likely that each of the oarsmen in the trieres, like those in the pentecontor, pulled his own oar. This likelihood is proved correct by a passage in Thucydides to which brief reference was made in the last chapter (p. 111). He is describing an incident in the winter of 429 when the fleet which Phormio had twice defeated in the gulf of Corinth earlier in the year withdrew to Corinth. There the crews of 40 of the ships were transferred to the other side of the Isthmus to man 40 Megarian ships at the port of Nisaea for a surprise attack on Piraeus. Such a move was quicker and attracted less attention than if they hauled their own ships across by the *diolkos* (above p. 50 n. 1). Each man was to go on foot 'taking his oar, his cushion and his oarloop', items of gear apparently personal to the oarsman. The cushion has an interesting implication. Assuming that it was tied firmly to the seat, its presence implies that (in the absence of a sliding seat) the oarsman moved his body backwards (i.e. towards the bows) during the stroke as he straightened his legs, having previously bent them as he moved his body forward (i.e. towards the stern) in preparation for the stroke. This point was made by John Hale (1973) commenting on the raised knees of two oarsmen in the Lenormant relief (p. 21 and below, pp. 139–51: fig. 13). Such movement is confirmed by a passage in the *Frogs* of Aristophanes (236) where the god Dionysus, made to row across the Styx by Charon, complains of blisters, presumably because he had not brought his cushion with him. The purpose of the oarloop or grommet is more obvious. Made of leather, according to Homer (*Od.* 4.782) and probably also in the fifth century, it was looped over the tholepin and held the oar to it during the stroke. The mention of the cushion and the oarloop is interesting, but the main value of the Thucydidean passage is to show beyond doubt that in the fifth century the oars in a trieres were pulled each by one man.

We have already referred briefly to the naval inventories.[7] Inscribed on stone slabs found in Piraeus and covering a number of years mostly after the middle of the fourth century BC, they contain lists of ships and gear in various categories and provide the most important and authoritative source of information about the classical trieres and its equipment, recording as they do the contents of the dockyards which the overseers of one year handed over to their successors in the next. In the previous chapter we were concerned to deduce from the record of 170 oars for each ship that since 170 oars implied 170 oarsmen and the total number of each crew was 200, the *hypēresia* must have numbered thirty. Here we are concerned with the detailed classification of the oars in these inscriptions into 62 thranite, 54 zygian and 54 thalamian oars. There are, as we have seen, literary references to thranite and thalamian oarsmen, and we have seen reason to infer that the latter, working oars through oarports, sat in the lowest part of the ship below oarsmen seated on the *zyga*. The category of zygian, as well as thranite and thalamian, oars occurring in the inventories justifies the conclusion that there were oarsmen called *zygioi* as well as those called *thranitai* and *thalamioi*, although there is no literary reference to them. The name suggests that these were the oarsmen seated on the *zyga*, the thwarts or cross beams in the ship's hull.[8]

We may now address ourselves to the question of the relative positioning of the three categories of oarsmen. The inference that the thalamians occupied the lowest part of the ship is confirmed by a passage in Aristophanes (*Frogs* 1074ff.) where a character speaks of one of the crew of the *Paralos*, one of the two crack state triereis, as 'making wind in the face of the *thalamax* and getting excrement all over his messmate'. *Thalamax* is a colloquial equivalent for *thalamios* (cf. *stuppax* below, p. 186), who must, therefore, have sat below at least one of the other two classes. The greater number of thranites

7. *IG* 2² 1604–1632: p. 5.
8. Modern writers (e.g. Anderson (1962) pp. 6, 7, 12, 14) continue to speak of zygite oarsmen (the latest example *The World of Athens* (1984) p. 265). *Zygitēs*, like *thalamitēs*, occurs only in the scholiast on Aristophanes, *Frogs* 1074, no doubt on the analogy of the correct *thranites*. *Zygios*, like *thalamios*, is used of oars in the naval inventories, as is *thranitēs*. *Thalamios* is used of oarsmen in Thucydides, and it is reasonable to suppose that *zygios* was also so used in the fifth and fourth centuries. Zygian and thalamian then seem to be the correct anglicisations.

(62) than the number (54) of the other two classes, i.e. four more on each side of the ship, is an indication that the thranites sat higher in the ship, since thus they would be less affected by the reducing beam and depth of the hull at bow and stern (below, p. 217).

The general assumption has been, and still often is, that if, as it appears, the thranites sat highest and the thalamians sat below and between the zygians (these latter two classes seated like the oarsmen in a two-level pentecontor), the oars in each unit of one thranite, one zygian and one thalamian oarsman would have had to be of different lengths, and that the difference would have created insuperable difficulties, in harmonising the oar-beat (above, pp. 21-2). It can however be shown that there was no necessary difference in length between the oars in any one such unit. The naval inventories provide the vital piece of information by recording the number and length of the spare oars carried.[9] There were thirty of these, of 9 cubits (3.99 m) and 9½ cubits (4.2 m), and a reference to this small difference can be found in Aristotle (*PA* 687b18). Speaking of the fingers of the hand he says: 'the outermost finger is short for good reason and the middle finger long, like the oar amidships'. Galen (*UP* 1.24) is a little more explicit:

Why are all the fingers of unequal length and the middle finger the longest? Is it for any other reason than because it is better for their ends to extend the same distance in grasping large round objects? . . . as I think in triereis also the ends of the oars extend the same distance and yet they are not all the same length; for in that case too they make the middle oars longest for the same reason.

And lest we should be led astray by Galen's word 'longest' Michael of Ephesus, the Greek commentator on Aristotle, is brief and to the point (22.118.15): 'the middle oars of ships are longer than those at each end'. This fact is likely to have been true of triacontors and pentecontors as well as of triereis. There is not much room for doubt: the spare oars in triereis are of two different lengths because in the bow and stern, where there was less room, shorter oars were used, but still in all but a very few units all the oars would have been of the same length.

It would, again, seem likely that the gearing of the oars (i.e. the proportion between the part of the oar outboard of the thole and the

9. E.g. *IG* 2^2 1606. 43–4, 1607.14.

part inboard of it) would remain the same throughout the ship irrespective of the oar-length. But the fourth-century work on mechanics attributed to Aristotle (4.850b10) is evidence to the contrary. Answering the question 'Why do the midships oarsmen move the ship most?', the author says: 'Amidships the largest part of the oar is inboard for the ship is broadest there.' It seems, then, that the half cubit (22 cm or 8½ ins.) by which the bow and stern oars were shorter came off the loom, or inboard part of the oar, so that 'the midships oarsmen move the ship most' because they have greater leverage, and, as Galen says, all the oars extend to the same distance from the ship's side although they are not (overall) of the same length.

With the help of the naval inventories and some literary sources it has been possible to establish the general nature of the oarsystem of the trieres fairly clearly. There is, however, still no indication of the suspected connection between the thranite oarsman and the *parexeiresia* or outrigger. We may now turn to the representations of oared ships which in the light of what we now know may be identified as triereis.

There are a few representations of galleys, deriving directly or indirectly from the fifth and fourth centuries, which are *prima facie* likely to depict triereis, but none show the whole ship or the sails and rigging.

(1) The most spectacular of these is the relief probably found by Lenormant on the Acropolis at Athens and published in 1859 (fig. 13).[10] It is dated in the last decade of the fifth century. Small and delicately cut in local pink marble, it portrays a midships section of the starboard side of a galley under oar. The painted colours which would have aided interpretation are now lacking and its surface is worn (for an interpretation by shading see fig. 36). The galley can nevertheless be seen to possess the characteristics which we have come to expect in a fifth-century trieres. On the deck are the lower parts of figures half-lying or sitting. Supporting the deck are successive curved stanchions (the curvature possibly indicating perspective), which descend outside the hull and rest on the upper wale, and in between them eight figures are visible pulling oars. Their oars pass through two heavy horizontal timbers, which are connected by short uprights (tholes and stiles) and seem to be in

10. For the literature see Beschi (1969–70) p. 117 no. 5.

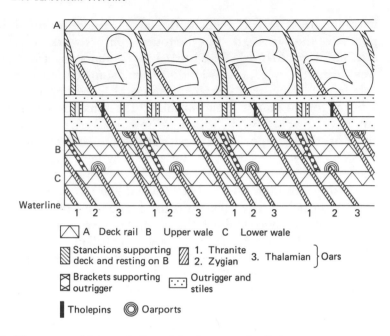

36. The proposed interpretation of the Lenormant relief.

higher relief than the two horizontal wales beneath them on the ship's side. Cartault (above, p. 19) rightly recognised these upper horizontal timbers as an outrigger and the visible oarsmen as thranites, since he also recognised two lower levels of oars emerging from the ship's side, thus happily identifying and connecting to each other the two features which distinguish the trieres. Cartault's recognition is the key to the interpretation of the relief and one of the two remaining unidentified features of the ship's side in the relief is thereby explained. The longer slanting semi-vertical timber resting on the lower wale is a bracket supporting the horizontal timbers which stand out from the ship's side as an outrigger through which the thranite oars are pulled. (The shorter such timber is to be recognised as the lower part of the deck stanchion resting on the upper wale.) From under this structure of the outrigger emerge the zygian oars, probably through ports originally picked out in colour. Thalamian oars emerge above the lower wale, again through ports originally picked out in colour and fitted, as will be seen, with sleeves (*askōmata*: pp. 169–70) as a precaution against water splashing in.

Thus the relief illustrates the relative position of each of the three oarsmen in the unit: the thranite somewhat higher and, thanks to the outrigger, further outboard than the other two. The zygian and thalamian are in the same positions relative to each other as those which they held in the two-level pentecontor. The trieres in fact, at the time covered by the naval inventories, is a ship with 27 oarsmen a side at each of two levels on which has been superimposed on each side a third file of 31 oarsmen, sitting virtually on the gunwale and pulling oars through an outrigger supported at two-cubit intervals away from the ship's side by a bracket resting on a horizontal wale. It is possible that the word *thranos* (from which the name *thranites* comes and which has the general meaning of a longitudinal beam in, e.g., a roof) in the nautical context denotes the 'gunwale'.

(2) A small fragment of relief[11] which by reason of the marble of which it is made, and the style and subject matter of the sculpture, is certainly part of the monument from which the Lenormant relief comes, shows part of the side of a galley with a thranite oarsman visible and traces of two figures seated on deck (fig. 14). It was found in 1876 in a spoil heap from the earlier excavation of the Acropolis at Athens.

There are two further representations in the same general style and showing galleys on the same scale as the galley on the Lenormant relief. One depicts the bow and the other the stern (in both cases the starboard side, as in 1 and 2) of a ship which can likewise be identified as a trieres.

(3) One of a folio of drawings made for the Cavaliero dal Pozzo in Rome between 1610 and 1635 and now in the British Museum (fig. 11)[12] shows the starboard bow of a galley with five oarsmen pulling oars in the same position as those in the Lenormant relief. It is then a reasonable assumption that the ship is a trieres. The scale is also the same, since in both the oarsmen measure about 4.4 cm from seat to the crown of the head. Again, as in the relief, the oarsmen are framed fore and aft by the aft-curving deck-stanchions and above and below by the deck and by the upper outrigger timber. In the drawing the heads of the oarsmen slightly overlap the deck, suggesting that the artist thought that they sat outboard of it (pp. 143–5). A figure wear-

11. See Beschi (1969–70) p. 121.
12. See C. C. Vermeule (1964) p. 27. Also Beschi pp. 123ff.

ing a high cap, drawn rather larger than the oarsmen, lies propped on one elbow at the forward end of the deck, and looks and signals aft with one hand. He can be recognised as the bow officer (*prōratēs* or *prōreus*). The deck has a low bulwark which conceals some of the bow officer's body, and would conceal more if his size was not exaggerated.

On the ship's side there are the same horizontal timbers of the outrigger and wales, and tholes and stiles between the former, as have been seen in (1). The artist has, however, not recognised that the deck-stanchions are to be seen continuing downwards between the horizontal outrigger timbers and resting on the upper wale: these continuations are inserted, but incorrectly aligned. The thalamian and thranite oars are shown correctly, but the zygian oars although appearing in their correct positions below the lower wale have not been recognised as continuing upwards across the lower end upper wales to the point where they disappear inside the ship under the outrigger, but the artist inserts, again incorrectly aligned, what in the original were the upper parts of the zygian oars between the wales and between the upper wale and the outrigger. The early seventeenth-century artist, ignorant of galleys with oars at three levels, very naturally has failed to understand what he is copying, but it is not difficult to see the nature of his mistakes and penetrate to the original with the help of the Lenormant relief. One thing is clear. The original showed the bow unit as consisting of a single thranite oarsman while the next units aft were shown complete, containing thranite, zygian and thalamian oarsmen.

The form of the trieres prow which the dal Pozzo drawing shows, i.e. with a foredeck continuing forward to the stem, is corroborated by two vases of a ritual character (rhyta) which are dated respectively in the latter part of the fourth and the third century BC. The earliest (fig. 37) is Apulian.[13] It shows clearly the ram and above on both sides of it the laterally projecting *epōtides* (below p. 166) or 'ear-timbers'. Above and in between the handles (which of course have nothing to do with the ship imitated in the vase's shape) is the hint of a superstructure, a deck such as that on which the *prōratēs* lies in the drawing. This deck superstructure is more clearly shown in the later

13. See *GOS*, p. 178.

37. Apulian rhyton in the shape of the bow of a trieres, 400–322 BC.

rhyton (fig. 38), in which a figure is placed on it. Still more clearly but in two dimensions the foredeck appears on a Cian coin of the end of the fourth century (fig. 39). The screens which box in the sides of the space below the foredeck are shown in the coin giving place further aft to a deck-stanchion curving aft in just the same way as the deck stanchions do on the Lenormant relief and its associated fragment, the dal Pozzo drawing and the Aquila relief – (1), (2), (3) and (4). This screened area underneath the foredeck may have formed a cabin for the bow officer corresponding to the cabin underneath the quarterdeck in the stern. The suggestion made by the artist of the dal Pozzo drawing that the foredeck did not extend laterally over the

38. Rhyton in the shape of a trieres' bow, third–second century BC.

39. Coin of Cius in Bithynia showing a trieres' bow, 340 BC.

thranite oarsmen is not elsewhere corroborated for the late fifth century and is unlikely to have had support in his original.

(4) A piece of a marble relief, now at L'Aquila in Italy (fig. 12),[14] shows part of the starboard side of the stern of a galley under oar. The style and aspect of the representation is similar to that of (1), (2) and (3). The stroke oarsmen and the three others visible have the same posture, and measurement shows them to be on the same scale, as the oarsmen in the other three representations. The marble is Greek but shows none of the transverse veining of (1) and (2), and cannot therefore come from the same monument as those. Compared with them the surface has suffered less weathering and the relief is higher, but severe damage round the edges, particularly at the bottom, makes interpretation difficult. When first published[15] it was thought to be a Roman copy of the monument from which (1) and (2) come. But the provenance of the marble makes this unlikely. A recent suggestion[16] that it is a contemporary Greek copy of the monument made for exhibition at a second site in Athens seems unlikely and is ruled out by certain differences between it and (1) and (2). It may come from a separate but broadly similar monument, brought to Italy, like the original of (3), by a Roman visitor to Athens interested in Greek warships.

Part of the up-curving line of the keel is visible in the relief, as well as the top of the aft-slanting steering oar on the starboard side, and the lower part of a figure seated on a deck which has no low bulwark. Of the first (stroke) oar unit there is recognisable a thranite and zygian oar but no thalamian, and there is no outrigger bracket.

14. See Beschi (1969–70) p. 121.
15. By A. Rumpf (1935) p. 14.
16. Beschi (1969–70). Rumpf and Beschi regard the original of which the Aquila relief is a copy, the Lenormant relief and the original of the dal Pozzo drawing as parts of the same monument. Beschi reconstructs the whole as a votive relief to which he attaches a fragment (Acropolis Museum 2544). He regards this fragment as showing the head of a figure which appears seated in the upper part of the dal Pozzo drawing, and identifies it as Paralos, the eponymous hero of the state trieres of that name depicted at the foot of the relief. The added fragment has features which date it, like the Lenormant relief, to the end of the fifth or the beginning of the fourth century BC. O. Walter (1932), on the other hand, connects the Lenormant relief with the picture of the Paralos trieres in the Pinacotheca of the Propylaeum at Athens, which Pliny (*N.H.* 35.101) and Cicero (*Verr.* 4.135) speak of as painted by Protogenes of Caunus at the end of the fourth century BC. It is doubtful, however, whether a relief, even if coloured, could be described as a painted picture.

In unit no. 2 a thranite and a zygian oar are recognisable but again no thalamian, and there is again no outrigger bracket. Unit no. 3 shows first an outrigger bracket then thranite and zygian oars. The outrigger bracket appears to have a continuation below the lower wale, although the state of the stone is such that no conclusion is certain. If there is a continuation there, the stonemason has made one of two possible mistakes. Either, as is more likely, he has simply treated the bracket as if it were an oar and continued it downwards, or he has merged a thalamian oar (which stands next to the bracket in (1), (2) and (3)) with the bracket. In unit no. 4 only a thranite oar survives the break in the stone, but this unit is likely to have contained also a zygian and a thalamian oar. Stiles and tholes appear between the upper and lower outrigger timbers, and so do the lower parts of the deck stanchions, which are not shown as continuing downwards to rest on the upper wale. The looms of the thranite oars are noticeably thicker than the outboard parts (see below, p. 173 n.22).

The most significant difference between the Aquila relief and (1), (2) and (3) is the absence of a waterline. In the Lenormant relief the waterline is plain and no part of the hull or oars below it is shown. The deck stands 13.5 cm above it. There is a most realistically drawn waterline in the dal Pozzo drawing, the deck standing 14.5 cm above it. The additional height is at least partly caused by the clearly drawn low bulwark, higher than any bulwark which may possibly be intended in the Lenormant relief. In the Aquila relief the clearly marked keel is visible to a point 16 cm below the deck surface, where a break in the stone cuts it off. Now the practical requirements of pulling an oar make it certain that at each of the three levels the oarsmen in a trieres must have sat throughout the ship at the same height above the water. The oarsmen in the stern could not have sat higher, at each level, than those in the rest of the ship in relation to the waterline; and it must be remembered that measurements of the oarsmen show that the stern on the Aquila relief is drawn on the same scale as the midships section and bow in (1), (2) and (3). The waterline in the Aquila relief should, then, be a horizontal line crossing the keel at the point where the stroke thranite oar crosses the keel (and in fact is not shown continuing) about 14 cm below the surface of the deck. It seems clear, therefore, that the monument from which the Aquila relief comes depicted a trieres, but, unlike the Lenormant relief and the original of the dal Pozzo drawing, did not show a waterline.

The conclusions to be drawn from this examination may be briefly stated. Material, provenance and detail make it reasonably certain that (1) and (2) represent a fifth-century trieres. Community of scale and detail, in spite of some errors of execution, make it likely that (3) and (4) also represent such a ship. The original of (3) might well have been a part of the same monument of which (1) and (2) were parts, but (4), although a broadly similar picture of a similar ship, shows differences of material and detail which indicate that it came from a different monument of the same type.

The ship of which we have the bow and stern depicted in (3) and (4) has one more thranite than zygian oarsmen on each side, and three more zygian than thalamian oarsmen, a different distribution from that which the naval inventories attest, where the zygian oarsmen and the thalamian oarsmen are the same (27), and the thranites are four more (31) than the other two classes. Since the crew of a trieres remains constant at 200 throughout our period, it seems likely that the total number of oarsmen was 170 in the fifth century, as it was in the fourth. If that is so, the distribution of the 85 oarsmen on each side attested by our four representations is 30 : 29 : 26 in contrast with the distribution 31 : 27 : 27 attested in the naval inventories.[17] Such a relatively small change could have been dictated by an alteration in the shape of the hull. The distribution shown in the four representations deriving from the fifth century is set out diagrammatically in fig. 40.

	UNITS	1	2	3	4	5-28	29	30	
	Thranite	.	.	.	.	24 complete units	.	.	= 30
STERN	Zygian	.	.	.	.			.	= 29 BOW
	Thalamian			.				.	= 26

40. Distribution of oarsmen in the Lenormant Relief trieres.

17. *IG* 2² 1615–18. See *GOS* p. 272 n. 16. Beschi's reconstruction enables the height of the relief to be estimated at 95 cm. Taking it as a rule that the breadth of such votive reliefs is twice the height, he reaches 1.90 m for the breadth. In this breadth a ship with only 25 thranite oarsmen a side can be fitted. He says (p. 129): 'the maker of the relief was an artist not a geometer, and the number is sufficient to give an impression of the real thing to the eye'. I find it difficult to believe that the artist who so meticulously represents each detail in the relief can have been so careless in something which any Athenian observer would see at once to be wrong. A simple adjustment of the scale would have enabled the right number of thranite oarsmen to be shown.

(5) The Talos vase in the Jatta collection in Ruvo (S. Italy), which is dated to the end of the fifth century, can also be seen, by comparison with the Lenormant relief, to show a trieres (figs. 41a and b).[18] The painting gives a very detailed and precise picture of the port side of the stern. The ship is beached, i.e. slightly on its side, with the stern slanting away from the eye. There are three human figures, all enormously out of proportion to the ship, two sitting on deck and a third descending a ladder which is leaning against the lower horizontal timber of the outrigger. The deck is supported, as in the Lenormant relief, by stanchions with an exaggerated curvature, the lower ends of which rest on the upper wale; and the outrigger, again as in the Lenormant relief, is supported by a bracket resting on a lower

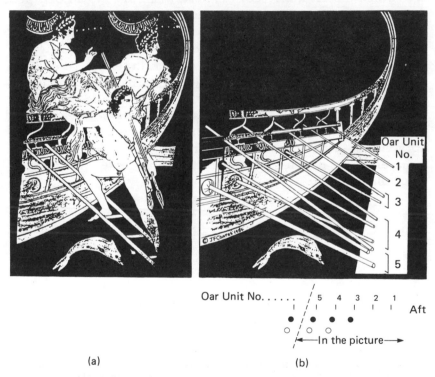

(a)   (b)

41a. Attic red-figure volute krater by the Talos painter showing the stern of the
    Argo portrayed as a trieres, end of the fifth century BC.
41b. Interpretation of fig. 41a.

18. See *GOS* pp. 173–6.

horizontal wale. In a beached ship, naturally, the oars have been shipped, but below the outrigger and above the upper wale there is a row of three oarports and between the upper and lower wales a single, larger, thalamian oarport covered by a sleeve of some kind (see above, p. 41 and p. 40) to which we shall return. Two thranite tholes are visible and one is implied by the corresponding zygian oarport. The figure with his foot on the ladder conceals part of the stern, so that it is impossible to tell whether the thranite tholes and zygian oarport continue aft. The thalamian oarports plainly do not. If, as is quite possible, two further thranite tholes and two further zygian oarports are concealed, the arrangement is such as is set out above in fig. 40. If on the other hand only two further thranite tholes (and no zygian oarports) are concealed, then the arrangement would fit the distribution between the classes of oarsmen attested by the naval inventories as shown in fig. 42 (the arrangement has been converted to starboard side for comparison). Since the greater part of our detailed knowledge about the trieres comes from the naval inventories and the oar arrangement they imply appears to be the result of a refinement of hull shape, this is the distribution that we have adopted in the reconstruction. Other arrangements than that shown in fig. 42 would of course satisfy the distribution 31 : 27 : 27, but the Talos vase stern, as far as it goes, is consistent with the arrangement in fig. 42, and provides further reason for our following that pattern.

	UNITS	1	2	3	4	5–28	29	30	31		
	Thranite	.	.	.	.	24 complete units	.	.	.	= 31	
STERN	Zygian		.	.				.		= 27	BOW
	Thalamian			.				.	.	= 27	

42. Distribution of oarsmen in the Talos vase trieres.

(6) There remains a small fragment of red-figure pottery to be considered (fig. 43).[19] It antedates (1), (2) and (5) by about fifty years, and represents part of the side of a trieres comparable with what is shown in them. Like (5) it shows no oars, and since the bunched 'foot'[20] of a sail is visible above the deck it is possible that the ship is under sail.

19. See *GOS* p. 176.
20. See *GOS* pp. 299, 312.

43. Fragment of a red-figure cup: part of the side of a trieres, *c.* 450 BC.

There are minor differences. The absence of tholes and stiles in the outrigger as well as of the bracket supporting it, and the similar size of the zygian and thalamian oarports, are probably the result of rough drawing, but the presence of a substantial rail to the deck indicates a difference in practice which may imply that this ship was a troop-carrier with hoplites on deck. Instead of the two heavy wales seen in (1), (3) and (4) there are here two pairs of light horizontal timbers with the oarports in between each pair. The deck stanchions in (1), (3), (4) and (5) curve towards the stern. On this fragment they curve from left to right. This fact, and the decorative roundel[21] partly

21. The only evidence for decoration on the side of a trieres' hull that I know of is the
    passage in Hipponax (see above) which speaks of a snake painted 'on the many-
    benched side of a trieres fleeing from the ram towards the helmsman'. Apart from
    the eye (e.g. *GOS* Pl. 21 e) and the boar's head (*GOS* Pls. 13–20) which are common
    on the earlier ships but forward of the oarsystem, there are the two dolphins on
    the famous Exekias cup (*GOS* Pl. 13).
        The eye which is a regular decoration of the prows of earlier oared ships (See
    GOS, General Index s.v.) in triereis of the fourth century was apparently a piece
    of marble shaped and painted to resemble an eye. Some have been discovered in
    Zea (Chrysoula Saatoglu-Paliadele 1978) and provide an explanation of the
    enigmatic entries in one of the naval inventories (IG 2² 1604.68 and 75: *GOS* p.
    288 note 26) that the eyes of a ship 'are broken', and in another (*IG* 2² 1607.24:
    GOS, ibid.) that in a certain ship 'there is no gear and even the eyes are missing'.

visible on the ship's side, suggest that a section towards the port bow of a trieres is shown. The vertical lines apparently passing through a slot in the deck may be rigging ropes of the 'boat' sail, the 'foot' of which is visible, or possibly weapons which in earlier ships were often stacked in the bow.[22] If the break in the sherd on the left-hand side conceals a second thalamian oarport, then the oar arrangement may be that in fig. 40 with units nos. 28 and 29 (partly) shown and unit no. 30, consisting of a single thranite place, also invisible by reason of the break on the left-hand side.

The evidence for a slot in the deck is unique. There is a necessity for such a narrow opening in the deck above the keel-line to enable the mast to be raised and lowered, and this feature will be present in the reconstruction. There is no other evidence of any kind, for or against it.

There is a final observation to be made about the general form of the trieres as it appears from the evidence given in this chapter. Although the oarsmen were protected to a certain degree from weather and in battle from enemy missiles by a light deck, whether 'overall' or not, the trieres was open at the sides above the gunwale. This weakness was exploited by the Syracusans in the early battles in the Great Harbour. They employed small boats to get close in among the enemy ships and enable missiles to be thrown in among the oarsmen (Thuc. 7.40.5). There are screens of linen and hair among the gear of triereis in the naval inventories.[23] The latter were presumably for protection against such attacks and against javelins thrown from the decks, while the first were for protection against the weather. In Xenophon (*HG* 1.6.19) screens are said to have been used to conceal the manning of ships planning to make a dash for the open sea. The introduction of catapults in the Hellenistic navies made necessary the permanent and solid 'boxing in' of the oarsmen.

Types of trieres

In the accounts of the Salamis campaign distinctions are made between the performances of different triereis to which we should now give our attention.

22. E.g. *GOS* pls. 2c and d, 6a and 12c.
23. *IG* 2² 1605.40–43; 1609.85, 86, 113; 1611.244–9; 1612.73–9 (two *pararrumata* to each ship); 1627.348. Screens put up before battle (*parablēmata*) Xen. *HG* 2.1.22.

In the first place, in giving the numbers of the two fleets Aeschylus says that the Greek fleet was made up of 300 ships of which ten were 'outstanding' (*ekkritous*), while the total of the Persian fleet was 1,000 of which 207 were especially fast (*Persians* 338–40). Our other contemporary authority, Herodotus (7.89, 184) speaks of a total of 1,207 for the Persians, probably having added the 207 fast ships to the total of 1,000 instead of including them in it as Aeschylus does. He says that the Phoenician ships were the 'best movers in the water' (*arista pleousas*) (7.96) and that there were 300 of them (7.89). In his two accounts of the Greek naval force before Artemisium (8.1.1–1) and before Salamis (8.43–8) no number or group of ships is said to be specially fast, but after Salamis (8.22.1) he speaks of Themistocles taking the 'best moving' Athenian ships on a special mission.

In the second place when Herodotus comes to describe the engagements at Artemisium he characterises the Persian ships as a whole as moving better in the water than the Greek ships (8.10.1), and when he comes to the account of the Greek council of war on the night before the battle of Salamis he gives Themistocles the words (8.60a): 'if you engage them at the Isthmus you will fight a battle on the open sea, which is least advantageous to us who have ships heavier and fewer in number [than they].'

It seems that there are two quite different ratings in these two groups of passages. In the former group the rating rests on specific inbuilt characteristics of the hull, i.e. some ships are built to be faster than others, whereas in the latter group the better performance or the greater heaviness derives from some other factor which affects all the ships in the fleet whatever their build. For the clue to this latter factor we must go once more to the letter Nicias wrote to the Athenian Assembly in 414.

The Athenian ships in Nicias' fleet were the 100 empty hulls, 40 fast and 60 troop-carriers (Thuc. 6.31.3 cf. 4.3.1) which the city had supplied for the expedition. The ratings 'fast' and 'troop-carrier' depend, here at least, not on their function alone – for they were empty hulls – but on some inbuilt characteristics. A Syracusan speaker (Thuc. 6.34.3), talking of the expected invasion, mentions a fast squadron of the Athenian fleet which could keep together on the crossing from Corcyra to Italy. On arrival at Syracuse the fast ships were moored together under the forts at the harbour's entrance. But in the letter from Syracuse a year later (Thuc. 7.12.3) Nicias says:

'Our fleet was originally in first-class condition, the ships dry and the crews unimpaired, but now the ships are leaky and the crews have deteriorated. It is not possible to beach the ships and dry them out because the enemy fleet . . . keeps us constantly on the look-out for an attack.' The Syracusans on the other hand 'have a greater opportunity of drying out their ships'. It is clear from these words that the second kind of rating is here explained. Regular maintenance of these wooden ships was of the greatest importance if they were to be kept in efficient condition, and this involved a lengthy procedure of beaching and 'drying out' which would have included careening and caulking of seams as well as, in all probability, giving the underwater hull a coat of pitch.

We may compare the Persian and Greek fleets before Salamis in the light of this crucial maintenance factor. Herodotus tells (7.59.2–3) how the Persian fleet, on its voyage from the Hellespont, came to a wide beach at the mouth of the river Hebrus near Doriscus, where 'they hauled their ships up on to the beach and dried them out'. This was in the early summer of 480. The Greek ships on the other hand appear to have been mobilised and at action stations since the previous autumn. They would not have been able to risk immobilising their ships for the time taken for the maintenance operation, because they too, by the time 'drying out' became necessary were, like Nicias, 'constantly on the look-out for an attack'.

The 200 triereis, which the Athenians built just before the battle of Salamis and which fought there, were, in Thucydides' words (1.14.3) 'not decked overall', and the 'Decree of Themistocles' shows that these, like the fast triereis in use later, carried only ten *epibatai*. If on the other hand we look at the ships in the Persian fleet we find that, according to Herodotus (7.96), they all had, in addition to the native *epibatai*, 30 Persian, Median and Sacan *epibatai* on each ship as well. Since the rest of the Persian army was proceeding to Greece by land the reason for the additional *epibatai* being on board was not because this was the only means of getting them to their destination, but, probably to ensure the loyalty of the ship's company, and for that reason they were also carried in battle. All the ships therefore, whether technically 'fast' or not, would qualify as troop-carriers in the sense in which Thucydides uses the term, and thus be, *prima facie*, slower than the ships which carried no extra troops. Nevertheless, in spite of the extra weight of the additional 30 soldiers on deck and the probable structural modifications entailed, it appears that the favourable condition of the ships as regards maintenance was a powerful enough factor to override the disadvantage of the extra men, etc., as far as speed was concerned.

Since it appears that at Salamis, irrespective of the maintenance factor, which was of great importance, all the Athenian *triereis* were 'fast' in the sense that they did not carry extra troops, and all the Persian ships were in Thucydidean terms troop-carriers in the sense that they did, in what sense were ten of the Greek ships 'outstanding' (*ekkritoi*) and 207 of the Persian ships 'especially fast' as Aeschylus says? At the beginning of the Peloponnesian War the Athenians set aside each year 100 *triereis* in reserve against emergencies. These ships are called by Thucydides (2.24.2, cf. Andocides 3.7) *exairetoi*, and the same word is also used in the fourth century for a category of *triereis*, many of them new, in the naval inventories, where other categories of ships are first, second, and third class and 'old'.²⁴ It seems then that within the overall Thucydidean categories of 'fast' ships and troop-carriers *triereis* could also be placed in categories according their date of construction, building standard (possibly in respect of the timber used, see below, p. 181), hull design (see above, p. 152) or some other factor.²⁵

At this point we must enquire whether there are any clues to the structural difference between the 'Themistoclean' fast *trieres* with 10 *epibatai*, and with a correspondingly restricted deck, and the *triereis* in the Persian fleet with 40 *epibatai* (and the necessarily larger deck). A larger deck for at any rate some of the non-Athenian *triereis* of the time is implied by Thucydides' remark that the Athenian *triereis* 'did not yet have decks overall' (1.14.3). There are two relevant passages from Plutarch, who wrote in the first/second century AD but is likely to have derived his information from a reliable source. He says (*Cimon* 12.2) that the Athenian general Cimon in command of a fleet of the Delian League operating in 467 in SW Asia

---

24. *IG* 2² 1611.
25. Thuc. 8.62: 'the troop-carriers carrying hoplites' and Xen. *HG* 1.1.36 'troop-carriers rather than fast'. In *IG* 2² 1623.284 four hulls are specified as 'fast', and of these three are in fact said to be new. In *IG* 2² 1611.65–128 there is a special class of *exairetoi*, 'selected' ships, which are mostly new. The earliest mention of troop-carriers is probably *IG* 1³ 499 (435–410 BC) *strat*]*iōtides*. See Appendix I, below.

Minor 'set out with two hundred ships which had been originally very well built by Themistocles for speed and easy turning and which he had then made broader and given a (greater) deck span, so that they might proceed against the enemy with the greater fighting power exercised by many hoplites'. There is the implication that, so modified, they were slower and less easy to turn. If these were in fact the triereis built by Themistocles, they would have been getting on for 15 years old and would have been ready for conversion to troop-carriers. This is what Cimon appears to have done and we are told how he did it: 'by making the hulls broader and giving the decks greater span'. Similarly we hear later of old triereis being made into horse-transports by what must have been a major conversion.

The second passage (*Themistocles* 14.2) is from Plutarch's account of an incident in the battle of Salamis which he uses to illustrate Themistocles' qualities as a naval commander:

He seems to have been as much aware of the right time as of the right place [to start an engagement], and to have been careful not to send his triereis in to attack the enemy's ships until the moment arrived which usually brought a stiff breeze from the sea and a swell through the straits. This did no harm to the Greek ships, which were nearer water-level and lower, but did affect and confuse the enemy's ships with their towering sterns and high decks, and offered them broadside to the Greeks, who were in fact bearing down on them and keeping an eye on Themistocles as he was watching for the right time to make his attack.

Plutarch describes the moment when the two Persian squadrons were coming up the straits several ranks deep in line abreast (above, p. 58) and the Athenians on the Greek right wing were waiting for the right moment to turn into line ahead and launch their attack aimed at a breakthrough. Plutarch preserves a tradition that Themistocles, like Phormio later in the gulf of Corinth (pp. 68–71), used his knowledge of local weather conditions to attack at precisely the right moment, when the following breeze and swell caused enemy ships to broach to and present themselves broadside to the Athenian rams, thus enabling the breakthrough to be effected. Plutarch's story concerns only a brief, if vital, moment in the action. It emphasises an important characteristic of the ships of the Persian fleet, all of which were built to carry 40 soldiers on deck as opposed to the Athenians' 10.

It has already been seen that troop-carriers had to have broader hulls and wider decks than triereis of the Themistoclean type. The second passage from Plutarch shows that they also had higher sterns and decks, offering greater wind resistance and making the ships heavier. In what sense could they have been higher? The oarsystem of the trieres will be seen to be such that the oarsmen could not be arranged lower or higher in one trieres than in another (see fig. 45) without changing the length of the oars, and no reason is discernible for such a change. On the other hand there is very good reason for troop-carriers to have bulwarks at least 1 m high if 40 men are to be accommodated on deck. Such bulwarks are visible on the oared ships taking part in the evacuation of Tyre in 701 and depicted on the relief from Sennacherib's palace (fig. 24). They are also seen on the oared war-ships of the first century AD in Pompeian wall-paintings, in particular on the ship in the House of the Priest Amandus the deck of which is packed with armed men[26] (fig. 44). If the few rep-

44. Wall painting in the House of the Priest Amandus at Pompeii showing the bow of a three-level oared ship, probably a quinquereme, with high bulwarks and many armed men on deck, AD 54–68.

26. Her oarsystem resembles that of a trieres, but as a Roman ship it is perhaps likely to be a penteres or 'five', with two of the oar-levels double-manned. The ship has high bulwarks to the deck and many *epibatai*.

resentations of triereis which we possess show only a minimal bulwark or none at all (figs. 37 and 38) the reason must be that they are all representations of fast triereis. There is good reason to think that the Lenormant relief and its associated representations come, or are derived from, a monument showing the *Paralos*, which was certainly a fast ship.[27]

Plutarch probably exaggerates the differences between the Persian fleet and the Greek fleet in 480 in order to make his point. Herodotus (7.194.1–3) tells how some Persian ships, as they were coming in to Aphetae after their voyage down the coast of Magnesia, mistook the Greek fleet at Artemisium for their own in the evening light, went over and were captured. The difference was not such as would be obvious under those conditions.

Besides fast triereis (including some that were outstanding) and troop-carrying triereis there is a third category, the horse-transport (*hippagōgos* or, for short, *hippegos*: pp. 226–9). Horse-carrying vessels are mentioned in Herodotus' accounts of Darius' and Xerxes' invasion fleets (6.48.2, 7.21.2, 7.97); but they seem not to have been modified triereis, since in speaking of Pericles' expedition against the Peloponnese in 430 Thucydides (2.56.2) mentions 300 cavalry in horse-transports 'which then for the first time were made out of old triereis'. And Aristophanes in the *Knights* (595–610) speaks of horses being regularly transported by sea in the Peloponnesian War. There was one horse-transport in the Sicilian expedition (Thuc. 6.43) carrying 30 horses, and an inscription[28] shows that such transports were pulled by 60 oarsmen. It is a natural inference that the horses occupied the space in the hull vacated by the thalamian and zygian oarsmen, and that there were 30 thranite oarsmen on each side of the ship instead of the regular thirty-two.[29] These horse-transports are in fact called triereis in Demosthenes and in an inscription.[30]

The naval inventories record the numbers of triereis in the dockyards at Piraeus in 357/6 as 283.[31] In 353/2 the triereis in the dockyards and on commission numbered 349,[32] and in 330/29 there were

27. Since she went on errands for the state. Her crew were punished by being transferred to a troop-carrier.
28. *IG* 2² 1628.154–5, 161–2, 470, 475, 480.
29. As JFC has discovered, in his drawing of a possible replica (below, p. 227).
30. Dem. 4.16, *IG* 2² 1627.241.   31. *IG* 2² 1611.1–9.   32. *IG* 2² 1613.284–302.

even greater numbers: 392 triereis in the dockyards and 7 at sea including horse-transports, and 8 'fours' in the dockyard and 10 at sea.[33] The inventory of 326/5 records 360 triereis and a number (erased) of 'fours'; and it also gives the number of ship-sheds, 372 all told, 82 in Munychia, 196 in Zea and 94 in Cantharos.[34] In the following year there are the same number of triereis and in addition 43 'fours' and seven 'fives'.[35]

In this chapter all the evidence from various sources has been assembled relative to the more general features of the trieres, the hull, the accommodation of the trierarch, the *hypēresia* and the oarsmen, and the various types of triereis which were built. In the following chapter important particular features of the ship will be considered – her deck, outrigger and ram – and then certain articles of gear which are relevant to the reconstruction.

33. *IG* 2² 1627.268–9.
34. *IG* 2² 1628.481,553. Fig. 71 (p. 229) gives a reconstructed view of Munychia.
35. *IG* 2² 1629.801–11.

9

THE SHIPS II

The ancient evidence for the main structural features of the trieres will be our first concern in this chapter – the deck, the outrigger and the ram; and we shall look at various items of gear – the oarport sleeve, the oars for pulling and steering, and the masts, sails and rigging – all of which are particularly relevant to the making and navigating of the replica.

The deck (in Greek *katastrōma*, or plural *katastrōmata*)

The oared ships depicted in the earlier vase-paintings have platforms at bow and stern (*ikria*) and probably, in some, a connecting gangway between these platforms (fig. 21). These are twenty-, thirty- or fifty-oared ships, in the case of the latter two sometimes with oars at two levels. None has a deck. Speaking of Homer's ships in the *Iliad*, Thucydides (1.10.4) remarks that they were unlikely to have taken on board many men, apart from the leaders, in addition to the oarsmen (who were, as he has said, also the fighting men), since the ships were not *kataphrakta*. This word is here taken to mean 'decked' since, as we have seen, it would have been on deck that the additional men were accommodated.

A fourth-century picture of the stern of the *Argo* (starboard side) engraved on the bronze Ficoronian chest in the Villa Giulia in Rome (fig. 27) shows two levels of oars and a deck supported by curved stanchions continuing forward from the stern platform at the same level. The *Argo* was traditionally a pentecontor. The Talos vase-painting described above (pp. 148–9: fig. 41) gives a very similar picture of the *Argo*'s stern, this time port side, but the presence of the outrigger indicates that the ship represented (anachronistically) is a trieres. Here again a deck, supported by curved stanchions, continues forward at the same level as the stern platform. The outward edge of the deck, which has no bulwark or rail, appears to be vertically above the horizontal outer planks of the outrigger. The Vienna fragment (pp. 149–51: fig. 43) shows a deck with a deck-rail, the deck having a slot in it on the middle fore-and-aft line of the ship through which lines are drawn representing rigging ropes, javelins, or poles. The Lenormant relief with its associated fragment (pp. 131–41: figs. 13 and 14), giving the midships section of the starboard side of a trieres, shows a deck on which men are lying, and which, like the deck of the Talos vase ship, has no bulwark or deck-rail. The Aquila relief (pp. 145–6: fig. 12) shows the starboard side of a trieres stern with the deck continuing forward at the same level and men seated on it, as in the Lenormant relief. The dal Pozzo drawing (pp. 141–5: fig. 11), probably taken from the same monument as that from which the Lenormant relief derives, shows the bow of a ship, starboard side, in which the deck continues into the bow where it joins the bow platform at an identical level. On this bow platform a man, probably the bow officer, reclines and signals aft (to the helmsman). We may draw the following conclusions from this evidence: (1) in the fifth century triereis had a deck connecting bow and stern platforms; (2) this deck extended laterally to the same width as the outrigger; (3) the deck was supported by outward-curving (or outward-leaning, if the curve is an attempt at perspective) stanchions; (4) the deck in some cases had a rail and in some cases had not; and (5) the deck had a slot in it running fore and aft on the ship's median line.

Such, then, was the deck of the trieres in the later fifth century. It can be seen at once that the slot would have been necessary for managing the main mast and, further forward, the 'boat' mast (pp. 176–7). It is likely that both were stepped into tabernacles built around the keel, possibly between *parastatai*, 'mast-partners', which occur in the naval inventories,[1] like a modern flagpole. How does this account fit what Thucydides says about Themistocles' triereis at Salamis (1.14.3), that 'they were not decked overall'? The phrase 'overall' (*dia pases*) is not at all explicit. It could mean 'throughout the length' or 'throughout the breadth' or both.[2] It seems so unlikely as

1. As LSJ s.v. and Torr (1894) p. 83. In the naval inventories they appear regularly as important items of the wooden gear of a trieres. In *GOS* p. 293 I called them shores, but since mast-partners are clearly needed and *parastatai* is a very suitable word for them, I am now inclined to follow Torr. In *IG* 2² 1611.38–41 there are two *parastatai* for each ship.
2. Torr (1894) p. 50 n. 118. See also Casson (1971) ch. 5 p. 52.

to be virtually impossible that the trieres could have had no deck at all, not even a narrow one, connecting the bow and stern platforms. The presence of the *epibatai* and the necessity of managing the masts and sails, with the hull packed with oarsmen, make a deck imperative. On the other hand, if, as the history of the trieres makes clear, the prime consideration of the shipbuilder was lightness, it is reasonable to suppose that Themistocles' triereis at any rate had as narrow a deck as possible in contrast to the ships of the Persian fleet, all of which were, in Thucydides' parlance, carriers of troops and would have needed not only a wide deck and bulwarks but also a more heavily built hull. And that is the contrast which Thucydides is making. His remark fits well with Plutarch's statement (above, p. 154) that Cimon converted Themistocles' triereis 'built for speed and easiness of turning' into troop-carriers with wider hulls and broader decks. It looks as if, by the end of the century, Athenian fast triereis, as well as the troop-carriers, had adopted the wider deck, but only the troop-carriers had the wider and heavier hull and a deck-rail, a lighter version of the deck-bulwark which we have inferred for the Persian ships at Salamis (above, p. 156).

It is an interesting fact that on the Lenormant and Aquila reliefs (figs. 13 and 12), the associated Acropolis fragment (fig. 14) and the dal Pozzo drawing (fig. 11), representing the fast trieres *Paralos* under oar, the men on deck are all seated or reclining. In this connection we may recall the speech of the Spartan general Gylippus before the final battle in the Great Harbour at Syracuse (7.67.2). He is addressing the Syracusan and Corinthian seamen and soldiers who are about to join battle: 'When the Athenians . . . have many hoplites on their decks contrary to their established practice and many javelin men, landsmen so to speak, Acarnanians and others, on board, who will not have learnt the knack of throwing javelins in a sitting position, this factor will surely put their ships at risk and everything will be in confusion from the unaccustomed movement.'

The reason for the Athenian practice of taking only a few hoplites on deck is here shown clearly. Their prime consideration was pulling efficiency, and this was jeopardised if there were many men moving about on deck and inevitably causing the ship to roll. Anyone contemplating the oarsystem of a trieres (fig. 45) with this possibility in mind can see at once that even a small rolling motion of the hull would 'put everything in confusion' as far as the oarsmen were con-

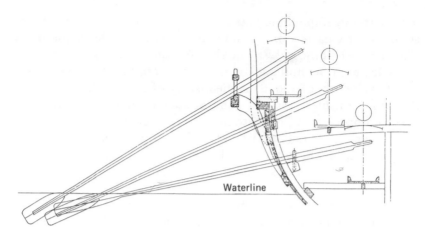

45. The oarsystem of a trieres.

cerned. The effect of javelin-men standing up and moving from side
to side of the ship to hurl their missiles would be even more disturb-
ing and dangerous. Gylippus' words are evidence that naval javelin-
men, not landlubbers like the Acarnanians, would be taught to
throw their missiles sitting down. Indeed it is pretty clear that
everyone allowed on deck during a battle, the hoplites included,
must have been ordered to sit or lie down while the ship was moving
under oar. When the ship had come to a stop locked into an enemy
ship and expecting boarders, the hoplites would of course have done
no harm by standing up and moving. We must assume that any
movement on deck, entailing a rolling movement of the ship, was
'unaccustomed' for Athenian oarsmen, and would spoil the stroke.

The other reason for carrying few men on deck is revealed by the
Athenian general Nicias in his speech before the same battle (Thuc.
7.62.2). He says: 'Many archers and javelin-men will be on deck and a
mass of hoplites, which we would not employ if we were fighting a
battle in the open sea, because they would hinder us through the
weight of the ships in exercising our skill.' Weight, particularly on
deck, prevented them bringing off the breakthrough, the circling
movement and the engagement of the ram amidships, all of them
manoeuvres in which speed and agility were essential.

The outrigger (*parexeiresia*)

The Greek word *parexeiresia* suggests some part of the ship concerned with pulling the oars (*eiresia*) outboard (*ex-*) and alongside (*par-*). Tarn wrote (1930 p. 65): 'The meaning of the word was Assmann's discovery (*Seewesen* in Baumeister's *Denkmäler*) and is the most illuminating thing discovered in modern times about these warships.' Two passages in Thucydides throw some further light. The first is part of the account of the Spartan attempt to dislodge the Athenian general Demosthenes from his foothold on Spartan soil at Pylos. Early in 425 an Athenian fleet, sent partly as a training exercise round the Peloponnese to Corcyra and from there to Sicily, was driven by bad weather into the large bay on the west coast of the Peloponnese now known as Navarino Bay, sheltered on the west side by the island of Sphacteria. Demosthenes was not one of the generals in command of the fleet but had accompanied it and at his own request had received permission from the Assembly to use the 40 ships at his discretion in their journey round the Peloponnese (Thuc. 4.2.4). He saw to it that, during the fleet's enforced stay, a small promontory (Pylos) at the northern end of the bay was fortified; and when the rest of the fleet continued on its way, he stayed there with four ships. In the course of Spartan attempts to dislodge the small Athenian force, Brasidas, who on this occasion was serving as a trierarch on one of the Peloponnesian ships sent to the scene, was among those detailed to try to effect a landing on the side of the fort facing the sea, where the defence was weakest. Thucydides (4.11.4–12.1) describes the attack:

Being a trierarch himself and noticing that the trierarchs and helmsmen, because the shore was rocky wherever a landing was possible, hung back and were afraid of damaging their ships, Brasidas shouted out to them . . . to run the ships aground [bow first] and make a landing in any way they could . . . And he . . . compelled his own helmsman to run his ship aground, and went to the landing ladder. As he attempted to get ashore he was beaten back by the Athenians and was wounded in many places. He lost consciousness and as he fell into the outrigger his shield slipped off his arm into the sea.

This picture of a trieres in action is unique even if the action itself is untypical. The ship is driven ashore bow first.[3] A 'brow' (*apobathra*),

3. See *GOS* p. 211. *Okellein* has the meaning of grounding a ship bow first.

i.e. a gangway on which a man could get down from the deck of a ship facing the shore,[4] was run out and the trierarch began to advance down it, but he was beaten back and fell unconscious into the outrigger. As he fell his body was caught in it, but his shield slipped through and rolled into the sea. The passage shows that the outrigger projected from the side of the ship at a lower level than the deck and was so constructed that a man going down from the deck could fall into it and be prevented from falling further, while a shield could fall through it. These are important hints for the reconstructor.

Before proceeding to the second of the two relevant passages in Thucydides, it is worth while looking at two devices attributed to the fourth-century Athenian naval commander Chabrias by the historian Polyaenus, writing in the middle of the second century AD. The first (3.11.14) was a device to assist steering a trieres in bad weather.

For voyages in the open sea and rough weather he fitted to each ship two pairs of steering oars and employed the normal single pair[5] in calm weather, but if there was a swell he ran out the second pair through the outrigger beside the thranite oars with the upper ends [of the oars] and the tillers above the deck [instead of above the stern platform as would be the case with normal steering oars], so that when the stern came out of the water [as it would in a swell, with the result that the normal steering oars would be ineffective], the ship was steered by the second set.

The other device (3.11.13) consists of sidescreens to protect the oarsmen in bad weather. The text is very uncertain, but it is clear that the sidescreens were in some way hung from the deck to the outrigger.

These passages give reliable information about the trieres. In them the outrigger appears to extend along the side of the ship from the bow, where Thucydides shows it to have been, to the stern, where auxiliary steering oars could be run out through it. The further important point made is that the auxiliary steering oars run out through the outrigger were beside the thranite oars, which must then also have been worked through the outrigger. The normal function of the outrigger becomes plain. The proposition may now

---

4. *Apobathrai* were used similarly in the opposed landing at Mycale (Hdt. 9.98.2).
5. *IG* 2^2 1611.23–7.

be put forward that the structure of the outrigger made possible the addition of the third class of oarsmen to the two-level pentecontor to form the trieres.

The second passage in Thucydides illuminates the relation of the outrigger to the bow-structure and at the same time gives interesting information about the efforts made by Athens' enemies to overcome the advantage which the speed and lightness of her ships gave her in the normal course of fighting at sea.

In the spring and early summer of 413, when Demosthenes' fleet of 50 ships was on its way to reinforce Nicias, ten of the fastest were detached to join Conon, Phormio's son, who was then in command at Naupactus, and had asked for reinforcement. When next we hear of the Naupactus squadron it had increased to 30 ships under Diphilus, and the Corinthians had raised their opposing force on the other side of the gulf of Corinth to nearly the same number. The ensuing engagement (Thuc. 7.34) had a considerable bearing on the fate of the Athenian fleet at Syracuse.

The Corinthian ships put to sea and formed line abreast in a crescent-shaped bay on the southern shore of the gulf at Erineus in Achaea (map 15). Their land forces occupied the horns of the crescent, the projecting headlands on each flank. The Athenians pulled out to meet them from Naupactus on the other side of the gulf and to the west. The Corinthians remained where they were, to draw the Athenians out and to avoid exposing their wings to encirclement if they came out beyond the protecting headlands on each side. Then, when they judged the moment to be right, they raised the signal and attacked the Athenian ships.

For a long time neither side gave ground. Three Corinthian ships were put out of action, and of the Athenian ships none was completely swamped, but some seven became unmanageable, having been rammed bow-to-bow and having their outriggers smashed by the Corinthian ship's bow-timbers which had been specially strengthened for just this purpose. There was an indecisive battle, in which both sides claimed victory, but the Athenians got possession of the wrecks because the wind drove them out to sea and the Corinthians refused to come out after them. Then the two sides separated, and there was no pursuit nor were any men captured on either side. The Corinthians and Peloponnesians easily escaped since they were fighting near the shore, and none of the Athenian ships was swamped.

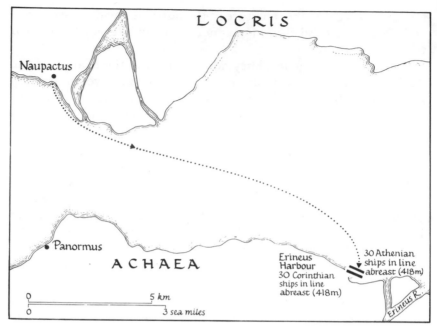

Map 15 The battle of Erineus.

Two features of this battle have already been noticed on other occasions: the planned role of land forces and the fact that triereis holed and consequently abandoned by their crews nevertheless continued to float and were towed away by one side or the other. The interest of the battle lies here in the evidence it provides of a serious attempt by the Corinthians to devise an answer to the tactic of breakthrough and encirclement. The answer was for their opponents to seek a combat situation in which head-on, bow-to-bow, collisions would inevitably occur, and previously, without regard to weight, to reinforce the bow-timbers of their ships so that when bow-to-bow ramming did occur the bows of their opponents' ships, being more lightly built, would be smashed and the oarsystem disrupted. More precisely, what would happen would be this: the ram of a strengthened ship would, after a bow-to-bow collision, slide along the ram of an opponent; and her bow timbers (one end of which projected on each side of the ship (fig. 46) at a higher level than the ram and covered the outrigger (above, p. 142)) would smash into and,

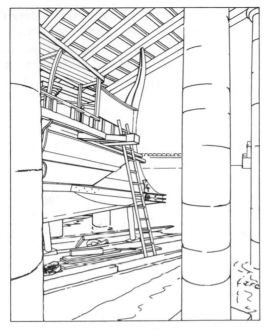

46. The bow timbers of a trieres (perspective). The anchor platform, here removed for rebuilding, would normally obscure the *epōtis* beam and its brace.

having been strengthened, break the bow-timber of the more lightly built opposing ship. These bow-timbers themselves were not particularly vital, but if one of them was broken the outrigger through which the thranite oars were pulled would be dislocated. The Corinthians' carefully planned tactical situation (in which bow-to-bow collision was inevitable), together with the structural modification of their ships, constitutes an intelligent response to the Athenian use of lightly built ships. This Corinthian innovation, tried out here for the first time, is significant not for its immediate results, which were negligible, but because it was adopted by the Syracusans in the Great Harbour, where the Corinthians were acting as advisers to them in the build-up of their naval force.

While the Athenian generals Demosthenes and Eurymedon were on their way to Syracuse with 50 ships, the Athenians already there lost possession of the three forts covering the approach to the Great Harbour, and were experiencing still greater difficulty in victualling their force by sea. The Syracusans were anxious to attack the Athenian positions by sea and land before their reinforcements arrived. Thucydides describes (7.36.2) how they, in preparation for a sea-battle, 'shortened the bows of their ships and made them stronger and placed stout timbers across the bows, taking brackets from them to the ships' sides to a distance of six cubits [2.64 m] both inside and outside, in just the same way as the Corinthians had modified their ships in the bow-to-bow fight against the [Athenian] ships at Naupactus'. The word used for bow-timbers both here and in the earlier passage is *epōtides*, literally 'ear-timbers'. The bow of an oared galley was often decorated to look like the head of an animal with the ram as its snout (e.g. fig. 26), so that timbers projecting on each side of this simulated head could be described as 'ear-timbers'. The strengthening of these in the way described would be effective in head-on collisions if ram slid alongside ram. The strengthening of the ram itself by making the bow shorter seems to imply ram actually hitting ram, an occurrence which was not envisaged in the earlier passage but seems now to be a possibility which had to be guarded against. The Athenian rams were designed for a much lighter – if more deadly – task: to penetrate the hull timbers of a trieres from the side.

The ram (*embolos*)

Hipponax (above, p. 36), the mid-sixth century poet who first mentions the trieres, is also first to mention the ram. Its first use in battle of which we have any account (above, p. 30) is at the battle of Alalia in 535, when the rams of the Phocaean pentecontors are said to have been twisted off. Aeschylus (e.g. *Persians* 415) speaks of the use of bronze rams at the battle of Salamis, and they appear in the lists of gear of the naval dockyards as returnable when a ship is broken up.[6] There is plain (if anachronistic) representation of a bronze ram in a late sixth-century vase-painting showing Odysseus' ship (fig. 47).

A large bronze ram with some structural timbers attached (fig. 33) has recently been found in the sea off Athlit in Palestine. It cannot be the ram of a trieres since it is far too heavy, about 400 kg compared with the 200 kg which is an appropriate weight for a trieres.[7] It prob-

6. *IG* 2² 1623.11–13, 1628.498.
7. *MM* 68.1.3–7, 69–3.229–49.

47. Attic red-figure stamnos showing Odysseus and the Sirens, 500–480 BC.

ably belonged to one of the large new types of oared warship which are known to have been built in Cyprus at the end of the fourth century.[8] Nevertheless, the discovery provides useful information about the mounting of a ram which is of indirect relevance to the trieres. The shape of the ram is also likely to be common to the earlier triereis and seems to have been designed to cause maximum waterline damage without penetrating the hull too far and making it difficult for the attacking vessel to back off.

This chapter may be concluded with a brief consideration of certain items of gear[9] which are relevant to the making and working of the replica.

The oarport sleeve (*askōma*)

In the earliest naval inventory, of 377/6 BC,[10] it is noted against each

---

8. See *IJNA* 13.2
9. For the gear of the trieres in general see *GOS* pp. 289–307.
10. *IG* 2^2 1604 e.g. 33 ('the dockyard has them'), 38 ('fitted to the ship'), 42, 91 ('the trierarch has them').

of the ships listed what the position is with regard to her *askōmata*. They are either already fitted, or someone named has them, or the dockyard holds the money for them (43 dr. 2 obols), or they are missing. Plainly they are important fittings. There is reason to believe[11] that they are leather sleeves through which the thalamian oars were worked as a precaution against water coming in through the lower, and larger,[12] row of oarports when the sea was choppy or the ship was under sail. There is some indication of them on the Lenormant relief but the clearest representation is in the stern on the Talos vase (fig. 41). It is possibly more than a coincidence that the number of thalamian oars inferred for the oar-arrangement in fig. 40 (above, p. 147) is 52 (2 × 26) and that the money held for the *askōmata* in the inscription of 377/6 is easily divisible by 52. *Askōmata* work out at five obols each. The triereis of 377/6 seem to have retained the earlier distribution of oarsmen between the classes.

The undergirdle (*hypozōma*)

The undergirdle of the trieres has long been a puzzle. It is the first named and hence the most important and considerable of the ship's ropes (called 'hanging gear'). A decree lays down the minimum number of men to be employed in fitting it to a ship (but unfortunately the number is not preserved).[13] and ships fitted with them are regarded as being in commission.[14] Four were the regulation number carried, a further two being added for a squadron sent in 325/4 to suppress piracy in the Adriatic.[15] It would appear then that they wore out fairly quickly. 'Pieces' of them are listed.[16] By a happy chance the weight of four is given in an inscription[17] and from that weight the rough length of one can be calculated, viz. 280–340 ft (85–108 m), according to the type of rope chosen – twice the length of a trieres, with a good deal to spare.

11. See *GOS* pp. 283–4.
12. They appear larger in the Talos vase stern, which is our most accurate piece of evidence. See pp. 148–9. The reason for their being larger appeared during the making of the mock-up (below, p. 172).
13. *IG* 1³ 153: *c.* 440–425 BC.
14. *IG* 2² 1627.29.
15. *IG* 2² 1629.11f.
16. *IG* 2² 1610.26.
17. *IG* 2² 1479 B 49 and 58. Since the date of the inscription is after 314/13 the *hypozōmata* could have been part of the gear of a 'four' or 'five'.

The *hypozōma* features most enigmatically[18] in Plato's *Republic* (616B–C) where a story is told of Er's journey as a soul in the country of the dead. At one point with other souls he came to a place where they could see

> from above stretched over the whole heaven and earth a straight light, like a pillar but resembling most of all a rainbow. Arriving at this light after a day's journey they saw there in the middle of this light stretched from heaven the ends of the bonds of it [i.e. of the light] for this light is the constricting bond of heaven like the *hypozōmata* of triereis thus holding together the whole revolution [i.e. this light ties the heaven together just as *hypozōmata* tie triereis together]. And from the ends [of the bonds of it] is hung the spindle of necessity.

The third-century Alexandrian poet Apollonius of Rhodes (*Argonautica* 1.367–9) describes the launching of the *Argo* and the fitting of it with a *hypozōma*: 'the first thing they did was to girdle the ship strongly with a well-twisted rope from within, putting a tension on each extremity, so that the planks should fit well together with the dowels and withstand the opposing force of the sea'. In the representations of parts of the hull of a trieres which have been noticed earlier in this chapter there is no trace of an external rope. It seems that we must accept that the rope ran from stern to stem and back again within the hull, where alone it can be structurally significant (pp. 197–8). Plato (*Laws* 945C) and inscriptions,[19] both in the fourth century, speak of braces (*tonoi, entonoi*) of *hypozōmata*, and Plato speaks of them as adding to the ship's seaworthiness, confirming Apollonius' explanation of the purpose of the 'girdle'. A *hypozōma*, then, can be taken to be a doubled rope in tension 'tying together' bow and stern of a trieres and situated within the hull. The purpose of the rope and of the braces which applied the tension was to preserve the seaworthiness of the ship. Further explanation of Plato's 'straight light' is not relevant here, but it may be noticed that his braces were in the middle of it, i.e. equidistant from both extremities, and that its bonds (i.e. braces) had ends to which a spindle was attached. This spindle may reflect the twisting device situated in the middle of the ship which applied the necessary tension, through the braces, to the two parts of the *hypozōma* there running parallel to

18. See JSM (1955) for an early attempt to solve this baffling problem.
19. *IG* 2² 1610 23, 1613 280–2, 1673 12.

each other, the rope having passed round anchoring posts at bow and stern. Its name 'undergirdle' suggests that it was placed low down in the ship.

Oars (*kōpai*)[20]

A full-scale mock-up (figs. 2, 3) of part of the three-level oarsystem based on the Lenormant relief and the Talos vase was built by John Coates and David Moss in the winter of 1982/3, successfully demonstrated at the National Maritime Museum in April 1983, and subsequently improved by some adjustments. The oars used were 4.2 m in length at all levels. The mock-up was designed to combine a suitable hull shape and beam on the waterline with the need for the tholes of each level of oars to be well outboard of those in the level below. To achieve this it was necessary to set the thalamian tholes in carlings mounted on the inboard facings of hull frames. This was made possible because the larger oarports used at the thalamian level allowed the proper movements of the oar as it passed through the hull shell. The existence of larger oarports demands a compelling reason for what would otherwise be an unnecessarily hazardous feature. Such a compelling reason is provided by the need to set the thalamian tholes a few inches inside the hull shell.

The oars used in the mock-up were of the naval pattern with blades 150 cm × 15 cm (pierced for pulling in a static structure alongside a pool), and it became apparent that the varied angles at which they were pulled required a different-shaped blade in each category (fig. 48): i.e. where the angle was largest a short broad blade, and where the angle was least a narrow long one (similar to the oar actually being used in the mock-up). It happens that there is an inscription in

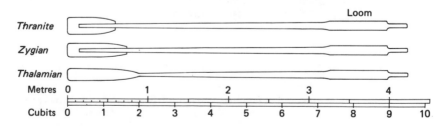

48. The oars of a trieres.

the naval inventories[21] which records that 'the inspector declares that of these thranite oars four are zygian'. As we have seen, the difference between the thranite and zygian oars was not in length. It could be either in the shape of the blade or in the nature of the loom. Experience at Greenwich and at the Boat Show at Earl's Court in January 1984 where the mock-up was demonstrated again, suggested that the former is likely.[22] This conclusion is confirmed by Dr Nooteboom (1949) who mentions and illustrates a 'model of a merchant ship of the ordinary South Celebes type, but with two rows of oars. The lower row has its tholes on the gunwale and consists of five oars *with long and narrow blades*. The upper row has its tholes on a bulwark which rises from the ends of beams projecting from the hull planking. It consists of six oars *with rectangular blades*.' He mentions and illustrates other models of Indonesian ships pulled at two levels and with similar differences between the oars (fig. 49).

49. Indonesian two-level oared ship.

20. The substance of this and the following sections appeared in *IJNA*, JSM (1984).
21. *IG* 2² 1604.56. See my note (1978) in reply to a query by M. Lucien Basch.
22. It is possible that thranite oars were also different as having looms which were heavier than the looms of the zygian and thalamian oars, since the need to balance them would have been greater because they were pulled at a steeper angle.

To return to ancient Greece. There are several representations of ships being pulled by oars at two levels (figs. 25 and 26) which show no difference between the oars. These pictures are not, however, carefully drawn. The earliest oars shown, in the ships illustrated on late Geometric vases of the Dipylon group (760–735 BC),[23] have triangular blades, a shape repeated in later pictures.[24] Others from the same century are spade-shaped[25] or paddle-shaped.[26] From the sixth century there are a large number of Attic black-figure vases showing warships with one or two levels of oars. These oars are depicted by an incised line for the shaft and a broader brush-stroke for the blade. The only carefully drawn oars appear at the end of the sixth and the beginning of the fifth century on the well-known red-figure vase in the British Museum (fig. 47) depicting Odysseus and the Sirens. These oars have short, broad spade-shaped blades, with round shoulders, apparently spliced to the oar-shaft which tapers towards the outboard end. As far as is known there are no further representations of oar blades until the Roman period, when the ships depicted are certainly pulled by oars manned by more than one oarsman, e.g. the Palestrina relief in the Vatican museum.[27] These oars are massive affairs shaped from a single timber and growing gradually broader towards the outboard end, which is pointed. A composite oar made up of a tapering shaft and a short broad blade spliced to it might conveniently have a blade of a different shape according to the angle at which it was pulled, long and narrow for the thalamian position, shorter and broader in differing degrees for the zygian and thranite.

Steering oars (*pēdalia*)

There is a problem about the steering oars of the trieres,[28] whether they were turned on their axis or moved from side to side. It was suggested in *GOS* (pp. 291–2) that the tiller (*oiax*) was a connecting bar between the tops of the two steering oars which were thus ganged for lateral movement, and a phrase in Plato, 'moving the tiller in or out',

23. *GOS* pls. 3 and 4.
24. *GOS* pls. 8b and 22a.
25. *GOS* pls. 7b and bc.
26. *GOS* pl. 7d.
27. First century BC: see JSM (1980b) pl. 27.
28. L. Th. Lehmann (1978) pp. 94–104.

was cited (*Alc.* I 117C–D) in support. This phrase could, however, equally well be used of the movement of the handle of a tiller set at right angles to each steering oar in an arc either outward or inward. The function of a tiller is to enable the helmsman to operate the steering oar with greater control. A tiller attached to the single steering oar with a pin is shown in one of the earliest pictures of a Greek oared galley, the Mycenaean ship, probably of 50 oars, since it has 25 thwarts, on the Pylos–Tragana pyxis (fig. 19). This tiller could as well have been used to turn the steering oar as to move it laterally. There are two very carefully drawn pictures showing the stern of smaller oared vessels, one of Theseus' ship on an Attic black-figure vase by Cleitias (fig. 50) and the other on a fragment of a similar vase of the same date (fig. 51). The first probably belongs to a triacontor and the second is closely similar. In both cases the helmsman sits in a narrow stern seat with the ends of the steering oars rising conveniently on either side. On the Cleitias vase the 'fins'[29] on the after edges of the steering oars suggest that the oars were designed for turning rather than for lateral movement. On the fragment, the tops of the steering oars are given ball-shaped 'caps'. John Coates has suggested that these are more likely to be the ends of tillers than caps, the ends being enlarged and rounded to embrace the shaft of the steering oar. Pindar, Aeschylus and Euripides, all of whom wrote in the heyday of tricres use, speak consistently about 'turning the steering oar', and it seems very unlikely that they would have used that phrase if in the most commonly used ship of their time they knew that the steering oar was moved laterally. The conclusion then is that the steering oar

50. Scene from an Attic black-figure volute krater painted by Cleitias showing the stern half of a one-level oared warship, *c.* 570 BC.

29. The word for this 'fin' is *pteryx*, 'wing', which is recorded sometimes as 'broken' in the naval inventories (*IG* 2² 1607.74 cf. 1608.14–15).

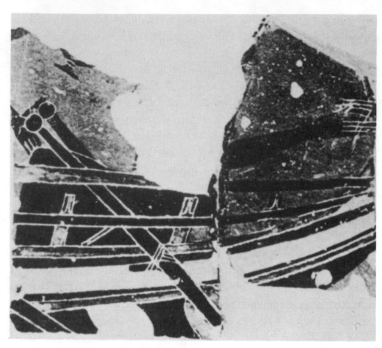

51. Attic black-figure fragment in the Acropolis Museum Athens showing the stern of an oared warship, *c.* 570 BC.

in long ships was, in all likelihood, turned on its axis, and that a tiller was used to help the helmsman control both oars effectively. Whether such steering equipment was sufficient, without the help of the oarsmen, to make the sharp turns (*anastrophai*) which are said to be the mark of a well-trained ship (Thuc. 2.89.8) is a question which can only be resolved in the sea trials of the replica.

Masts, sails and rigging

There are no extant representations of the trieres under sail, or even of one with masts up. There are two masts for each ship recorded in the naval inventories[30] – the main mast and the 'boat' mast. The position of both must be guessed, but pictures of some later ships (e.g. fig. 52) can give some clues. The main mast is probably stepped

30. *IG* 2² 1604.23, cf.48, 50, 60, 66.

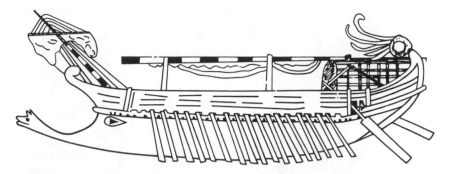

52. Roman oared ship on a mosaic from Themetra, AD 225–250.

about amidships, and the boat mast is probably raked and stepped forward. The height of neither is known. There are similarly two sails, the main sail and the 'boat' sail. The main sail was regularly left ashore before battle.[31] There is no evidence for the size or shape of these sails. It is reasonable to assume that they were rectangular, like the sails of pentecontors and other ships depicted on sixth-century vases (e.g. fig. 53). Two sorts of sails occur in the naval inventories, light and heavy, and it seems that the light ones were more expensive, possibly reserved for specially fast ships. There was a yard, called in Greek *keraia*. It was hauled up by halliards, working through a truck probably of metal at the top of the mast, clearly visible in vase-paintings of smaller ships (e.g. fig. 47). Sails were brailed up to the yard when the ship was moving under oar but the sails were kept ready for use (see again fig. 47). Brailing ropes are also shown (fig. 47) coming over the top of the yard and led aft where they are belayed near the helmsman. There are also braces attached to the outward ends of the yard, and brought back aft. Herodotus (2.36.4) says that while other peoples attach rings and *kaloi* to the far (i.e. forward) side of the sail, the Egyptians attach them on the near (i.e. after) side. *Kaloi* must then be the Greek word for the brailing ropes, and they must be carried over the yard and down the forward side of the sail and attached at regular intervals to the bottom edge of it. Some of these rings have been found with wrecks on the sea-bed (fig. 54a). A vase-painting shows brailing ropes passing over the yard

31. E.g. Xen. *HG* 2.1.29: Lysander left his main sails on the promontory of Lampsacus before the battle of Aegospotami, and Conon carried them off after it.

53. Attic black-figure cup showing a pentecontor under sail, *c.* 500 BC.

54a. Leaden rings used as fairleads for brailing ropes.

through special fittings which look as if they were made of metal (fig. 54b). It appears that these brailing ropes were not only used for shortening sail in the normal way, but could be used to alter the size and shape of the sail in a variety of ways. The height of the yard was also varied to suit the needs of navigation.

Such is the information which can be extracted from the sources about the means of navigation with triereis under sail. About the practice of such navigation virtually nothing is known,[32] and all will have to be discovered in the replica's sea trials. This will be not the least interesting part of them.

32. See *GOS* pp. 312–13.

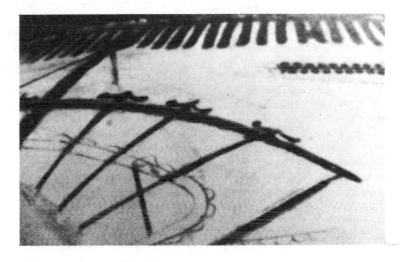

54b. Detail from an Attic black-figure jug showing the fittings through which the brailing ropes passed over the yardarm, 500 BC.

10

THE MATERIALS[1]

Wood for the planks of the hull

In Aristophanes' comedy the *Knights*, acted in Athens in 424 BC the chorus (1300–10) tells a story. 'The triereis came together for a meeting, and one of them, rather older than the others, got up and spoke':

'Maidens, are you not aware of what is talked of in the city?[2] There is a man asking for a hundred of us for Carthage, a wicked, sour-tempered man, Hyperbolus.' The rest of them thought it shocking and intolerable, and one, who had never been near a man, exclaimed: 'Lord save us, he will never be my master. If it comes to that, I'd rather become an old maid here and be eaten by ship-worm.' 'And he won't be master of Nausiphante, daughter of Nauson, either', said another, 'no, in God's name, so long as I, like you, am built of pine (*peukē*) and joinery (*xula*).'[3]

The 'pine and joinery' of which these two Athenian triereis of the last quarter of the fifth century are built are given a little more definition in the literature of the next century. Plato, who deplored the effects of a maritime economy on a city's life, makes the Athenian stranger in the *Laws* (705C) ask a question natural to an Athenian: 'How is the environment of our colonial city off for ship-timber?', and get the answer: 'There is no fir (*elatē*) to speak of, nor pine (*peukē*), and not much cypress; nor is much larch (*pitys*) or plane to be found, which shipwrights normally have to use for the inner parts of ships.' Theophrastus, a younger contemporary of Plato and a pupil of Aristotle, wrote an *Enquiry into Plants* in which he says a good deal about the timber used for building ships – triereis in particular. In one passage (5.7.1–5) he gives three principal ship-timbers – mean-

---

1. In this chapter I am constantly indebted to Meiggs (1983), in particular chapter 5.
2. This line is a quotation from Euripides.
3. The Budé translator rightly here gives 'bois charpenté' for *xula*.

ing, like Plato, timbers for building the hull. They are fir (*elatē*), pine (*peukē*) and cedar (*kedros*). The last had now become more readily available from Syria as a result of Alexander's conquests. Theophrastus had earlier (5.1.5) compared the fir and the pine: 'The latter is fleshier and has few fibres, while the former has many fibres and is not fleshy. That is why the pine is heavy and the fir light.' The later passage continues: 'Triereis and long ships [i.e. oared ships] are made of fir for the sake of lightness, whereas round ships [i.e. ships in which, not being oared, weight was not important] are made of pine because it resists decay.' Elsewhere (5.4.4) he says that pine (*peukē*) is more liable to ship-worm (*terēdōn*) than fir, but presumably what he means in the passage quoted is that, apart from fir, which no one would think of using for round ships, *peukē* is more resistant to decay than other woods.

Theophrastus continues:

Some make triereis also of *peukē* [like the two in Aristophanes] because they cannot get fir (*elatē*). In Syria and Phoenicia triereis are made of cedar because pine (*peukē*) also is in short supply. In Cyprus they use coastal pine (*pitys*) since this is indigenous and it has the reputation of being superior to their pine (*peukē*). The rest of the hull [i.e. other than the keel, the planking] is made of these woods, but the keel is made in the case of the triereis of oak to stand up to hauling ashore, and in the case of merchantmen (*holkades*) [i.e. round ships which when not under sail are towed rather than pulled and ride at anchor in port], of pine. If the latter have to be hauled ashore a false keel of oak is fitted. For smaller craft beechwood is used for the keel and in general the breastwork [of the bows] is made of beech.

It may be noted here that the wood found in the Kyrenia ship (above, p. xvii) was mostly pine, beech and oak.[4] An interesting point arises from these remarks of Theophrastus. *Peukē* was, he says, second best timber for triereis because it was heavier. Yet two of Aristophanes' triereis hulls were made of *peukē*. It seems then possible that the timber used, *elatē* or *peukē*, may have had some bearing on the rating of triereis. For example, 'fast' triereis may have been made of *elatē*.

The mention of oak prompts Theophrastus here to digress with an observation. 'Oak-wood does not join well in a stopped joint to pine (*peukē*) or fir (*elatē*); for the one is of close and the other of open grain,

---

4. H. W. Swiny in Colston Papers no. 23 p. 356.

the one has a consistent texture, the other not. Things which are to be made into one piece should be of similar and not opposite character like wood and stone.' The implication of this passage is that some stopping was used, as well as other means, to join planks together edge to edge in the hull-structure but that this stopping material was not found satisfactory in fixing the garboard strake of pine or fir to the rabbet of the keel which was made of oak. The reason for the failure of the joint would probably be the differing movement of timbers with changing moisture content. The method of joining the planks will be considered later in this chapter (below, p. 183).

Wood for internal structure

From the timbers used in the hull Theophrastus passes to the 'joinery'. The word he appears to use for this is *torneia*, which is probably a textual corruption of *enteroneia*[5], signifying the 'woodwork', which Plato opposes to the planking with the phrase 'the inner (*entos*) parts of ships' and Theophrastus elsewhere calls the *enkoilia* of a ship, when he speaks of the Egyptians using *acantha* (acacia) wood for this part in shipbuilding (4.2.8):

In merchant ships the internal woodwork is made of mulberry or ash or elm or plane since it must be cheap and tough. Plane wood is the worst, because it rots quickly. Sometimes the internal parts of triereis are made of coastal pine (*pitys*) as well, because of its light weight. But the stempost, which adjoins the breastwork, and the bow timbers are made of ash and mulberry and elm, since these parts have to be tough. This is about all there is to say about ship-timber.

Which is a pity because, as every builder of wooden boats knows, there is a great deal more to say. However, the emphasis on light weight for the timber both for the hull and for the rest of a trieres is to be noted.

5. In Aristophanes, *Knights* 1183–5, Demus, a character representing the Athenian people, is offered tripe (*entera*). 'What shall I do with this tripe?' he asks; and the reply comes 'The goddess (Athena) sends it you as *enteroneia* for your triereis', i.e., as the lexicographers say, internal woodwork. Of *torneia* the word in fact preserved in the text of Theophrastus A. F. Hort said: 'The word is perhaps corrupt: one would expect the name of some part of the vessel', and, one might add, of some part of the vessel opposed to the hull planking, which has just been described. *Enteroneia*, as alternative to *enkoilia*, is just such a name, i.e. for the frames, beams and the rest of the furniture (*not* ribs as *GOS* p. 279).

Joints

Theophrastus then turns to woods used in house-building, but shortly afterwards returns to ship-timber.

For carpentry the oldest wood is best, provided it is not rotten; for old wood is suitable for craftsmen of all sorts. But for shipbuilding, because of the need for bending, it is necessary to use sappier wood (though when it is a case of stopped joints the drier the wood the better). The fact is that (hull) planking shows gaps [between the planks][6] when it is new, but when the ship is launched the planks absorb[7] water, close up and are watertight, except in the case of timber which has been completely dried out. In that condition planks do not make a close joint, or not as well as they would if the wood was not completely dried out.

The text of the foregoing passage is uncertain in places, but the general meaning is clear. A number of interesting practices are attested: in the first place, the bending of planks (instead of carving them) where possible to bring them to the required curve; in the second place there seem to be two ways in which watertight joints between the planks of the hull are achieved: (1) by stopping of some kind and (2) by the selection of timber which is dry enough to swell and make a completely watertight joint, but not so dry that it will not take up water when immersed.

Vegetius also speaks about the use of green wood in shipbuilding, but makes rather a different point (4.36). 'When ships which have been built with green timber sweat out their moisture [i.e. in hot weather] they contract and develop cracks. There is nothing more dangerous for sailors.' Theophrastus was saying that when completely seasoned wood is used it does not swell at all or not enough to close up the inevitable gaps between hull planks in a new ship, so that it is better to use wood with a little moisture left in it. Vegetius' point is that if completely green wood is used and the wood is allowed to dry out (e.g. in the sun) the resulting cracks and open seams could endanger the ship.

6. The reading of the manuscripts *histatai*, 'stands', makes no sense. *Dihistatai*, 'shows gaps', is what is required.
7. The text translated is that of the Aldine edition.

Method of construction

Study of the remains of ancient merchant-ships found on the sea-bed of the Mediterranean, and of the timbers adhering to the ram discovered at Athlit (pp. 168–9), leaves no doubt that in those waters in antiquity shipwrights built their hulls from the keel up with planks joined to each other edge to edge to form a shell. This method seems to be indicated by the verb *pēgnunai* (to fix together), the root of which is embodied in the noun *naupēgos*, a shipwright.[8] There is no detailed description of the process in literature of the classical period, but the building of Odysseus' makeshift boat as described by the eighth-century poet of the *Odyssey* (5.243–61) can be recognised as true shipbuilding now that underwater archaeology has shown us how ancient ships were built.

Calypso, having provided Odysseus with an axe and an adze, first told him 'where tall trees grow, alder, poplar and lofty fir (*elatē*), dry long ago, well seasoned, which would float lightly in the water'. She left him to it, and he quickly got on with the task of cutting the planks.

He felled twenty [dead] trees in all, and adzed them with the bronze tool. He cleverly planed them and made them straight to the line. Then Calypso brought drills and he drilled them all and fitted them one to the other (*harmozein*). He hammered the ship (together) with dowels (*gomphoi*)[9] and mortice-and-tenon joints (*harmoniai*).[10] As broad a bottom (*edaphos*) as a man skilled in carpentry will round out (*tornousthai*) for a wide merchantman, so broad a bottom did Odysseus fashion for his wide boat.

The structural importance of the *harmoniai* is revealed later, when a storm hits Odysseus' improvised ship, and he declares (5.361–2) 'as

8. The root meaning of sticking something into something else is most appropriate for the mortice-and-tenon method. The word is used of shipbuilding in, e.g. *Iliad* 2.664 and Herodotus 5.83.
9. Aristotle gives the ways by which things can be joined together in his usual comprehensive manner (*Physics* 5.3.227a): 'by *gomphos* or glue or contact or organic union' and (*Metaphysics* 10.1, 1052a): a thing is a whole either naturally or 'by glue or *gomphos* or by tying together'. The words *gomphos* (noun) and *gomphoun* (verb) are used in connection with shipbuilding and general carpentry, where *gomphos* is a wooden dowel (in particular Hdt. 2.96). The Attic word for it may have been *tulos*, since in the description of the naval preparations in the dockyard in Aristophanes, *Acharnians* 552–3 there is said to be 'a din of oarblades fitting, *tuloi* hammering, etc.'.
10. In Aristophanes, *Knights* 532 *harmonia* appears to be a joint in a 'wooden' lyre which gapes apart when the lyre is old and in disrepair.

long as the planks are held fast in the *harmoniai* so long will I stay aboard and suffer the worst that comes'. These *harmoniai* are mortice-and-tenon joints regularly found in excavated hulls in Greek waters from the bronze age onwards. The mortices were probably made by drilling, finished by chisel, and the tenons hammered home. The next plank was then carefully marked and morticed correspondingly, to fit over the protruding tenons, and driven home to make a close seam. Finally, each tenon was locked firmly in place by a pair of dowels. Holes were drilled for the dowels through the plank and tenons, and the dowels hammered into place from the inside of the plank. The poet of the Odyssey has named the tools, axe, adze and drill, and described in general terms the process, involving dowels (*gomphoi*), mortice-and-tenon joints (*harmoniai*), hammering and fitting together, which we can now recognise as the means and method which produced the hulls whose remains have been found.

Stopping and caulking

There is no direct evidence about the stopping or caulking of ships' planking in the fifth and fourth centuries BC, and it is possible that shipwrights relied on the slight swelling of planks on immersion to effect a tight joint. There is nevertheless a certain amount of indirect evidence. Speaking of Egyptian shipbuilding Herodotus says (2.96.2) that the Egyptians caulk the joints between their short planks with papyrus from the inside. Since he tends to make the point that the Egyptians do everything in just the opposite way to the Greek practice, we may possibly infer that the Greeks caulked their ships from the outside (as one might expect) and used flax as opposed to papyrus which was the Egyptian alternative to the flax of the Greeks and Phoenicians (see below, p. 191). Pliny (*NH* 16.158) speaks of the reed used by the Belgae for caulking their ships and says that it is more adhesive than tar (*gluten*) and more reliable than pitch for filling the seams between the planks (or possibly, cracks in the planks). Pliny writes in the first century AD and provides no strong evidence for practice in earlier Greek warships, but although the ships of the Belgae were built to the north European pattern, he is contrasting them with the ships he knew in the Mediterranean. If seams there were stopped with pitch some fibre would have had to be soaked in pitch for it to be held in the seam effectively. Only fibre soaked in pitch is analogous to the adhesive reed the Belgae used.

There is a good deal of evidence for the existence of such a fibre in the fifth and fourth centuries BC, and it plays an important part in naval contexts. We should call it tow or oakum. In the *Knights* (129)[11] a seller of *stuppeion* is mentioned, and in a fragment (696) of Aristophanes a contemporary, Eucrates, is given the nickname *stuppax*.[12] In a speech of the next century (Dem. 47.20) we read: 'It happened that there was a dispatch of triereis and an emergency expedition speedily mobilised. There was not enough gear in the dockyard . . . What was more there was not available for purchase in Piraeus a supply of sailcloth and *stuppeion* and ropes, all of which are needed for getting a trieres ready for sea.' In the fourth-century naval inventories[13] *stuppeion* again appears with cords in between *askoi* (= *askōmata*: pp. 169–70) and timber for oars (*kōpeis*). In another list payment is made to a *stuppeioplokos* ('tow-splicer') for splicing a rope which had parted. *Stuppeion* would then seem to be raw flax as opposed to *linon*, an article made of flax. It appears in Herodotus and frequently later (8.52, Xen. *Cyr.* 7.5.23, Aen. 33,35, Diod. 14.51.2) as an incendiary material used in sieges for defence and attack, often in association with pitch. *Stuppeion* could also describe old rope material.[14]

To be classed with sailcloth and ropes *stuppeion* was clearly an important naval commodity. After the earthquake at Rhodes in 224 BC Ptolemy promised (Polybius 5.89) the Rhodians, among other things, timber for the construction of ten 'fives' and ten triereis, 40,000 cubits of squared pine planking, 3,000 talents of coined bronze, 3,000 talents of *stuppeion*, and 3,000 pieces of sailcloth (e.g. 130 pieces for each trieres, 170 for each penteres).

The seams of newly built warships and of older ships undergoing maintenance may have been caulked with flax soaked in pitch. There is also a possibility that a substance was inserted between the planks during the process of construction – resin (pine tar) or, again, pitch. However, the planks of warships were thin and there was very

11. Cf. *IG*² 1570.24 and 1572.8.
12. The termination -*ax* is colloquial, like *thalamax* for *thalamios* (p. 137).
13. *IG*² 1629.1151–2; 1631.336.
14. As its occurrence with cords in the inventories shows.

little depth of seam outside tenons into which to drive caulking. The apparent absence of any caulking in the wrecks yet found may well be true evidence of its actual absence. Of stopping and bedding compositions made of tar, pitch, lime, hair and no doubt much else there is much evidence in the seams of wrecks as well as under hull timbers. There is no doubt that the outside of the hull of oared ships was coated with pitch, as we shall see below.

Theophrastus (9.2) speaks of the methods used to obtain pitch and resin from trees: *elatē*, terebinth, *pitys*, Phoenician cedar and *peukē*. These substances appear to have been imported into Greece from Macedonia, Asia Minor, and Syria. Bitumen (*asphalton*) is known to Herodotus (1.179.2) as used with bricks in building Babylon; the fifth-century author of *Airs, Waters, Places* speaks (7.50) of it as being collected from springs, and Herodotus (6.119) mentions a well near Sardis which produced bitumen, salt and oil. It is sometimes said[15] that the Greeks and Romans, like the inhabitants of Mesopotamia,[16] used bitumen on the hulls of their ships, but there appears to be no evidence for this practice in Greece of the fifth and fourth centuries.

The principal enemy of wooden-hulled ships in Mediterranean waters was ship-worm. Merchant-ships were as a rule lead-sheathed, but the weight of the lead in vessels constructed for maximum lightness and the practice of hauling ashore made lead sheathing highly undesirable for oared warships. The maiden trieres in Aristophanes resigned herself to a worm-eaten old age. Theophrastus remarks (5.4.4) that *peukē* was more liable to the *terēdōn* than *elatē*, and that the harm done to a ship's planks by the *skōlēx* and *thrips* is easy to cure, for when the ship has been smeared with pitch and immersed it is watertight, but that the damage done by the *terēdōn* is impossible to repair. That may have been true, but caulking of worm-holes during the regular process of maintenance, and a coating of pitch, would have gone some way to remedying the effects of *terēdōn* on the hull provided that the planking was not too much weakened. Items of wooden gear in the inventories are frequently labelled 'worm-eaten'.

15. E.g. by R. J. Forbes (1936) p. 87.
16. E.g. the Gilgamesh epic 117 where Utnapishtim coats his ship inside and out with bitumen.

Coating with pitch, etc.

The most common epithet for ships in Homer after 'swift' is 'black'. It is reasonable to assume that the blackness is the result of the application of pitch. It was certainly also used on Athenian triereis in the fifth century. In Aristophanes' play the *Acharnians* (190) an envoy comes back from Sparta with a five-year truce, but the hero Dicaeopolis, who is keen to end the war, does not like it because 'it smells of pitch and naval preparations'. It seems that ships preparing for an expedition were given a coat of pitch. Pitch was on the contraband list and export of it was forbidden in the war (Aristophanes, *Frogs* 364). In the next century an inscription of 330 BC[17] lists four items in a miscellaneous inventory of naval stores: '*hypaloiphē* [i.e. substance for application to a ship's bottom] in a cask, black; another kind, in an amphora, black; another kind, white, in a cask; in two amphoras, white'. The black substance is likely to be pitch of two varieties. The white is likely to be resin, probably mixed with lime. When Theophrastus speaks about the extraction of resin from trees (9.2), he says that some is 'most pitch-like' and another kind of pitch is 'whiter'. Indeed the names resin and pitch seem to be coterminous, with the blacker sort being called pitch and the 'whiter' called resin. Plutarch (*Mor.* 676A) confirms this, and shows that both were used on ships' hulls to make them watertight: 'The *pitys* and kindred trees, *peukai* and *strobiloi*, produce the wood most suitable for shipbuilding, and the pitch and resin paint (*aloiphē*) without which shipwright's work is useless in salt water.' The words rendered 'shipwright's work' (*ta sumpagenta*) suggest the edge-to-edge method of hull-building with pegged mortice-and-tenon joints, and Plutarch's words do not rule out the possibility that resin was used between the planks as a kind of stopping. If that were to be so the white bottom paint (*hypaloiphē*) of the inscription could be wax, for which there is some evidence in this connection. Hipponax (p. 46 Diehl[3]), in the middle of the seventh century, speaks of a trieres' keel being waxed. The purpose of this treatment could be to make watertight the seam between the keel and the garboard strake, often a main source of

17. *IG* 2² 1627.313. Cf. also 1622.740 where it occurs in a list of gear for a ship, the *Amphitrite* (*hypozomata*, anchors, oars, ladders, poles), with the suggestion that it was carried on board for use when the ship was hauled up for regular maintenance when in commission.

leakage. Applied to the underside of the keel, particularly, it could have been a lubricant to facilitate slipping and hauling up in a ship-shed. There is however some further evidence for wax on a ship's bottom, where applied over the wetted surface of the hull it would reduce skin-friction and thereby the chief element in the ship's resistance as she moved through the water. Pliny (*NH* 16.56) speaks of pitch being produced from various trees and extracted by heat from a pitch pine (*taeda*) for the protection of warships; and then he adds: 'We must not omit the fact that among the Greeks there is a stuff, pitch mixed with wax,[18] scraped off seagoing vessels, which is called *zōpissa* (since experience of life teaches us everything) and is much more effective for all the purposes for which pitches and resins are useful, presumably because the hardness of salt has been added.' This curious piece of information suggests that pitch and wax were customarily applied, either successively or as a mixture, to the wetted surface of a ship's hull.

Materials for gear

We may now turn to what may be said about the material for the two kinds of ship's gear: 'wooden' and 'hanging'. Theophrastus (4.1.2) has something to say about the wood used for the sailyard, mast and oars.

Masts and yard

At a place in Arcadia the *elatai* and *peukai* are superior in height and girth, but the wood is not similarly dense or fine, rather the reverse, like pines that grow in shady places. These are not accordingly used for expensive work, such as doors, but rather for shipbuilding and house-construction. They provide the best roof beams and timbers, and sailyards, and again particularly tall, but not equally strong, masts. And sunny situations produce masts which, while being shorter, are of denser wood and stronger.

Elsewhere (5.1.7) he says that the best sailyards and masts come from the *elatē*, 'which is both the tallest and the straightest growing of trees', while Pliny (*NH* 16.195) says that the fir is preferred for these items of gear because of its light weight.

18. This stuff is used in medicine. See Hippocrates, *On Joints* 62.20, and 63.30 wax treated with resin, also Dioscorides 1.72.

Oars

Oars were a vital part of a trieres' gear. Each oar-shaft was made from a young fir-tree, very carefully prepared. Theophrastus (5.1.6–7) says: 'The fir has many skins like the onion. Underneath the visible skin there is always another, and the wood is composed of these skins. For that reason oar-makers (lit. 'shavers'[19]) do their best to remove the skins one by one evenly. By so doing they make the shaft strong, but if they deviate and take them off unevenly the shaft is weak.' As Meiggs points out, the naval inventories at Athens show how carefully the oars were inspected for faults, and those which were substandard were rejected. The procurement of suitable oar-timber was important to Athens. Thrace, in which she had a continuing interest throughout the period of her naval ascendancy, is noted by Herodotus (5.23.2) as 'having much ship-timber and many oar-shafts and silver mines'; and Perdiccas, the king of Macedon, signed a treaty with Athens, probably during the Peloponnesian War, engaging himself to export Macedonian oar-timber to Athens alone.[20] A little later Andocides (2.11) curried favour with the Athenian democrats in the fleet at Samos by using his friendship with the king of Macedon to secure oar-timber for them. The oar-shafts, prepared from rough young trees, had to be equipped with a blade, probably, as we have seen (pp. 172–4), of a different shape for each of the classes of oarsmen. The process of fitting the blades seems to be mentioned in a passage of Aristophanes (*Acharnians* 552–3: n. 9 above) which describes how when a fleet was preparing to put to sea the dockyard was full of a great variety of noises. Among these was the noise of oar-shafts being given blades (*kōpeōn platoumenōn*), either by carving the ends or by splicing on a separate blade (see above, p. 174).

Ropes and sails

The main 'hanging gear' consists of a great variety of ropes[21] and the sails. Information about the material used for ropes in the fifth century comes from Herodotus' account (7.25, 34, 36.3) of Xerxes' famous bridge across the Hellespont for the invading army in 480.

---

19. An inscription relating to Cos (*SIG* 1000.18) speaks of 'oar-shavers'.
20. *IG* 1³ 89.31 (440–415 BC).
21. For these in detail see *GOS* pp. 299–301.

'He prepared ropes for two bridges, of papyrus and white flax, giving the task (of making them) to the Phoenicians and Egyptians. The former made the bridge of white flax and the latter the one of papyrus.' These first bridges were carried away in a storm. The second pair of bridges was reinforced with boats and the kinds of rope were mixed. Each bridge had two ropes of white flax and four of papyrus hauled taut by wooden 'donkeys'. The two kinds of rope were eqully thick and handsome in appearance, but those of white flax were heavier in proportion, each weighing one talent for a cubit. The fact that there were twice as many ropes made of papyrus as made of flax may be an indication of their relative reliability. There is some evidence from Euripides[22] that ropes were made of flax in Athens in the later fifth century.

The same two materials, flax and papyrus, were alternatives for sails as well as for ropes. Theophrastus says (4.8.4) that sails were made of papyrus in Egypt, and in the previous century a comic poet (Hermippus fr. 63 Diehl[3]) speaks of sails and papyrus coming from Egypt, although Euripides (*Hecuba* 1081–2) calls a sail a 'cloth of yellow flax'. It is to be inferred from what Herodotus says about the relative weight of flaxen and papyrus ropes that sails made of papyrus were also lighter. The naval inventories[23] show that a trieres had two suits of sails, one of which was light. It seems reasonable to think that these were made of papyrus. Flaxen articles, i.e. ropes and sails, were on the contraband list at the end of the fifth century, like leather oar-sleeves and pitch (Aristophanes, *Frogs* 364).

In the third century BC material for the ropes made for a ship built for Hiero of Syracuse consisted of *leukaia*, a variety of esparto grass, from Spain, and hemp (*kannabis*) and pitch from the Rhône (Athenaeus 5.40.206). These fibres were presumably more readily available in Syracuse than the flax and papyrus which were the alternative materials for ropes, as they were for sails in the eastern Mediterranean.

22. Euripides, *Trojan Women* 537–8 'with swifters of woven flax', *IT* 1043 where mooring ropes are called 'bridles of flax'.
23. *IG* 2² 1627.65, 1629.371, 1631.415. There is a suggestion that light sails are more valuable.

11

THE RECONSTRUCTION: FUNDAMENTALS OF DESIGN

A reconstruction of an original whose design and whose techniques for building, operation and maintenance have been lost has to be redesigned. That is a process of deduction, calculation and spatial organisation utterly different from the slow step-by-step process by which the original was developed over a time-span running to decades, even centuries. Our better knowledge today of the laws of physics, of mathematics and of the properties of materials enables us to design a ship, for example, with a degree of discrimination and choice as to what we create which was almost totally denied to the ancients. However, our ability to design at will devices of practical use in wide variety does little, of itself, to help us to work back to deduce the 'design' of ancient artefacts. 'Design' is here given inverted commas because most ancient artefacts were not and could not have been 'designed' in the sense in which we use the word today. 'Design' here means only the description or definition of the thing. What our present knowledge enables us to do is to explore the physical consequences of surviving evidence in the sure knowledge that the natural laws have not changed.

In many cases this exploration may not succeed in discriminating between the physical feasibility of different 'designs', and so may fail in identifying the most likely actual design of an object in the past. Failure is more probable in the case of objects whose manufacture and use were comfortably within the limits of possibility, allowing scope for custom, fashion or irrational preference in the design. However, in the case of artefacts near the edge of practicability physical constraints bore heavily upon their design and there is less room for choice.

It has become evident in the course of the book that the trieres was an ancient artefact pushed to the limit of what was technically possible at the time. Exploring the physical consequences of the evidence about the ships revealed their design to be as intricate and interlocking in quality, though not of course in scope, as that of modern warships.

Fundamentals of ship design

The first step towards retrieving the design must be to marshal the ancient evidence, and this task has been done in the previous chapters. This evidence is the equivalent of the requirements for a ship which a naval architect sets out to satisfy. The next step is to consider particularly those pieces of evidence affecting the fundamentals of the vessel which are much the same in any ship, viz.

1. *Accommodation* of what must go in or on the hull.
2. *Propulsion*, power and speed.
3. *Weight* and *waterline*.
4. *Centre of gravity* and *stability*.
5. *Strength*.
6. *Feasibility* of building.

None of these is independent of the others: indeed it will be seen that they interact strongly in the tricres. However, some pieces of evidence may be regarded as primary determinants of one or more of the above fundamentals, as follows:

Fundamental requirement	Determined by
1. *Accommodation*	Spacing of oarsmen, number of fore-and-aft files and of men in each. Length of oars, number of men to each oar. Representations. Ship-sheds. Outrigger. Position of thalamians.
2. *Propulsion*	Ship-sheds. Outrigger. Build of ancient ships. Sustainable speeds.
3. *Weight* and *waterline*	Ship-sheds. Outrigger. Build of ancient ships. Number of crew. Floating when holed. Number of men required to haul ship up slip.
4. *Centre of gravity* and *stability*	Ship-sheds. Outrigger. Size of thalamian ports. Floating when

	holed. Build of ancient ships. *Askōmata*. Masts and sails.
5. *Strength*	Build of ancient ships. Length. Representations. *Hypozōmata*. Long timbers.
6. *Feasibility* of building	Build of ancient ships. Athlit ram.

Because the size of the trieres is for us virtually determined by the number and arrangement of oarsmen, and by the size of the ship-sheds (though of course in evolution the reverse was the case), it was the arrangement of oarsmen that had to be settled first, sufficiently at least for their arrangement to be a basis for designing the ship as a whole. In doing this, interactions between design fundamentals immediately arose: attested speeds demanded an arrangement with a high oar-gearing of about three (see Glossary) as in most fast-pulling sea-boats like gigs: likely available power required that the wetted area of the bottom be small and so there must be minimum beam on the waterline and minimum displacement. From that it followed that the height of the centre of gravity would be critical in achieving adequate stability without ballast. The high oar-gearing with oars of given length led to short looms, which did much towards enabling oarsmen to be closely arranged vertically and thus to lowering the centre of gravity of the ship. The normal method of ship-building in the ancient Mediterranean, as demonstrated by recent underwater archaeological work, required a ship of the fourth century BC to have a wineglass-shaped midsection. After much calculation and drawing, it turned out that a hull of overall beam fitting the ship-sheds and of that shape (fig. 55) with convex flaring sides and outriggers would

(a) house transversely without waste of space three files of oarsmen on each side tightly but workably packed by placing each man outboard of, and in height overlapping, the one below, provided that thalamian tholes were set inboard and their ports enlarged (as indeed they appear to have been) to allow oar movement;

(b) house longitudinally the required numbers of oarsmen in each file in a fine enough hull of overall length just less than the dry length of the slips, provided that the hull had a parallel middle body (fig. 56) and a large prismatic coefficient (see Glossary);

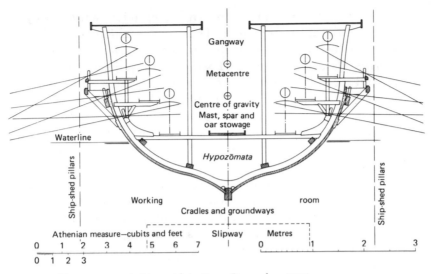

Gangway

Metacentre

Centre of gravity
Mast, spar and
oar stowage

Waterline

Hypozōmata

Ship-shed pillars

Ship-shed pillars

Working   room

Cradles and groundways

Athenian measure—cubits and feet   Slipway   Metres

55. Reconstructed ship: mid-section, December 1981.

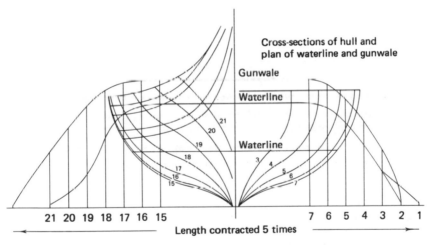

Cross-sections of hull and
plan of waterline and gunwale

Gunwale

Waterline

Waterline

21 20 19 18 17 16 15   7 6 5 4 3 2 1

Length contracted 5 times

56. Reconstructed ship: lines of hull form No. 3, December 1981.

(c) provide sufficient displacement volume to float the total weight
of the ship at the right waterline;

(d) have sufficient beam on the waterline to provide on that displacement adequate stability for sailing across a wind of about
15 knots, i.e. a metacentric height (see Glossary) of 0.5 to
0.7 metres.

Thus all the evidence about the trieres could be satisfied by a design of hull and an arrangement of oarsmen in which physical considerations of hydrostatics, fluid mechanics, physiology and properties of materials, acting together, fix the beam on the waterline very closely, and the height of the centre of gravity, the weight, and the hull form within fairly tight limits. It follows that any physically satisfactory reconstruction of a trieres conforming to the same evidence would have much the same values for these leading features. All are interlocked so that any other fundamentally different solution is difficult to imagine.

Speeds attested in antiquity seem only just attainable, so that any increase in weight or wetted area is out of the question. The centre of gravity could not be any lower without reducing the height of thalamian tholes above the water and thus rendering performance too sensitive to waves, heel or rolling. If the centre of gravity were higher the beam would have had to be increased to restore stability and that would have demanded either thalamian ports too large to fit between the necessary top timbers of the hull, or greater beam overall, too large for the sheds. If the prismatic coefficient were reduced to lessen wave resistance, without increasing the length, the foremost and aftermost thalamian oarsmen, despite short oars, could not have fitted inside the hull. If that coefficient were increased, wave resistance at high speeds would have risen to make it unlikely that the reconstructed ship could attain the attested speeds. Length could have been increased by a metre or two with possible gain at high speed but at a penalty at more usual speeds: in any case the ram would then have overhung the water inconveniently when on the slip.

The complete design

It was at this point in the exploration of the design of the trieres that it seemed worth developing the design of the whole ship. If all essential features could be determined, the puzzle of the trieres might be solved. But before designing individual features, we had to investigate the remaining more intangible fundamentals of structural strength and feasibility of building.

It had become obvious that the trieres hull was very shallow for its length and that longitudinal bending strength might be critical, particularly as the hull was not decked in the normal sense. Although triereis operated in coastal waters and normally had no need to ride out rough weather, they would nevertheless have been subjected to some bending by waves. With a depth of hull, keel to gunwale, of only 2.1 m (at that stage of the design), the length on the waterline (LWL) of 34 m was sixteen times the depth. That figure is more than one-and-a-half times the largest value admitted by the rules of *Lloyd's Register* for wooden ship construction in the last century, even though those ships would have been strapped with iron. But Lloyd's were concerned with ocean-going ships which, like all flush-planked ships since about AD 1000, were frame-built and without the benefit of having their shell planks tenoned together edge-to-edge to form a true shell in the engineering sense.

Calculations of the shear forces and bending moments generated when the hull was balanced on the crest of a wave of length equal to the LWL and whose height from trough to crest was 1/20 of its length, indicated a maximum bending moment in hogging of about 1300 kN m. Such waves could well be met in the Aegean Sea, and they would demand that the keel and gunwales carry stresses about 50% greater than acceptable. Actually a trieres would probably be swamped by such waves and a sea with waves half as high, 0.85 m from trough to crest, would be about as much as trieres could be expected to survive without being overcome. The hull should therefore be strong enough to withstand such waves with certainty. That would require the hull to carry shear forces up to 90 kilo-newtons and bending moments amidships of about 900 kN m. However, bending stresses would still be too high, and here the necessity for *hypozōmata* (above, pp. 170–2) becomes apparent.

The position and rigging of *hypozōmata* have been a particular mystery in triereis, but it is virtually certain that their purpose was to reduce bending stresses which would otherwise damage the hull. These would be the tensile stresses tending to open butt joints in the hull rather than the compressive actions which would keep them closed. To protect the hull structure against breaking its back by hogging, the *hypozōmata* should be stretched between points forward and aft high in the hull section where they would act like a hogging truss. Conversely, to protect against bending in the opposite direction, sagging, they should be low in the hull. Curiously, it was the development of the underwater profile of the stern that decided where the *hypozōmata* were to be rigged in the reconstructed ship.

Until that stage of the design the stern of the Phoenician ship found off Marsala (above, p. xviii)[1] had been adopted for the reconstructed ship. In that stern the straight keel ends well aft and the stern then rises at quite a steep angle. When launched from a slip such a ship would hinge, when the bow lifted to the buoyancy, about a point necessarily quite far aft, causing a large sagging bending moment made worse by such a steep declivity as 1 in 10. In the reconstructed ship that moment would have been as big as the hogging moment on a 0.85 m wave, but more to be avoided because it would open joints below water. With such a stern the best place for the *hypozōmata* would, on balance, be low in the hull.

However, one of the results of the Advisory Discussion (see above p. xvi) was to cast doubt on the validity of the Marsala stern for the trieres. Apart from the heavy sagging at launch, the waterlines of that stern were really too full for the fast trieres.[1] It was also scarcely the right shape for backing on to beaches, and the long straight keel would have greatly impeded the quick turning so important in a vessel whose principal weapon was the ram.

We therefore changed the stern to one with a longer and more gently sloping after-keel. The hinge point on the slip was moved forward by this change of stern shape far enough to reduce the sagging at launch to insignificance. Hogging then became the most severe bending condition (as it usually is in ships), and the proper place for the *hypozōmata* became high in the hull section. In that position they were much easier to rig and tighten by twisting. Simple and safe anchorages forward and aft to carry the tension in the *hypozōmata*, which could be equal to more than half the weight of the ship, could also be more easily arranged.

The keel was made deeper[2] and, following the structure of the Kyrenia ship (see above p. xviii and fig. 5), the lower three strakes were made heavier to accord better with the practice of the time. That had the advantage of stiffening the hull section as a whole and making the keel into a more substantial girder on the middle line to distribute local loads from slips and beaches and increase the flex-

1. *IJNA* (1973) p. 40. In writing of the remains of the stern, Honor Frost observes that 'the lines of the ship widened abruptly after [*sic*] this extremity'.
2. *The Greek Trireme of the 5th Century B.C.* (1984) p. 35. On the advice of Richard Steffy.

ural stability of the whole bottom in hogging. The midship arrangement had by the end of 1983 assumed its final form as shown in fig. 57. It is compared with the Lenormant Relief in fig. 58 (see also Appendix 2).

On evidence[3] of the use of long timber in building warships, butt joints in longitudinal timbers have been avoided amidships near keel and gunwales, where bending stresses will be high when the replica is in waves. This measure will contribute greatly to the stiffness and longevity of the replica. The *hypozōmata* have, after resolving the shape of the stern, been placed about 0.5 m above the neutral axis of bending of the hull section. If they carry a total fore-and-aft tension of 300 kN, hogging bending stresses will be, as maxima, about half the largest allowable working stress (5.5 N/mm²) for pine structures in tension and near to the corresponding compressive stress in the garboard strake. Without the *hypozōmata* the gunwale stress would be one-third greater, while those in the keel would fall by about one-fifth.

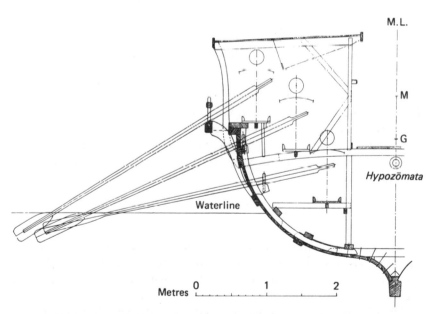

57. Reconstructed ship: mid-section, October 1983.

3. Mainly from Meiggs (1983).

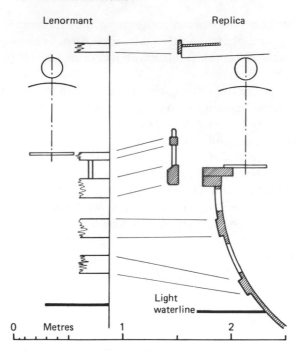

Lenormant   Replica

Light
waterline

0   Metres   1   2

58. Comparison of the reconstructed ship with the Lenormant relief.

An important additional advantage of *hypozōmata* and similar devices in wooden ships and boats built with mechanical joints between their shell planks arises from preventing stress reversals, from tensile to compressive and vice versa, except in fairly extreme conditions which occur relatively rarely, thus reducing working at joints and therefore leakage.

Building feasibility

This design fundamental is of a different nature from the others. It has two aspects: the feasibility of building such an intricate and sophisticated ship in fifth- and fourth-century BC Greece, and the feasibility of building it today.

Greek building of all kinds at that time shows a high degree of sophistication and craftsmanship, and the wrecks that have been examined show that shipbuilding was no exception. The fact that triereis, wooden ships lightly built and roughly used, lasted as long as twenty years[4] indicates the highest standards of care and accuracy in building and maintenance.

The feasibility of building a trieres today has raised some doubts and has had to be proved at some expense. Besides much calculation and design, tests and trials of several kinds were needed. Together they amounted to a research and development programme costing over 10% of the cost of building the ship herself.

The mock-up

The arrangement of the oarsmen, originally demonstrated by Sinclair Morrison about 40 years ago with a small working model, has had to be modified and proved at full scale with live oarsmen. That required a mock-up (fig. 2), already described, which not only served that purpose but also enabled the experience of working the oars to suggest an important improvement in placing the thranites, canted at an angle to the middle line of the ship, and more nearly alongside (though higher than) the zygians.[5]

Model of the ship

While the mock-up was being built, a model of the whole ship was made in a simple style to 1/25 scale by Norman Gundry (fig. 2) to give a general idea of the proposed replica and to stimulate discussion of its main features and proportions. That model played an essential part in demonstrating the unsuitability of the Marsala stern, and it was later given the new stern.

4. L. Casson, *Ships and Seamanship in the Ancient World* (1971) p. 90.
5. The heels of the thranites were thus able to occupy the spaces between the envelopes swept out by the looms of the zygian oars. By that means the thranites could be lowered by 0.2 m and the angle of their oars to the water reduced by nearly 5°, greatly easing their inboard wrists at the finish of the stroke. The centre of gravity of the ship was also lowered by about 0.05 m. The arrangement of the oarsmen that was finally adopted would certainly not have been achieved without the working mock-up and its exposure to criticism at the Advisory Discussion. At a cost of £500 for materials and of about two man-months of labour, the mock-up was of great value to the project.

Stern planking

In the early stages of the project the run of planking at the stern below the lower wale as well as at the bow was a puzzle. Eric McKee, an expert on shell building in the northern tradition, whom we had asked to advise on planking, made a 1/20 scale model before the Advisory Discussion. After his sudden death, that work was continued with models of the stern to ensure that planking the final shape was practicable. These models, by James Paffett, also helped the builder to reproduce on full scale the upswept stern unfamiliar to shipwrights for centuries.

Tank test of hull form

In collaboration with the Hellenic Navy, a model of the finally-adopted underwater hull form was made in Greece and towed in the ship-model tank of the Athens Polytechnic to find its wave resistance. This step was advisable because the form combined slimness with high prismatic coefficient to such a degree as to put it outside the range of forms for which data are available. These experiments ensured that the proposed hull would not be too bluff at the ends to achieve attested speeds, a principal aim of the project. The final lines are shown in fig. 59.

Material of tenons

The appreciable bending stresses expected in the reconstructed ship will be accompanied by high shearing forces in the shell and therefore in the tenons joining the planks together. In the round Kyrenia ship, 14 m long, tenons were only 6 mm thick, pitched at intervals of about 150 mm. In the Marsala long ship they were 9 mm thick, pitched 100 mm, reflecting heavier stresses in the longer and more slender hull. In the trieres, tenons pitched 90 mm would in some parts of the shell be subjected to shearing loads acting on their sides of about 2.5 kN. Would tenons of the same size as those in the Marsala ship be sufficient in a trieres?

This question could not be answered without experiments. Norman Gundry stepped in again to make a test piece in which the tenons were of boxwood and, following the Marsala ship, 9 mm

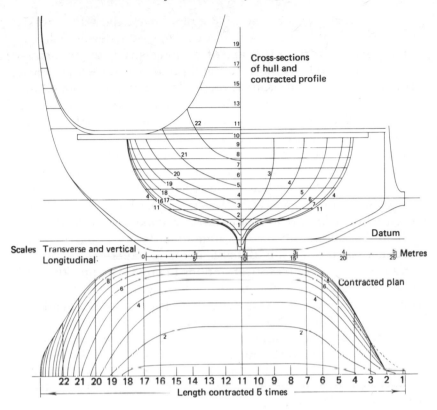

59. Reconstructed ship: final lines of hull.

thick. Under load they began to crush appreciably at about 1 kN per tenon, less than half the maximum expected load on tenons in the trieres. When dismantled, the tenons looked as though someone had tried to cut them in half with a gigantic pair of blunt shears. It was remarkable that the end-grain at the mouths of the mortices in the Douglas Fir planks had scarcely crushed at all. This test seemed to reveal the likelihood of leakage in long and slender ships of the ancient Mediterranean. Here also, however, was a dilemma about authenticity.

We had tested tenons as thick, relative to shell planking, as any yet found by archaeologists – in the only discovered wreck of a long ship. Those tested were made of the most resistant wood to crushing across the grain available in the Mediterranean area and known to have been used for such tenons. We may have exposed the reason for the structural limits to which long ships were developed.

It was decided that for the sake of the longevity of the replica and to promote confidence in her operation at sea, we would depart from authenticity in the dimensions and the material of the tenons. There is no direct evidence about the dimensions of tenons in trieres. We decided to increase their thickness to one-third of the plank thickness and to employ woods hard enough across the grain at least to match the end-grain strength of the plank. We chose to use either Greenheart (*Ocotea rodiaei*), or, even better, American Live Oak (*Quercus virginiana*) which would be harder as well as more akin to the Mediterranean Turkey Oak (*Quercus cerris*), which was used by the ancients for making tenons for ships. In making this decision we took into account present-day unfamiliarity with the old leaky wooden ships and the servitude of sailors to bailer and pump.

In a second test, of Greenheart tenons 12 mm thick (fig. 60), crush set in at a load per tenon of about 2 kN m, a much more adequate figure, and it appeared that the end-grain strength of the plank had been matched. This test also showed that the oak pegs (*gomphoi*) locking the tenons in place should be stronger, so they were increased in diameter from 8 mm to 12 mm. Leon Neel of Georgia, USA, has very kindly supplied Live Oak for tenons, so the shell seams of the ship should be as stiff under shear loading as the plank timber allows with the tenon type of joint.

The trial piece

The largest feasibility question of all was whether people today could build a trieres hull to the necessary specification, and it called for the project's most costly preparatory step. A Trial Piece of hull was built (figs. 7 and 8), 5.5 m long and just over half the hull in breadth, to the specification of the ship herself. To elicit as many building problems as possible, a difficult part of the hull was chosen, including the scarf between the straight and the rising stern keel, the ends of the garboard and second strakes and an area of shell where all planks are curved. The aim was to find, and then be better able to avoid, snags that would hold up the construction and add to the cost of building the ship. A long and light wooden ship would be liable to

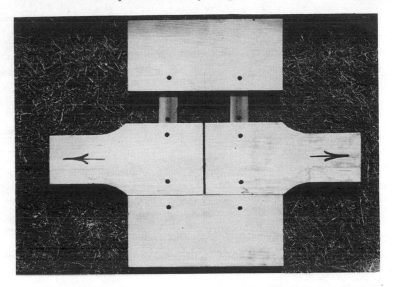

60. Reconstructed ship: second test of tenons. The four tenons of the test piece are loaded in shear by pulling in the directions of the two arrows. The test piece is shown here after being subjected to loads rising to 4.3 kN m, at which load the tenons had crushed to allow a slip between the planks of about 1 mm. The upper plank has here been separated to reveal two greenheart tenons with holes to receive *gomphoi*.

warp out of shape if left for long in an incomplete and unbraced state.

Ram

The timber structure of the ram, shown by the remains found at Athlit[6] to have been intricate and well made, has been designed on the evidence of those remains to join on to the hull proper. Authenticity had to be combined with practicality and strength. To prove the design of that part of the reconstruction, Norman Gundry made a 1/5 scale model including the forward end of the hull shell (fig. 61). That model, besides demonstrating the design generally, is intended to give the builder of the vessel much guidance in cutting and fitting complicated timbers.

6. J. R. Steffy (1983) pp. 229–46.

61. Model of the ram structure proposed for the reconstructed ship. The ram upper planking, which would be fitted above the ram wale piece, is shown in one piece lying beside the model. The ram lower planking may be seen in place below the ram wale piece: the upper of these two planks is dark-, the lower light-coloured. The metal sheath fitting over the forward part of the ram structure has been omitted.

Hypozōmata tension

The behaviour of these ropes had to be investigated to find out how torque, tension and angle of twist are related when the ropes are twisted together to be tightened as in a Spanish Windlass. It may be assumed that these 40 mm diameter ropes in a trieres would have been tightened according to experience to the maximum that they could safely bear. In the absence of such data we undertook 1/8 scale experiments to discover whether *hypozōmata* could be of polyester (a stronger, safer, more readily available, but also more elastic material) or whether we should have to stick to hemp to keep the torque to be applied within practical limits. The choice would make no difference to the structural effect of the *hypozōmata* on the hull, which is determined only by the total tension and the position in which it is rigged.

Timber

Choice of timber and details of fastenings had to be carefully considered in view of the highly stressed nature of the trieres. The materials of the originals have already been described, but timber of the required structural quality and sizes is now scarcer in the regions and in the species from which it could be obtained in ancient times. The Trust decided with the agreement of the Hellenic Navy and after consulting the Building Research Establishment in Britain to specify Douglas Fir (*Pseudotsuga menziesii*) otherwise known as Oregon Pine and Columbian Pine, instead of the botanically authentic species such as silver fir, larch or several of the many pines which grow around the Mediterranean and Black Seas. All true firs, though advantageous in being light for their strength, were rejected because they are prone to decay. Triereis often had oak keels (above, p. 181) but seasoned straight-grained oak in the section and length required is now virtually impossible to obtain. The keel could have been laminated from oak but Iroko (*Chlorophera excelsa*) is structurally satisfactory, cheaper and available in a stable state: it is also very resistant to decay. We chose it in preference to oak.

As another exception from authenticity, we decided to allow long timbers to be formed by gluing shorter ones together.

Watertightness of seams

On the rather humdrum but important matter of caulking or stopping the seams to make them watertight, literary and archaeological evidence is too vague for any particular processes to be identified as authentic. It was therefore decided with the agreement of the Hellenic Navy to build on the firmness it is hoped to achieve in shell seams and to make the ship as watertight as possible by stopping the seams below the lower wale with a modern two-part curing polysulphide sealant. No aspect of the performance of the trieres or of its investigation with the reconstructed ship will have been lost as a result of this step: loss of 'fast' qualities by prolonged immersion could not have been properly reproduced with any confidence no matter how carefully the 'most authentic' stopping had been selected or applied. All effects of increasing roughness and fouling with length of immersion will be experienced with the reconstructed ship in the course of trials and operation.

12

~~~~~~

THE RECONSTRUCTION:
MAIN FEATURES

Having discussed the fundamentals underlying the design, we can properly turn to the main physical features of the vessel, starting with the main hull and then progressively building up the complete ship in much the same order as she would actually be built.

The builder of a trieres in ancient times would almost invariably have been adding to an existing and uniform fleet. He would have worked to a set of traditional scantlings, rules and key measurements of which only the *interscalmium* (0.888 m, p. 134) has survived. He would therefore have been perfectly clear about what he was to produce. His concepts and methods, handed down and guarded by generations of master shipwrights before him, are almost certainly lost for ever and probably impossible to reconstruct. As a modern but very incomplete substitute we can do no better than to offer a drawing of the general arrangement of the proposed ship (fig. 62).

Building starts by cutting and setting in place a long timber, 17 m in length, to which are scarfed the forward and after keels rising gently to stem and stern. The three pieces are joined end-to-end by *trait de Jupiter* scarfs (fig. 63) which, in a number of variations, seem to have been universally used in ship keels in the ancient Mediterranean. This scarf is an ingenious and intricate piece of carpentry in itself, being self-locking and, if well fitted, strong in end compression though less good in tension.

To the keel are fitted the first, or garboard, strakes of the shell. Being heavy strakes, wide and thick, to reinforce the keel as the central girder of the hull, these have to be carved to shape at each end to bend into the rising keels fore and aft. In shorter, round, ships that curve would extend over the whole length of the strakes and to simplify their shape the keel would be rockered – that is, curved upwards like the sheer of a boat. In long ships rocker is needed only at each end of the length. The garboard strakes are fastened to the keels by tenons, already discussed, about 10 to every metre of seam.

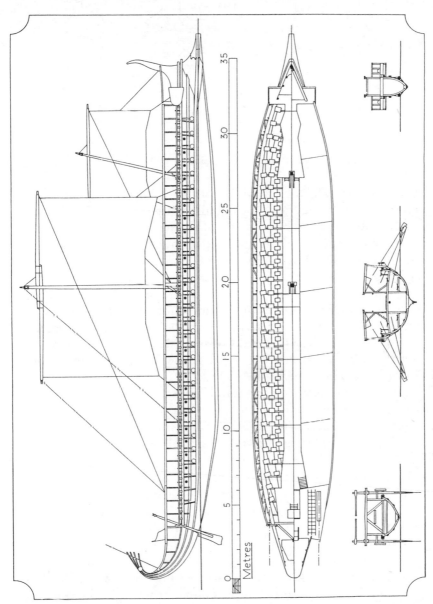

62. General arrangement of reconstructed ship.

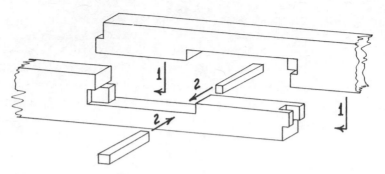

63. Reconstructed ship: *trait de Jupiter* scarf.

The shell is thus formed, strake by strake, according to some rules or methods governing the shape of hull to be generated. The builder works by adjusting the bevel angle of the plank edge and so of the mortices cut perpendicularly into it to receive the tenons. Seams are close, carefully fitted before being finally tenoned in place. As the shell grows, transverse stiffening timbers two or three metres long are then progressively fitted to the inside of the shell in overlapping tiers to reach the gunwale (fig. 64). These timbers are fastened to the planks by wood dowels driven through bored holes and then locked by copper spikes driven up the dowels and clenched over, the points being driven back into the face of the timber to form a square hook out of the inboard ends of the spikes.

The ancient Greek terms for the stiffening timbers have been lost, so more recent English equivalents are adopted here. Those in the bottom and lying across the keel are called floors: those laid on each side, ends overlapping the floors to reach the lower wale, are called futtocks, and the shell stiffening is completed up to the gunwale by top timbers whose lower ends overlap the tops of the futtocks. In a trieres, top timbers have to be carefully placed in the spaces which there will be between the oarports, later to be cut in the ship sides in a zigzag pattern, one port in each space between top timbers.

The top edge of the hull shell is capped by the gunwales, upper and lower, heavy members forming two layers of timbers in the reconstructed ship to give strength to the long, shallow hull. Stiffening is completed by internal longitudinal stringers in the bottom, riding over the transverse timbers, three on each side of the keel, and by beams across the hull, one to every other top timber at the level of the middle wale, to hold the sides of the hull at their proper distance.

The result is a shell, in the main little thicker in relation to its curvature than a plastic bucket, lightly stiffened over its general extent but with substantial members at the keel and, like the bucket, round its rim. The weight of this basic shell is only about 15 tonnes. The addition of outriggers, seats etc. for oarsmen, decks, stanchions and braces to complete the hull adds another 10 tonnes or so to make a weight of 25 tonnes, a little more than half of the total weight of the fully manned and equipped trieres.

When the basic hull had been finished by the shipwrights the greater part of building a trieres was done, though they would probably also have fitted the more important features closely connected with the hull structure, namely the outriggers and the *thrēnus* and

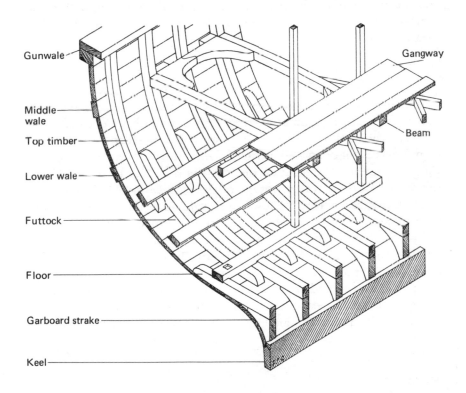

64. Reconstructed ship: hull structure (isometric).

epotis beams forming the ends of the outriggers. Building would then in all probability have been handed over to other trades: carpenters for furniture and decks, ram-fitters for the ram, spar-makers for oars, masts and yards, and other items would have been made by cordwainers, sailmakers, ropemakers, riggers, smiths and metal-founders.

Outriggers

Each outrigger consists of a heavy main rail, very slightly above the gunwale and one-third of a metre outboard of it, supported on curved brackets (see fig. 57), one to every oarsman, secured to the hull and extending down to be lodged into the top edge of the lower wale. The rail is braced between brackets to the gunwale to prevent fore-and-aft movement and into it are set vertical stiles supporting the lighter upper rail of the outrigger. The two rails together hold the thranite tholepins in place.

Thrēnus and *epōtis* beams

The aftermost of these two special beams, which for convenience may be called by its Homeric name, *thrēnus*, and whose ends pass out through the shell under the upper gunwale, performs three functions besides that of a hull beam: it forms the after end of each outrigger as already stated, it carries the main rudder bearings, and it forms part of the after anchorage of the *hypozōmata*. The *epōtis* beam in the bows, laid across the lower gunwale, extends 0.8 m outboard on either side. It is heavily braced aft to the gunwale, as may be seen in fig. 46, to withstand nearly head-on collisions with opposing ships and so protect the outrigger from being sheared off. The *epōtis* also provides support for platforms beside the fo'c's'le from which anchors are let go and hove up clear of the ram. The side bulwarks of these platforms are ear-shaped, while their forward bulwarks incorporate fairleads for the anchor cables mounted directly over the *epōtis* beam.

Oarsystem

The furniture for the oarsmen – seats, foot stretchers, tholepins and oarports – have to be set correctly in relation to each other to give each oarsman the proper posture and room for pulling his oar. Some further explanation of the arrangement (see fig. 45 above) and design of these items in the reconstructed ship is appropriate. To any oarsman wishing to apply appreciable power to his oar the position of his foot-stretcher is vital. In the trieres with beams spaced, in accordance with evidence, every 0.888 m and the need for the smallest possible vertical separation of files, the feet of thranites and zygians could only have been immediately under the seats of the adjacent oarsman aft. That is also a suitable position for hard pulling. For hard backing down (going astern) foot straps are essential.

Foot stretchers

The foot stretchers[1] are a crucial element affecting the whole design because the heights of files of oarsmen above each other and hence the height, stability and beam of the ship, hinged upon the vertical space needed by the stretchers to give a reasonable clearance from the oar looms below them, allowing for some vertical movement of looms caused by roll of the ship.

It has been suggested that oarsmen in triereis could have sat on broad, rounded fore-and-aft stringers and slid upon them on greased cushions. Their feet could have been supported by stretchers built on either side of the stringers. However such a scheme would have been practicable only if the line of the stringers could have run continuously from one oarsman to the next, but the mock-up has shown (see below) that that could not be the case with thranites or thalamians, and a mixed system is improbable.

Canting of oarsmen

The mock-up demonstrated that the thalamians' heads moved through nearly the whole space between beams when oar stroke was long. Their tholes were fairly closely restricted in position between the adjacent top timbers if their oars were to have their required movement within the oarports, which were already as large as could be conveniently accommodated between the same top timbers. To reconcile thole position, head movement and the necessary hull structure, it became necessary to cant the thalamian oarsmen in plan

1. For advice on foot stretchers we are indebted to Tim Watson, an experienced oarsman who has studied the design of oar rigs.

by 3°, to face slightly towards the middle line of the ship. That angle, though small, throws the thalamian blades about 0.15 m aft, which is enough to put them nearly evenly between the oar blades of the zygians sitting at beam positions and facing directly aft. Even spacing of the blades of these two files accords with the historical evolution of the trieres from two-level pentecontors by the addition of thranites and their outriggers. Canting of oarsmen, applied to thranites, enables their height in the ship to be minimised, as already explained. By canting the thranites 9°, their blades are thrown into the best gap between the blades of the two lower files, considering all parts of the stroke. The arrangement of oarsmen in the reconstructed ship, as seen through the eyes of a thalamian, is shown in fig. 65, while the view from the seat of a thranite is shown in fig. 66.

Tholes

Thalamian and zygian tholes are set into carlings, respectively mounted on and set between top timbers as shown in fig. 57, while thranite tholes are dropped through holes in the top rail of the outrigger and seated in the main rail to enable them to be set in place after rigging the thranite oar-loops. Owing to the width of thranite blades and the presence of the upper rail these loops cannot be rigged while the thranite tholes are in place.

Tholes can be either forward of or abaft oars. Early pictorial evidence of hooked tholes, with the hooks on the aft side of the thole (fig. 22a), makes it virtually certain that they were aft of the oars in early Greek oared ships. In that position the oar hung from the thole during the pulling part of the stroke and the loop took the whole force on the thole. Wear would be concentrated on the loop, and for oars worked over an open gunwale that arrangement has the advantage that the oar will trail alongside when not manned, as is demonstrated in fishing boats all over the Mediterranean today. However, when worked through ports from which they cannot trail, oars may be better bearing on their tholes during the pulling part of the stroke: failure of loops in battle would be less serious and oar-ports can be a shade smaller. On the other hand, oars and tholes probably wear more quickly. In the reconstructed ship, tholes are aft of oars, but the design is not much affected in either case.

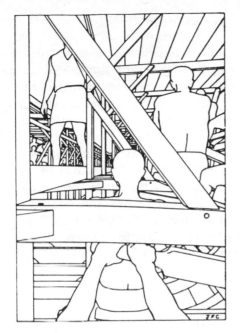

65. Reconstructed ship: a thalamian oarsman's view.

66. Reconstructed ship: a thranite oarsman's view.

Oars

The oars of the replica conform to evidence as to length (above, p. 138). The cramped space in the hull towards bow and stern has made it necessary to resort to oars with shortened looms at the ends of some files of oarsmen. The author of the *Mechanics* has recorded the employment of that expedient in triereis, providing supporting evidence for the hull shape in those places. The three aftermost and foremost pairs of thalamians and the three foremost pairs of zygians pull short oars, a total of 18 short oars or 10% of the total number in the ship. The mock-up showed that the blades of the oars in the three files needed to be of different shapes: shorter and therefore wider for thranites and long and narrow for thalamians. The reason is to equalise the angles by which they have to be raised and lowered to leave and enter the water on account of the differing heights from which they are worked. This accords with written evidence that thranite and zygian oars could be differentiated, but by implication could also be confused (above p. 172). We believe that the difference lay in the shapes of their blades and the similarity (apart from length) lay in both types having built-up blades – while thalamian oars were carved from one pole.

The oars have been given thick looms to help to reduce the handle force needed to lift the blade from the water (see p. 196 above). This was a common feature of high-geared oars in fast sea-going boats of the past: sometimes looms were even weighted with lead.

Askōmata

A particular feature of the trieres was a leather sleeve, *askōma*, fitted to every thalamian oarport to prevent water from slopping through them (pp. 169–70). These sleeves must have been essential to the seaworthiness of the vessel. They show that there was a clear necessity to place the lowest tholes as near to the water as they were, since only a compelling necessity could force acceptance in that position in any craft of the large fragile covers and the openings calling for them. In the reconstructed ship, *askōmata* are fitted inside the hull to enable their replacement or repair at sea.

Oarsmen's seats

All oarsmen's seats in the replica are flat rectangles (400 mm × 300 mm) with edge bolsters to prevent their occupants from sliding sideways on a roll, and to help them to keep their seats when the ship is under sail in a gusty beam wind. All files of oarsmen extend towards bow and stern as far as hull space allows. The resulting arrangement of end oarsmen happens to be the only one which appears to accord with fourth-century evidence (above, p. 149). The forwardmost thalamians on each side meet shoulder to shoulder. The foot-stretchers of the aftermost thalamians nearly touch the bottom timbers of the hull, as these rise towards the stern. The zygian files have to end in the bow two places short of the others because the zygians are squeezed out between the top and bottom files as the hull narrows. In the stern zygians extend as far as the increasing slope of the ship's side allows. Thranites extend from the rudders to a point near the bow where there is just room between them for a gangway 0.6 m wide to give access to the fo'c's'le. That all six ends of files should be determined by sound spatial reasons in relative positions which accord with evidence lends support to the correctness of the hull dimensions and form of the reconstructed ship.

Access

Easy movement of men is important in a ship as densely manned and whose crew embark and disembark as frequently as they did in the trieres. Clear fore-and-aft access is essential, and is provided by a gangway at beam level on the middle line. It is 1.2 m wide to enable two men to walk nearly abreast or to pass with reasonable ease by the standards of a crowded ship. However, the forward ends of the thalamian files have to converge with the hull, making a gangway at that level impossible near the fore-end. There is therefore a step up to a higher level to allow the fore-ends of the thalamian files to converge below it. The step in the gangway also allows it to broaden into a lower foredeck as wide as necessary elbow room for zygians and thranites permits.

In this chapter, decks and the like are described according to nautical practice. A gangway is predominantly a passage to give access. In the trieres there is one gangway. A deck is an area serving several purposes to do with working, defending or fighting the ship, or as accommodation. A platform is a small area for one or two special purposes. A canopy is of lighter construction than a deck or a gangway, sufficient to protect what is underneath it, often from sun and rain only. Canopies in ships commonly take the form of canvas awnings.

Canopy

The oarsmen on either side of the gangway and lower foredeck are protected by a light wooden canopy, whose main purpose would have been to stop javelins and arrows from plunging into the oarsmen as well as to carry sitting or reclining *epibatai* and to provide some shelter. It is strong enough to support a few seamen handing ropes while sailing, but not any dense mass of men, for whom it would be unsafe even if strengthened to take the weight unless fitted with guardrails, at least at the ship's sides. It must be remembered that the reconstructed ship is designed as a 'fast' trieres.

The canopy is built in six sections on each side of the ship to allow them to move longitudinally relative to each other as the ship flexes. No such light deck carried on stanchions could contribute to the longitudinal bending strength of the main hull, so it must be prevented from carrying hull-bending stresses.

Other decks and platforms

Proceeding forward along the lower foredeck to the end of the canopy on either side, one steps up to the level of the *epōtis* platforms; and immediately forward again is the fo'c's'le deck continuous with and at the same level as the canopy. There is room for a small cabin under the fo'c's'le deck.

Going aft from the step between lower foredeck and gangway, one walks between canopies at shoulder or chin height. Abreast the aftermost thalamian the gangway broadens into the afterdeck at the same level. A pair of ladders lead up to the quarterdeck, which is at canopy level. Under the quarterdeck to port and starboard are small accommodation spaces on the afterdeck, 2 m long and about 0.6 m wide, enough for a few seats or a narrow cot. The afterdeck ends at the *thrēnus*.

The quarterdeck (see fig. 67), whose main purpose is to support the upper bearings of the rudder stocks, also provides the command point for the trierarch and helmsman, as well as access for embarking the crew by ladders over each quarter up from the beach. The quarterdeck is constructed and braced to carry rudder forces and the tramp of a rapidly embarking crew, whose static weight on it could be as much as 5 tonnes. At the after end of the quarterdeck is the trierarch's chair, with the helmsman's position just forward of him and below his sightline so that both can see ahead. Aft of the quarterdeck and 0.9 m below it is a small platform for stern mooring to beaches and for archers to provide covering fire over the beach from a position shielded by the stern of the ship rising up to the stern ornament (*aphlaston*). At the command of the trierarch signals may be hoisted from the platform to the head of the staff (*stylis*), held aloft by the *aphlaston*.

Rudders (Steering oars)

The two rudders, 5 m long with their stocks, are each carried in two bearings in which they are turned by tillers lying athwartships. The ends of the tillers are close together so that each can be conveniently grasped by the helmsman standing on a small platform in the middle-line slot in the quarterdeck (fig. 67). The platform's height allows him also to brace himself on the end of the slot as on a misericord. To turn the ship to starboard the helmsman pulls the tiller in his right hand towards him and the other the same distance away from him. The rudder blades are balanced so that both tillers can be handled by one man in normal conditions. The rudders can be operated one at a time or together, if necessary by one man to each. Each rudder has a lower bearing mounted on the *thrēnus* and an upper bearing in the rudder slots in each side of the quarterdeck. These slots and both bearings are designed, by Dorian Dymoke, to allow the rudders to hinge on their lower, main, bearings to bring the blades out of the water for beaching. There are also two intermediate positions for rudders, one in which they can be operated in shoal waters with their lower ends no deeper than the keel, and the other in which the blades

67. Reconstructed ship: the quarterdeck.

are just clear of the water and ready for use. In their fully housed position the rudders are turned so that the tillers are vertical and the blades in a nearly horizontal plane as shown in fig. 35b.

Hypozōmata

The *hypozōmata* (above, pp. 170 and 197) are two lengths of heavy (40 mm diameter) ropes, each rather more than twice the length of the ship. They are rigged by being formed into two loops stretched between strong anchorages in the hull structure, one near the stem and between the middle wales and the other right aft in the form of a post lodged at its base in the keel and whose head is shored to the *thrēnus* and thence to the gunwale. The *hypozōmata* thus run nearly the full length of the ship on the middle line and just below the beams. The two loops, making four passes of rope, are tightened together by twisting with a stout bar of wood amidships, at first by hand and then with levers pulled round by hauling tackle. When the required tension has been obtained, the bar is safely locked in place. This tightening gear, the *entonos*, which needs a fair number of men to work it, has been designed by Dorian Dymoke.

Hypozōmata must always be rigged and tightened on the slip, before any bow or stern shores are knocked away, to ensure against hogging. They cannot be kept tight permanently, because natural fibres stretch under great tension. While the ship is afloat, *hypozōmata* have to be further tightened to maintain their tension. A spare pair of *hypozōmata* are carried on board to replace those first rigged when they have stretched too far to be effectively tightened further.

Ram

The principal weapon of the trieres, the ram, is a strong timber structure built on to the bow of the hull proper (see figs. 46 and 61) and coming to a point on the waterline about two metres in front of the stem. The forward part is sheathed with a tightly fitting bronze casting, thin but armed with three horizontal cutting blades at the foreend. A bronze sheath is visible in the ship shown in fig. 46. The structure of the ram consists essentially of a massive horizontal central member with two pairs of buttressing or bracing timbers, one pair, the wale pieces, bracing the ram sideways while the other, in the vertical plane, is composed of the brace sloping upwards to the stem of the ship and the ram keel piece buttressing it from below. The spaces in between are filled, or sheathed with planking and the casting covers the joints of the main members to each other. The design of the bronze sheath, which in the reconstructed ship weighs about 200 kg, and of the timbers within it closely follows that of the remains found at Athlit (above, p. 130) the upper planks of which indicate that the ram was built on to the hull rather than formed from the stem structure itself. The lines of the Athlit timbers, extended aft, mate with the principal forward members of the hull remarkably well to transmit ramming forces to the ship as a whole.

The order of magnitude of ramming forces may be estimated roughly. A ramming ship of mass 50 tonnes if brought to rest from 10 knots in a distance of one metre by a constant force would suffer a retardation of 13 m/sec.² and the force would be

$$\frac{50 \times 1000 \times 13}{1000} \text{ kN} = 66 \text{ tonnes force}$$

that is, one-third more than the mass of the ship. The rammed victim, especially if hit near one end, would herself move sideways from the blow, so two or three metres would be a more likely travel before coming to rest. However, the force with which the progressively breaking structure would resist the ram would not be uniform, so the 66-tonnes estimate can be expected to be of the order of the maximum force experienced. To speak of vast shocks upon ramming a light hull is mistaken.

Transverse forces could have been more destructive to rams and were probably the main cause of their loss in battle. Such a force could be quite large if the victim had an appreciable velocity across the path of the attacker at the moment of impact. The ram, on penetration, would immediately have to acquire the sideways velocity of the victim, but the consequent side force on the ram would be limited to that required to tear the point sideways through the victim's shell structure. That force could well be about 40 tonnes, quite sufficient to pull the ram off sideways, indeed about twice what may be estimated to be necessary. Ramming a target moving at more than a few knots must therefore have been dangerous, and trierarchs may have reduced the risk to their own rams by initiating a sharp turn in the direction of their victim's motion just before impact.

In the reconstructed ship, if the ram were to be torn off, there is a fair chance that the hull would remain watertight or leak at no more than a controllable rate. Most lost rams would have been easily salvaged because battles were usually fought near the shore and the buoyancy of a ram's structure is sufficient to keep the bronze casting afloat pointing downwards, if the structure came away fairly complete. The after ends of those that did sink would point upwards and often be quite near the surface, so it is not surprising that there seem to be so few left to be recovered today.

Sails and rigging

The sail and rigging plan is shown in fig. 68. Owing to lack of evidence, the rig is necessarily somewhat conjectural, though possible positions, shapes and areas of sails are restricted by the design and sail-carrying capacity of the ship. The rig has been designed by Owain Roberts, who has made a study of past European single square-sail rigs.

The sail plan follows the pictorial evidence from both earlier and later centuries. In accordance with the naval inventories (above

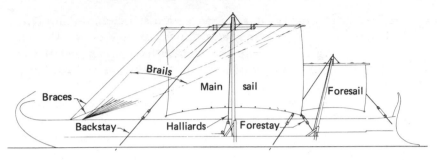

68. Reconstructed ship: sail and rigging plan. Forward rigging (not shown) is similar to the main.

p. 176), it includes a 'boat' mast and sail. Later pictures of Roman ships under sail suggest that this was a foremast and sail, the mast being raked forward (see above, p. 177). The area of the main sail, 95 square metres, and its height accord with nineteenth-century AD criteria of square sail carrying capacity when applied to a vessel with the characteristics of the trieres. Under main sail alone the ship can be expected to heel to about 7° in a steady beam wind of 14 knots: setting the foresail would add another degree or so to the heel. These angles are about one-third of the heel needed to immerse the zygian oarports (21°) and so swamp the ship. They are however sufficient to put the sills of the thalamian oarports very near the water, so that in all but very sheltered waters the *askōmata* will be called into action. It may be expected that sail would be shortened in winds stronger than about 14 knots.

As in all ancient Mediterranean rigs, sail can be reduced quickly in the reconstructed ship by means of 10 brailing ropes controlled from near the helmsman. These pass over the yard at equally spaced points and down the front (i.e. lee side) of the sail, through rings (see above, p. 177 and fig. 54a) sewn to every horizontal seam of the sail, to the foot. The main braces and sheets are also led to the helmsman's position so that he has immediate control of the main sail, probably through the stern deck party (see pp. 112–13) normally stationed near him.

The foresail, or 'boat' sail, in the reconstructed ship is about one-quarter the area of the main sail and is similarly controlled but from the fo'c's'le deck, a possible station for the bow deck party under the *prōrates* (see pp. 112–13) when the ship is under sail. The purpose of the foresail has long been a subject of discussion. Sailing the reconstructed ship (fig. 69) may show how it should be worked, its value in balancing the rig fore-and-aft and how it can be used to adjust the weather helm needed in various directions and strengths of wind.

Both masts are stepped in tabernacles with their heels at beam level. When lowered aft, they rest on portable bars placed between the canopies. Tabernacles consist of two main uprights, the mast-partners, secured to a deck beam and extending down to twin mast-steps each spanning several floor timbers. The masts are stayed fore-and-aft but not athwartships: when raised they are lashed into their tabernacles.

The main yard is made up of two spars fished together. It is held to the mast by a parrel and hoisted by twin halliards passing through eyes on each side of a bronze fitting or truck at the masthead (see fig. 47). Fairleads for braces, sheets and tacks are provided by wooden thimbles stropped with double rope tails for securing them to the ship where needed. Those for sheets and main tacks are passed

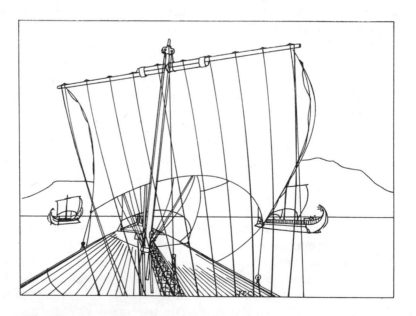

69. The reconstructed ship under sail.

through appropriate zygian ports and hitched to adjacent beams. All sails, yards and rigging can be carried ashore, as they normally were in clearing triereis for action before battle.

In beam winds the brails were used to furl the after part (leech) of the main sail, shifting the wind force on the sail forwards. In following winds it seems that the middle of the main sail (bunt) was brailed up more than the corners (clews). That was probably necessary owing to the proportions and rigging of the sail, but may also explain how the smaller and lower foresail could draw in such winds and, by moving the centre of effort of the sails forward, steady the ship against yawing in waves.

Hull paint

The hull will be black below the waterline and up to the lower wale because triereis, not being sheathed with lead like merchant ships, were frequently coated with pine tar or pine pitch or both. The upper parts of triereis were decorated with painted patches and devices[2], and a scheme for the reconstructed ship will be adopted in association with the choice of her name by the Hellenic Navy. The replica will otherwise not be painted: all her timbers will be treated with wood preservative as she is built.

Triereis as troop-carriers

From the earliest times oared ships carried soldiers, and triereis were no exceptions. There is room on the afterdeck of the replica to transport about 30 soldiers additional to the 10 normally on board, without interfering with the handling of ropes when under sail. They would, however, be very crowded on the afterdeck so it is not surprising that in representations men appear on the canopy, but always sitting or lying down.

The ability of a trieres to carry extra men is not limited so much by their weight and a consequent rise in the ship's centre of gravity, as by the available space and, above all, the necessity to limit their movement athwartships at all times while the ship is under oars (pp. 161–2). The working of oars in any boat is much hampered by

2. Casson (1971) p. 212.

rolling. To reduce as far as possible their sensitivity to rolling, the oars in pulling sea-going boats in the past were arranged to give looms as much room as practicable to rise and, more especially, to fall, to enable oarsmen to cope with waves and the motion of the boat.[3] That called for looms to be at about shoulder height when the blades were immersed in still water: even so, among waves a 10° roll relative to the wave surface was generally near the limit for effective pulling. In a trieres that limit would probably have been about 4°, an angle to which the reconstructed ship would heel if 30 soldiers on board were to move 0.7 m athwartships simultaneously, a thing unlikely to happen so long as they were sitting down.

Triereis as cavalry transports

Some older vessels were converted to carry 30 horses, cavalrymen and grooms. The feasibility of converting the replica in this way has been investigated to seek support for the likely correctness of the design. Fig. 70 shows how such a conversion could have been carried out fairly easily. The furniture for zygians is removed, the canopies each side are cut back to cover the thranites only, the widened space so created is planked and the mast tabernacles removed. There is then room, as shown in fig. 70, for 30 horses forward of the quarter-deck, standing athwartships. With their rumps against boards on the stanchions at the inboard edge of the remaining canopy and their chests restrained by rails set up for that purpose, the horses would be in the best position to steady themselves against rolling motions of the magnitude likely to be experienced. To balance the ship, about half the horses would face one way and half the other, with a slight imbalance to offset the weight of the ramp which must be on one side of the ship. The ramp necessarily displaces two thranites, reducing the total number of oarsmen to the attested number of 60 (above, p. 157).

So converted and loaded, the horse-carrier would be about eight tonnes heavier than the fast trieres with her full complement of oarsmen. The centre of gravity of the cavalry transport would be 0.16 m higher than that of the trieres proper but owing to the flare of the hull at the waterline, the metacentre would rise too and stability

---

3. Rowing and pulling oars in sea-going boats is discussed more fully by Eric McKee (1983).

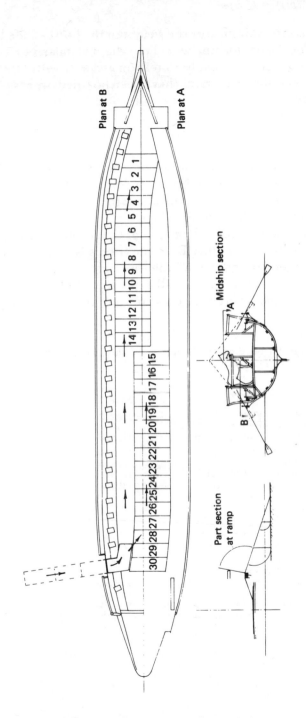

70. Reconstructed ship: conversion to a cavalry transport.

would be satisfactory in spite of the weight of the horses added high in the ship. The deeper loading would put the thalamian ports close to the water, too close probably to rely on *askōmata* with safety, so those ports would almost certainly have been boarded over as part of the conversion.

Conclusion

In this chapter features of the reconstructed ship have been explained and described in their broad aspects only. Readers wishing to have complete design information about the vessel are referred to the building specification and drawings.[4]

Fig. 71 is an imagined reconstruction of the Athenian harbour of Munychia in the fourth century BC. One trieres is seen leaving the harbour. From left to right round the shore are: derelict triereis, a trieres being rigged, a fire barrier wall at the side of a block of sheds, and, inside the mole, triereis used for routine training afloat.

4. *Trieres Specification* for building the reconstructed ship, written for The Trireme Trust by J. F. Coates, 126 pp.

Building drawings

Plan no.	Title	Scale
1	General arrangement	1/50
7	Lines of hull, form 7 mod. 2	1/50 and 1/10
8	Arrangement of mid-section	1/10
9	Foot-stretcher	Full size
10	Arrangement of stern	1/10
11	Arrangement of fore-end	1/10
12	Stern profile and plan	1/10
13	Run of planking	1/10
14	Scheme of scarfs	–
20	Ram	1/10
21	Forward and forecastle decks	1/10
22	Lines of stern	1/10
23	Quarterdeck	1/10
24	Rudder bearings	Various
25	*Hypozōmata* tensioning gear	Various

Enquiries about supply of these drawings and the specification of the ship should be made to J. F. Coates, Sabinal, Lucklands Road, Bath, Avon BA1 4AU, or to Cambridge University Press.

71. Munychia in the fourth century, a reconstruction.

APPENDIX I
Fast triereis

The interpretation of Greek texts referring to triereis as 'fast' may be helped by some discussion of

1. The relations between the resistance to the motion of a ship through the water and changes in displacement and roughness of the ship's bottom.
2. Likely variation, between different crews, of propulsive thrust, of turning forces and of ability to perform efficiently in the various modes to manoeuvre on command. The last two would affect times taken to manoeuvre rather than attainable speed.

'Fast' could refer to excellence in any combination of the following:

Speed on a straight course attainable for a given period of time.
Acceleration from rest to reach a target in the shortest time, or retardation from stated speeds to rest.
Rate of turning with oars.

In a ramming action agility in manoeuvres over relatively short distances would have been more important than speed attainable over long periods, though triereis capable of high sustained speeds would generally have accelerated well and in many cases also turned quickly with oars, but that would have needed training and practice on its own account.

The resistance of a ship in water is broadly the result of two factors. The first is skin friction and the second arises from the continuous formation of surface waves as the ship proceeds. Since it is a long vessel, the resistance of a trieres is mainly due to skin friction, particularly at lower speeds. At 10 knots frictional resistance is only about half the total, while at 5 knots and less nearly all resistance is frictional. Wave-making resistance is unlikely to vary much from one trieres to another at any given speed because the elements of form upon which that resistance depends could not vary greatly, being constrained by limits of length and breadth on one hand and by the necessity of accommodating the given number of oarsmen on the other. Frictional resistance (R_f), however, depends upon the roughness of the wetted surface of the hull, its length, the area (A) of the wetted surface and the speed (V). The first two determine the size of the frictional coefficient (f) and, following Froude,

$$R_f = fAV^n, \text{ where } n = 1.825.$$

Now if the bottom becomes rough or fouled with marine growths, f can readily increase above its value for a well smoothed and painted or pitched surface by 50%. Over long periods of immersion without cleaning the value of f can double or treble. It could commonly have increased by 50%, however, between beachings of triereis to dry them out. In such a case and for the lower speeds (for which resistance is nearly all frictional), if oarsmen pull the ship with the same force as when the hull is smooth and freshly pitched, they will achieve only

$$\left(\frac{1}{1.5}\right)^{\frac{1}{1.825}} = 0.8$$

of the speed, a reduction of 20%. At high speeds where friction accounts for only half of the total resistance, the corresponding reduction in speed will only be about 10%, say 1 knot. The general effect will be the loss of about 1 knot over a wide range of speed.

The effects of roughness would have been very obvious in a fleet of nearly identical ships, so the application of mixtures containing wax to their bottoms to reduce f would have been quite natural.

Triereis undoubtedly tended to leak – not surprisingly in view of their slenderness and length – and their timbers would have soaked up water, especially those made of fir or beech, which are permeable woods. There is mention of ships becoming slow because they were heavy in the water from not having been dried out for some time. The likely increase in weight in those circumstances may be estimated by assuming as a worst case that all timbers in the hull below water were to be waterlogged and, owing to heavy leakage, bilge water were to rise to the top of the floors. It can be calculated that 1 tonne of water would soak into the timbers and that the bilge water would amount to about 6 tonnes, a total increase in displacement of about 7 tonnes, or 15% of the ship's dry displacement. That would cause the waterline to rise by about 70 mm, and increase the wetted area of the hull by 4.8 square metres, or 4%, reducing the speeds considered above by 4% and 2%, 1/5 of the effects due to roughness and fouling. These are likely to have been the maximum effects on speed at the ends of normal periods between drying out triereis.

It seems therefore that the need for drying out, as regards speed at least, was not so much to reduce weight and leakage as to make the hulls smooth again. But the required repitching could not have been done unless the timber had been dried. 'Heaviness' and roughness would go together, making it hard to discriminate between their separate effects on speed until the mechanics of fluid flow and friction had become understood.

Heaviness and hull roughness would have affected a ship's acceleration rather differently. This should be discussed because it was probably more important in a ramming battle than sustained high speed. Assuming for simplicity that while accelerating their ship, oarsmen exert a constant propulsive force, and noting that fluid friction is negligible at low speeds, increasing with about the square of the speed, we can deduce that acceleration from rest will be in inverse proportion to mass, and at higher speeds it will be reduced progressively as resistance rises at a faster rate owing to greater roughness. As the ship reaches its reduced maximum speed acceleration will sink to zero. Again taking as likely maxima the increases in the coefficient of friction and in weight given above, we would expect acceleration to be reduced when starting from rest by up to 15% until a speed is reached at which resistance becomes significant, say 5 knots, after which as speed rises acceleration diminishes. The time taken to ram an enemy ship from rest would be lengthened by more than 15%. The swiftness of that manoeuvre was probably most important to a trierarch and may well have been the most readily felt penalty of 'heaviness'. Unlike speed, its cause lay more in extra weight than in hull roughness. Poor acceleration could therefore have been what was mainly meant by being 'heavy in the water', and for which drying out and repitching was indeed the cure, albeit a temporary one.

Retardation would of course have been actually improved by greater roughness and frictional resistance, but reduced by extra weight.

Turning, as vital in battle as acceleration, would also be affected more by extra weight than by roughness because while water velocities round the hull when turning would generally be low, extra weight would increase draft by about 6%, and the resistance of the underwater profile to turning and the mass moment of inertia of the ship by about 10%. It may be estimated that a heavy ship would take about 8% longer to make a turn.

Irrespective of heaviness, the strength and skill of her oarsmen could clearly determine whether a trieres was fast or not. A tired crew might pull with only 70% or even 50% of the force of a fresh one. This was always a potent factor in galley warfare, and such reductions would diminish attainable speed by 18% or 32% respectively, while the more important acceleration would be reduced more catastrophically, in proportion to the propulsive force. Lack of training or skill could have an equally bad effect.

Wind and waves plainly affected triereis, as reported at Salamis. Ships which, whether by leakage or inaccurate building, had less freeboard than was desirable would have been the more sensitive to weather because oar blades would tend to dig in and catch the waves coming forward. Power would be lost, particularly if the crowded blades fouled each other.

The military effectiveness of triereis would, by these arguments, be more sensitive to the weather and the quality or tiredness of crews than to leakage or to roughness of bottom, though extra weight would have made them more sensitive to weather.

The admiral of a fleet of triereis could judge whether an opposing fleet was 'faster' than his own by the following means:

1. Intelligence, possibly before reaching the scene of battle, about
   (a) the time elapsed since the opposing fleet had been dried out.
   (b) the quality and training of the opposing crews
   (c) whether the opposing crews were likely to be fresh or tired.
2. Directly observing
   (a) the enemy's oarsmanship during preliminary manoeuvres
   (b) the waterline of enemy ships particularly by noting tell-tale features like rams and rudders.

There are references to ships within a fleet being 'fast' compared with others in the same fleet, which was presumably composed mainly if not entirely of ships of the line. These ships could either have been manned with picked crews to perform, for example, crucial roles in battle tactics, or they may have been built as 'fast' ships, which would in all probability also have been specially manned in order fully to exploit the high qualities built into them. From the foregoing discussion it may be inferred that such ships would have been extreme examples of the trieres, of exceptional lightness and workmanship. If, for instance, hulls had been built of fir throughout instead of pine and oak they would have been up to 15% lighter, though less durable. It would be reasonable also to suppose that their bottoms would have been smoothed with extra care. Such ships while new could well have had a 20–30% advantage in agility.

APPENDIX II
The Lenormant Relief in projection

The accuracy of the vertical proportions of the Lenormant Relief is open to doubt for the following reasons:

1. The ratio between the projected lengths of thranite looms and the projected lengths of shafts from tholes to the water is only about 1.7. Thranite oar gearing as sculpted is therefore at most about 2, whereas in actuality it must have been near to 3 at least. (See discussion of oar-gearing in chapter 12.)
2. The lower wale is surprisingly far from the water, and the space between it and the middle wale insufficient to accommodate circular ports of the diameter both required geometrically and indicated in the Talos vase.

The angle of the oars in the Relief to the vertical and the relative fore-and-aft positions of the tholes, shown or implied, in the Relief (fig. 13) also raise questions of interpretation. Following the general opinion that the Relief is a broadside profile, it would appear that the oars are at about 1/4 of the stroke past the catch. They all lie at nearly the same angle. If, however, one considers that oar length, stroke length and gearing are the same in all three levels of oars, one will appreciate that in any horizontal aspect of the vessel, and neglecting cant of oarsmen, oars at different heights, but keeping time together, can appear parallel in the course of a stroke only at the instant when they are pointing towards the viewer and therefore appear vertical. At all other times, oars whose tholes are close to the water will appear inclined more to the vertical than those higher up.

In the diagrams (figs. 72 and 73) are shown the oar angles in the Relief and what they are more likely to have been at the moment in the stroke when the sculpted position of the thranite oars is correct. It is most noticeable how much tidier the Relief is and how it gives a strong impression of the whole array working 'to a single beat'. The sculptor may also have wished to portray thranites as fully as possible and to convey the height of triereis. He may therefore have dropped the outrigger by say 0.2 m to reveal the lower torsos and the thighs of those oarsmen, while reducing the figures a little in scale relative to the vessel. That change would have upset the nearly equal spacing, vertically, of outrigger, middle wale and lower wale, which could have been restored either by lowering the middle wale or by raising the lower wale. He appears to have chosen the latter alternative, which certainly adds to the impression of height.

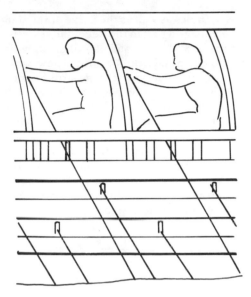

72. The Lenormant Relief: with probable thole positions.

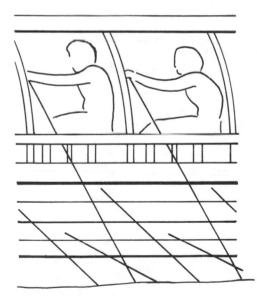

73. The Lenormant Relief: with oars at more realistic angles.

The fore-and-aft positions of tholes as well as the curve of the stanchions supporting the canopy strongly suggest that in the Relief the vessel is viewed from a direction 70–75° off the bow. The second pair of diagrams (figs. 74 and 75) show the replica broadside on and from 70° off the bow, with oars in both cases at the catch, the most natural moment of the stroke to portray. It will be seen that in fig. 75 the tholes at the three levels are in nearly the same relative fore-and-aft positions as they are in the Relief, but that in the broadside view in fig. 74 they are not. In fig. 75 the angles of the oars also accord better with the Relief.

The viewpoint suggested here is supported by the decreasing height between *katastrōma* and lower wale towards the stern. The decrease is 8% in 7 thole pitches or 6.2 m in the ship, from which one may infer a viewpoint 25–30 m from the middle of the ship which would subtend an angle of about 70°, appropriate for a close-up view of the whole ship.

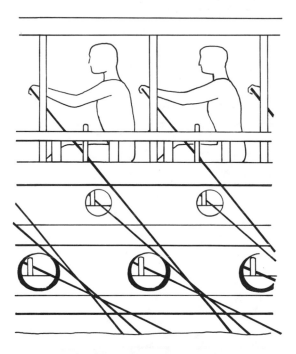

74. The Lenormant Relief: broadside on, with oars at the catch.

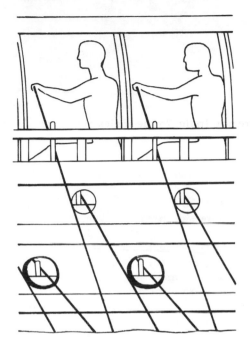

75. The Lenormant Relief: seen from 70° off bow, with oars at the catch.

GLOSSARY

I English

(a) Nautical

adze: a shipwright's tool, like an axe but with the cutting edge set at right angles to the haft.

beam: a term for the breadth of a ship. Also, a strong piece of timber stretching across the ship from side to side to keep the sides at their proper distance.

bending moment: the sum of the moments about the neutral axis of the cross-section in question of all the forces acting on the beam, on one side of the section. It is measured in newton-metres.

bevel: the angle by which one face of a plank or timber departs from the perpendicular with another face, or usually with parallel and opposing faces on either side of the one in question.

bireme: *see biremis in II.*

bitts: two strong timbers fixed vertically in the fore part of a ship, to which anchor cables are secured when the ship rides at anchor.

block coefficient: a measure of the slimness of a hull form. The block coefficient is the ratio of the volume of displacement to that of a rectangular block of sides equal to the waterline length, the waterline beam and the draft of the ship.

boatswain: a petty officer who summons members of the crew to their duty; *see keleustēs in II.*

bolt: a metal pin employed to connect timbers, particularly where liable to tension between them. Many bolts therefore have their ends clenched over broad rings.

bracket: an angular support.

brailing rope, brail: a rope to haul up the bottom of the sail to adjust, shorten or furl it.

brow: a gangway or ladder on which a man can face the shore while descending from a ship.

bulwark: a solid protecting screen at each outboard edge of the deck.

bunt: middle part or cavity of a square sail, extending over the two middle quarters of its breadth.

butt: a joint between the ends of timber forming a longer member.

cant: angle at which a timber or other item lies relative to its more usual direction.

careening: the process of cleaning a ship's bottom by heeling her over.

carling: a short piece of timber ranging fore and aft from one beam or timber to another.

catch: in the stroke of an oar, the instant at which an oarsman starts to pull.

caulking: the process of driving material into the seams of a ship's planking.

centroid: of a plane shape, the centre of gravity of a thin uniform sheet of material cut to that shape; the point at which if suspended the shape will balance in any position.

clew (or clue): lower corner of a square sail.

cutwater: the leading part of a ship's bow.

displacement: immersed volume of a body. The buoyancy force acting on such a body is equal to its displacement multiplied by the weight density of the fluid in which it is immersed.

dowel: a peg to make a fast joint between one timber and another.

draft: a depth of underside of keel below the waterline.

fairlead: an eye or ring to enable a rope to pass freely.

fished: two spars are fished when they are lashed together, one overlapping the other.

'five': an oared warship with five files of oarsmen ranging fore and aft on each side of the ship.

floor, floor timber: timbers placed across the keel and secured to the bottom planking.

fo'c's'le: the foredeck.

'foot': *see pous in II.*

foot, Athenian: 2/3 cubit, 0.296 m.

forefoot: the forward projection of the ship's keel.

'forty': a monstrous and unwieldy oared warship with forty files of oarsmen ranging fore and aft on each side of the ship.

'four': a ship with four files of oarsmen ranging fore and aft on each side of the ship.

frame: in a ship a frame is usually made up of several timbers, e.g. floors, futtocks and top timbers fitted at right angles to the keel.

freeboard: the height by which the gunwale stands above the waterline.

futtock: transverse hull timber stiffening the shell planking outboard of the floors and round the curve of the hull to its side (*see* frame).

galley: an oared vessel.

garboard: the first plank on either side of a ship's keel.

gearing: (of oars) the ratio a : b, where

> a = distance from the thole to the centre of pressure of the blade in the water, projected on to a horizontal plane, and
>
> b = horizontal distance of the thole from the plane of symmetry of the oarsman.

grommet: a loop of rope or leather.

gunwale: the uppermost edge of the ship's side, or the wale in that position.

halliard: rope for raising and lowering a spar (i.e. 'haul-yard').

heel: transverse angle from the upright at which a ship may float.

hog: bending or shearing of a ship's hull in the vertical plane, causing it to arch upwards in the middle and the ends to drop.

hoplite: *see hoplitēs in II.*

inch, Athenian: 1/16 Athenian foot = 18.5 mm.

Joule: SI unit of energy or work; symbol J. $1J = 1$ newton-metre.

leech: vertical edge of a square sail.

loom: (of an oar) the part inboard of the thole.

mast-partners: a pair of supporting timbers between which the mast stands.

mast-step: substantial timber into which the bottom of the mast or tabernacle post is fastened. It is laid on the floors, or onto the bottom, to spread the mast forces into the hull structure.

metacentre: the point in the middle plane of the ship through which the buoyancy force passes when the ship is inclined by a small angle.

metacentric height: the height of the metacentre above the centre of gravity of the ship; it is a measure of the ship's stability.

metic: *see metoikos in II.*

mock-up: a model, often full size, to find or demonstrate spatial relationships between parts.

moment (of a force) about a given point: the product of the force and the perpendicular distance of its line of action from that point. It is measured in newton-metres.

mortice: the slot cut in a plank or timber to take a tenon joining planks or timbers.

neutral axis of bending: the line passing through the centroid of a cross-section of a beam perpendicular to the plane of bending.

newton: the SI unit of force. It is the force required to accelerate a mass of 1 kg by 1 m/sec^2.

oakum: strands made from old rope and used for caulking.

oar-loop: the loop of rope or leather holding the oar to the tholepin.

oarport: the aperture in the hull of an oared warship through which an oar is pulled.

obol: the sixth part of a drachma.

outrigger: *see parexeiresia in II.*

parrel: rope holding a spar to a mast.

pentecontor: a fifty-oared ship.

pitch: angular motion (in waves) of a ship in the fore-and-aft vertical plane.

prau: Indonesian name for a vessel of local design and construction, employing sail and either oar or paddle.

prismatic coefficient: a measure of the fullness of the ends of a hull form. The prismatic coefficient is the ratio of the displacement volume to that of a prism of length equal to the waterline and of section identical with the immersed mid-section of the ship.

quadrireme: (Lat. *quadriremis*) *see* 'four'.

quarter: of a ship, that part of a ship's side which lies towards the stern.

quinquereme: (Lat. *quinqueremis*) *see* 'five'.

rabbet: a groove cut in a timber to receive the edge of a plank or the ends of a number of planks, to be fastened therein.

raked: a raked mast is one stepped to incline aft or forward.

rocker: vertical curve of a keel analogous to that of the upper edge of a hull.

roll: transverse angle from the upright to which a ship may oscillate.

room: (Lat. *interscalmium*) the space occupied by an oarsman or a group of oarsmen, seen as the distance between one tholepin and the next in a fore-and-aft file of oarsmen.

sag: longitudinal bending of a ship as if loaded amidships and supported at each end.

sailyard: the horizontal spar on which a sail is extended.

scantling: breadth and depth of a piece of timber in shipbuilding.

scarf: joint between timbers end to end in which they are shaped to overlap and fit into each other to give a uniform section when joined. *For 'trait de Jupiter' scarf see fig. 63.*

seam: a longitudinal joint between adjacent planks in the hull of a ship.

sea mile: 1.84 km, 1.15 miles (60 sea miles = 1 degree of latitude)

shear: state of force or stress in which successive planes in a material or structure tend to slide relative to each other.

sheer: curve seen in profile of the upper edge of a ship's hull.

shell construction: any method by which the hull of a wooden ship is built up on each side by successive planks joined edge to edge or by overlapping their edges, frames being inserted subsequently.

ship-sheds: the sheds in which oared ships were normally kept when not at sea.

shore: a prop to support a ship when slipped or beached.

'six': an oared warship with six files of oarsmen ranging fore and aft on each side of the ship.

Spanish Windlass: parallel ropes or chains twisted and so tightened by turning a lever placed between them at their mid-length.

spike: a pointed metal nail, with a head, for connecting timbers.

stability: measure of the tendency of a ship to return to the upright position.

stanchion: a vertical support or pillar.

stile: a vertical member in a wooden framework.

stopping, or bedding: the process of, or the material for, filling joints between planks as they are laid together.

strain: (in material) = $\dfrac{\text{loaded length} - \text{unloaded length}}{\text{unloaded length}}$

It is a non-dimensional quantity.

strake: a continuous row of planks, joined end to end, typically extending
from stem to stern.

stress: (in material) = $\dfrac{\text{force exerted on a given area}}{\text{the same area}}$. It is measured in
newtons per square mm.

stringer: an internal longitudinal timber riding over and fastened to floors,
futtocks or top timbers.

stroke: the aftermost man in a file of oarsmen ranging fore and aft in a
ship.

strop: rope passing round the body of a block to enable the block to be
secured where needed for use.

swifter: a constricting girdle of rope.

tabernacle: casing that encloses and supports the lower part of the mast, the
after part being open to allow the mast to be raised and
lowered.

tail: rope secured to a block, thimble or buoy with a free end by which it may
be hitched to anything as required.

'ten': an oared warship with ten files of oarsmen ranging fore and aft on each
side of the ship.

tenon: a tongue of wood fitting into a mortice, in ancient ships particularly a
rectangular tongue of wood fitting into an opposing mortice in timbers to be joined in the shell method of construction. In this form it
is also called a draw-tongue and (USA) a loose tenon.

thalamian: *see thalamios in II*.

thimble: ring of wood or metal, having a groove round its outer circumference to house a rope eye or cringle to protect it from wear.

thole, tholepin: the pin of wood forming, with the oar-loop, the fulcrum of
an oar.

thranite: *see thranitēs in II*.

'three': an oared warship with three files of oarsmen ranging fore and aft on
each side of the ship.

thwart: a seat or bench of a boat on which oarsmen sit to manage their
oars.

tiller: the lever on the head of the rudder oar by which it is turned.

top timber: (see 'frame') transverse, and generally vertical hull timber stiffening the planking from the gunwale to the futtocks.

tow: coarse hemp or flax.

treenail: long wooden pin employed to connect ships' planks and timbers,
especially where the joint is mainly subject to shear.

triacontor: a thirty-oared ship.

trierarch: the commander of a trieres.

trieres: see 'three'.

trireme: see 'three'.

truck: fitting at the top of a mast through which the halliards are worked.

undergirdle: *see hypozoma in II.*

wale: an assemblage of thick and broad planks along the outside of a ship's hull.

watt: SI unit of power (symbol W). 1 W = 1 joule/sec.

whaler: a naval oared boat.

yawing: swinging of a ship from her proper course or heading, particularly in following seas but also when riding at anchor: otherwise known as sheering.

zygian: *see zygios in II.*

(b) General

Archaic: a term applied to Greek painted pottery of the period 700–480 BC.

black-figure: a style of painted pottery with figures in black on an unglazed or slightly glazed red background.

cubit: an ancient measure of length; 1 attic cubit = 0.444 m.

'frying pan': the name given to the flat, fan-like terracottas with double-handles found in Syros.

Geometric: the term applied to Greek painted pottery with geometrical decoration of the period *c.* 900–*c.* 700 BC.

graffito: a rough drawing scratched on a wall or other suitable surface.

paean: a song of victory or praise.

red-figure: a style of painted pottery with figures left in the red of the pottery against a painted black ground.

scholiast: an ancient commentator on a Greek or Latin text, in most cases belonging to the Byzantine period.

II Greek (unless otherwise stated) and Latin

acantha: acacia.

acropolis: a citadel e.g. of Athens or Lindos.

aloiphē: substance applied to a ship's hull.

amphora: a high two-handled pot, the standard container for transporting oil and wine.

aphlaston: the ornament of a ship's poop in which the up-curving timbers of the hull terminate.

apobathra: *see brow in I(a).*

apostoleis: commissioners appointed by the Athenian Assembly to oversee the dispatch of a naval expedition.

arista (or *ameinon*) *pleousai*: a phrase describing ships as 'moving best (*or* better) in the water'.

askōma: a leather sleeve fitted to the lower oarports in a trieres to prevent water splashing into the ship.

asphalton: bitumen.

aulētēs: a member of the *hypēresia* in a trieres who gave the rate of striking to the oarsmen by playing a pipe; also called *trieraules*.

auteretēs: a fighting man serving as an oarsman in an oared ship.

biremis (Lat.): occurs in Horace and Livy (1st century BC); *see dierēs*.

chōma: the mole or hard in the dockyard at Piraeus to which triereis were brought round by their trierarchs, after manning and fitting out, for inspection by the *apostoleis*, followed by sea trials.

corvus (Lat.): 'raven', a kind of boarding bridge used by the Romans.

desmos: a bond or tie.

dia pasēs (*neōs*): throughout the whole (ship), overall.

diekplous: as t.t., the battle manoeuvre by which ships pulled through a gap made in the line-abreast formation of an enemy fleet, more generally the gap in a line of ships (e.g. in the bridge of ships at the Hellespont in 480) through which it is possible for other ships to pass.

dierēs: the term seems to have been invented as the Greek equivalent of *biremis*; an oared ship with two files of oarsmen ranged fore and aft on each side of the ship. The word is not recorded before Pollux in the second century AD.

dikrotos: adjective describing a ship (in one case a trieres) in which two files of oars were manned on each side.

dinos: round goblet.

diolkos: the tramway across the Isthmus of Corinth by which ships were transferred from one side to the other.

dipēchiake or *dipēchuia*: the unitary length of 2 cubits(*pēcheis*)=0.888m, which Vitruvius calls the *interscalmium*, between one tholepin and the next in a file of oarsmen ranging fore and aft in an oared ship.

dipylon: name for a group of vases (Late Geometric I: 760–735 BC), so called from the Dipylon cemetery at Athens in which they were found.

drachma (pl. *drachmae*): the standard Athenian coin. There were six obols to a drachma, and 6,000 drachmae to a talent. The drachma was also a measure of weight (4.36 g), as was the talent.

dromon: a two-level oared warship of the Byzantine navy.

elatē: silver fir.

enkoilia, entera, enteroneia: the internal woodwork of an oared ship.

entonoi: tackles for tightening the *hypozōmata*.

epibatēs, pl. *epibatai*: as t.t., a fighting man in full armour carried on the deck of an oared warship; or, generally, a passenger carried on deck.

epistoleus: (secretary) the title for the Spartan second-in-command of a Peloponnesian fleet.

epōtis: the 'ear timber' in the bows of a trieres projecting on each side of, and hence protecting, the outrigger.

galea (Lat.): galley.

gradus (Lat.): level, e.g. of oarsmen.

gomphoi: pegs driven through the planking to hold the tenons securely in the mortices; *see tuloi*.

harmonia (pl. *harmoniai*): either the tenon or the whole mortice-and-tenon joint.

hexērēs: *see* 'six'.

hippagōgos (or, in an abbreviated form, *hippēgos*): cavalry transport ship.

histion: sail.

histos: mast.

holkas (pl. *holkades*): (a towed ship) merchant ship, towed when not proceeding under sail.

hoplitēs (pl. *hoplitai*): fighting man in full armour.

hypaloiphē: substance applied to the under (i.e. wetted) surface of triereis.

hypēresia: (auxiliary group) a collective noun used for the 30 men carried on a fast trieres in addition to the 170 oarsmen and the trierarch (i.e. 4 archers, 10 hoplites, 6 petty officers and two groups of 5 deckhands, all being regarded as assisting the trierarch in various ways).

hypozōma (pl. *hypozōmata*): the undergirdle of a trieres. Two were regularly rigged.

ikria (pl.): poop and fo'c's'le.

interscalmium (Lat.): the two-cubit (0.888 m.) space between one thole and the next in an oared ship.

kaloi (pl.): brailing ropes which would pass over the sailyard and down the front of the sail through fairleads to the bottom edge.

kannabis: hemp.

katastrōma (pl. *katastrōmata*): the deck or canopy over the heads of the oarsmen.

kedros: cedar.

keleustes: the member of the *hyperesia* in charge of the oarsmen.

keraia: the sailyard.

kerkouros: an oared supply ship.

kommata (pl.): pieces (of rope).

kōpeus: a spar suitable for shaping as an oar.

kratēr: a big, deep bowl for mixing wine.

kratēr, column: a *krater* with column-like handles.

kratēr, volute: a *krater* with scroll-like handles.

kubernētes: helmsman, the member of the *hypēresia* equivalent to the master in a later sailing ship.

kuparissos: cypress.

larnax: a terracotta sarcophagus.

leukaia: esparto grass.

liburna (Lat.): light warship with oars at two levels employed in Roman fleets.

metoikos: a resident alien at Athens.

nauarchos: title of the Spartan commander of a Peloponnesian fleet.

naupēgos: shipwright, a member of the *hypēresia* in a trieres.

nautēs (pl. *nautai*): in general a seaman, in particular often an oarsman.

okellein: to drive (a ship) ashore bow first.

ordo (Lat.): a column or file of oars or oarsmen ranging fore and aft in an oared ship, sometimes used to denote all the oars on one side of a ship.

papyrus: plant grown in Egypt providing material for ropes and sails.

Paralos: the name for one of the two state triereis at Athens.

pararrumata: sidescreens.

parastatai: probably mast-partners.

paredroi: epithet for the archers carried on a trieres, possibly indicating that they sat beside the helmsman to protect him in battle.

parexeiresia: a structure built out from the side of the trieres to accommodate the tholes of the uppermost file of oarsmen, an outrigger.

pēdalia (pl.): the two rudder oars fitted on an oared ship.

pentēkontarchos: (commander of fifty) a member of the *hypēresia* in a trieres. His duties indicate 'purser' as the most appropriate English equivalent.

pentēkontoros: a ship of fifty oarsmen, 25 a side at one or two levels. *Pentēkonteros* is the spelling in the MSS of Herodotus, but in the MSS of Attic authors *triakontoros* and *pentēkontoros* are preferred.

pentērēs: see 'five'.

periplous: the battle manoeuvre of outflanking the defensive line-abreast formation of an enemy fleet.

peukē: the mountain pine (*see Meiggs (1983) p. 113*).

pinakothēkē: picture gallery.

pitys: the coastal pine (*see Meiggs (1983) p. 113*).

plērōma: oarcrew.

polemarchos: an Athenian official.

pous: clew

Propylaea: the building marking the entrance to the acropolis at Athens.

prōratēs: the member of the *hypēresia* in a trieres whose post was in the bows.

pyxis: casket.

rhyton: a type of two-handled cup with a hole in the bottom through which the wine was drunk, sometimes called a stirrup cup.

skōlēx: a species of ship-worm.

stamnos: jar.

stratēgos: an Athenian public official elected to command military or naval forces.

strobilos: a species of pine.
stuppax: a colloquial form of *stuppeioplokos*.
stuppeion: raw flax.
stuppeioplokos: rope-maker.
stylis: a staff in the ship's stern for display of flags and pennants.
syndesmos: a swifter.
syntaxis: a common contribution.
taeda: pitch pine.
talenton: *see drachma*.
taxiarchos: commander of a company.
taxis: as t.t., an oarcrew.
terēdon: the most harmful kind of ship-worm.
tesserakontērēs: *see* 'forty'.
tetrērēs: *see* 'four'.
thalamax: colloquial form of *thalamios*.
thalamē = *thalamos*.
thalamios: as noun, an oarsman in the lowest file of oarsmen in a trieres; as
     adjective, denoting e.g. something connected with such an oars-
     man, an oar or oarport.
thalamitēs: late Greek synonym for the noun *thalamios*.
thalamos: the hold of a ship.
thranitēs (pl. *thranitai*): a member of the file of oarsmen in a trieres who
     worked their oars through the outrigger (*parexeiresia*).
thranos: a longitudinal timber.
thrēnus: the seven-foot beam in the stern, on to which in the *Iliad* (15.728–9)
     Ajax steps back when driven from the poop (*ikria*) of a beached
     ship. A convenient name for the otherwise nameless stern cross-
     beam of a trieres. In the Homeric ship it is likely to have served as a
     foot-rest for the helmsman.
thrips: a ship-worm.
tonoi: tackles for tightening the *hypozōma*.
toxotai: archers.
triakontoros: a 30-oared ship.
triērarchos: the commander of a *trieres*.
trieraules: *see auletes*.
triērēs: *see* 'three'.
triskalmos: epithet describing a trieres as having three tholepins, presumably
     to each *interscalmium* or unit of two cubits.
tuloi: Attic synonym for *gomphoi*.
zōpissa: mixture of wax and pitch.
zyga (pl.): thwarts, beams.
zygios: noun, the oarsman who sat on a thwart in a trieres; adj., e.g. describ-
     ing the oar belonging to such an oarsman.
zygitēs: late Greek synonym for *zygios*.

BIBLIOGRAPHY

Alexiou, S. (1972) 'Larnakes kai Angeia ek Taphou para to Gazi Herakleiou', *Arch. Eph.* 1972:86–98

Anderson, R. C. (1962) *Oared Fighting Ships*. London

Andrewes, A. (1982) 'Notion and Kyzikos: the sources compared', *JHS* 102:15–25

Assmann, A. (1887) 'Seewesen', in Baumeister's *Denkmäler des klassischen Altertums* III, 1593–1639. Munich and Leipzig.

Babelon, E. (1901) *Traité des monnaies grecques*. Paris

Baif, Lazar de (1549) *Tractatus de re navali* (written 1536). Paris

Barras de la Penne, J.-A. (1727) *Lettre critique* . . . *au sujet d'un livre intitulé 'Nouvelles découvertes sur la guerre' par J. D. Foland avec des remarques critiques sur les trois systèmes de trirèmes*. Marseille

Barron, J. P. (1964) 'The sixth-century tyranny at Samos', *CQ* 14.2:210–29

Basch, L. (1969) 'Phoenician oared ships', *MM* 55.2:139–62 and 55.3:227–45

(1982) 'The Athlit ram', *MM* 68.1:3–7

Beschi, L. (1969–70) 'Relievi votivi attici ricompositi: il relievo della trireme Paralos', *Annuario Scuola Archeologica di Atene* NS 31–2:117–32

Blackman, D. J. (1968) 'The ship-sheds', Ch. 8 of *GOS*, pp. 181–92

Broadhead, H. D. (1960) *The Persae of Aeschylus*. Cambridge

Budé, G. (1514) *De asse et partibus eius* Vol. 5. Paris

Busley, R. (1918) *Schiffe des Altertums*. Berlin

Cargill, J. (1981) *The Second Athenian League*. London

Cartault, Auguste (1881) *La Trière athénienne*. Paris

Casson, Lionel (1971) *Ships and Seamanship in the Ancient World*. Princeton

Cawkwell, G. L. (1968) 'The power of Persia', *Arepo* 1:1–5

Chappelle, H. I. (1936) *The History of American Sailing Ships*. London

Cook, A. B. (1905) 'Triremes', *CR 119:371–6*, with remarks by Wigham Richardson, *ibid.* 376–7

Cook, R. M. (1979) 'Archaic Greek trade: three conjectures', *JHS* 99:152–3

Creuze, A. F. B. (1841) *Treatise on Naval Architecture*. Edinburgh

Davison, J. A. (1947) 'The first Greek triremes', *CQ* 41:18–24

Diehl, Ernestus (1952) *Anthologia Lyrica Graeca*, Ed. 3, Fasc. 3. Leipzig

Dragatzes, I. X. (1886) 'Report of the excavations in Peiraeus', *Praktika of 1885*: 63–8

Edmonds, J. M. (1957) *The Fragments of Attic Comedy* Vol. 1. Leiden

Fincati, L. (1883) *Le Triremi*. Rome

Forbes, R. J. (1936) *Bitumen and Petroleum in Antiquity*. Leiden

Forrest, W. G. (1969) 'Two chronographic notes', *CQ* 19:99–100

Foucher, L. (1967) 'Navires et barques', *Notes et Documents* XV (Institut Nationale d'Archéologie et Arts). Tunis

Frost, H. (1973) 'First season of excavation on the Punic wreck in Sicily', *IJNA* 2.1:33–49

 (1974a) 'The Punic wreck in Sicily', *IJNA* 3.1:35–54

 (1974b) 'The third campaign of excavation on the Punic ship, Marsala, Sicily', *MM* 60.3:265–6

Froude, W. (1879) *The Laws of Fluid Resistance*. London

Furtwängler, A. and Reichold, K. (1904–32) *Griechische Vasenmalerei*. Munich

Gomme, A. W. (1953) 'A forgotten factor of Greek naval strategy', *JHS* 53:16–24

Graef, B. and Langlotz, E. (1925–33) *Die Antiken Vasen von der Akropolis zu Athen*. Berlin

Graser, B. (1864) *De veterum re navali*. Berlin

Guilmartin, J. F. (1974) *Gunpowder and Galleys*. Cambridge

Haack, A. (1895) 'Über attische Trieren', *Zeitschrift der Vereins deutscher Ingenieure* 39

Hale, John R. (1973) 'Cushion and oar', *The Oarsman* 5.2 and 5.3

Hammond, N. G. L. (1945) 'Naval operations in the South Channel of Corcyra 435–433 BC', *JHS* 65:26–37

 (1956) 'The Battle of Salamis', *JHS* 76:32–54

 (1982) 'The narrative of Herodotus VII and the Decree of Themistocles at Troezen', *JHS* 102:75–93

Jal, Auguste (1861) *La Flotte de Jules César*. Paris

Joint Association of Classical Teachers (1984) *The World of Athens*. Cambridge

Jordan, B. (1975) *The Athenian Navy in the Classical Period* (University of California Publications, Classical Studies Vol. 13). Berkeley–Los Angeles–London

Jurien de la Gravière, J. P. E. (1878) 'La marine de l'avenir et la marine des anciens', *Revue des Deux Mondes* 30:746–81

 (1885) *Les Derniers jours de la marine à rames*. Paris

Kopecky, J. (1890) *Die attische Trieren*. Leipzig

Köster, A. (1923) *Das Antike Seewesen*. Berlin

Kourouniotes, K. (1914) 'The tholos tomb in Messenian Pylos', *Arch. Eph.* 1914:108

Landels, J. G. (1980) *Engineering in the Ancient World.* London

Lehmann, L. Th. (1978) 'The mystery of the Greco-Roman steering oar', *IJNA* 7.2:94–104

(1982) 'A trireme's tragedy', *IJNA* 11.2:145–51

Lemaitre, R. (1883) 'De la disposition des rameurs sur la trière antique', *RA* 3rd ser. 1:89–156

L'Illustration, 23 March 1861

Lloyd, A. B. (1972) 'Triremes and the Saite Navy', *JEA* 58:268–79

(1975) 'Were Necho's triremes Phoenician?', *JHS* 95:45–61

McKee, Eric (1983) *Working Boats of Britain.* London

MacKnight, C. C. (1980) 'The study of praus of the Indonesian archipelago', *The Great Circle*, vol. 2 no. 2 October 1980

Meiggs, R. (1983) *Trees and Timber in the Ancient World.* Oxford

Molmenti, P. G. (1906–8) *History of Venice in the Middle Ages* (Eng. trans.). London

Morrison, J. S. (1941) 'The Greek trireme', *MM* 27.1:14–44

(1947) 'Notes on certain Greek nautical terms', *CQ* 41:122–35

(1955) 'Parmenides and Er', *JHS* 75:59–68

(1974) 'Greek naval tactics in the fifth century BC', *IJNA* 3.1:21–6

(1978) 'Note on *IG* 2² 1604.156', *IJNA* 7.2:151

(1979) 'The first triremes', *MM* 65.1:53–63

(1980a) 'Hemiolia, trihemiolia', *IJNA* 9.2:121–6

(1980b) *Long Ships and Round Ships.* London

(1984a) 'Hyperesia in naval contexts in the fifth and fourth centuries BC', *JHS* 104:48–59

(1984b) 'Some problems of trireme reconstruction', *IJNA* 13.3:215–22

Morrison, J. S. and Williams, R. T. (1968) *Greek Oared Ships.* Cambridge

Napoleon III (1865–6) *Histoire de Jules César.* Paris

Nooteboom, C. (1949) 'Eastern diremes', *MM* 35:272–5

Owen, D. I. (1971) 'Excavating a classical shipwreck', *Archaeology* 24.2:127

Page, D. L. (1942) *Greek Literary Papyri* (Loeb Library). London

Robertson, J. A., ed. (1906) A. *Pigafetta: Magellan's Voyage round the World*, 2 vols. Cleveland

Robertson, N. (1982) 'The Decree of Themistocles in its contemporary setting', *Phoenix* 36:1–44

Rumpf, A. (1935) 'Römische Fragmente', *Winckelmanns Programm* 95:14–20

Saatoglu-Paliadele, Chrysoula (1978[1980]) 'Marble eyes from Piraeus', *Arch. Eph.* 1978: 119–35, pls. 40–1

Sainte-Croix, G. F. M. de (1972) *Origins of the Peloponnesian War.* Oxford

Salmon, J. B. (1984) *Wealthy Corinth.* Oxford

Savile, Sir Henry (1581) *The Ende of Nero and the Beginning of Galba: Foure Bookes of the Histories of Cornelius Tacitus*, p. 49 of the notes. Oxford

Steffy, J. R. (1983) 'The Athlit Ram, a preliminary investigation of its structure', with additional notes by Patrice Pomey, L. Basch and Honor Frost, *MM* 69.3:259–69

Swiny, H. W. and Katzev, M. L. (1973) 'The Kyrenia shipwreck', *Marine Archaeology* ed. D. J. Blackman (Colston Papers No. 23). London

Tarn, W. W. (1905) 'The Greek warship', *JHS* 25:137–73, 204–24
(1930) *Hellenistic Naval and Military Developments.* Cambridge

The Greek Trireme of the Fifth Century BC (1984) ed. J. F. Coates and Sean McGrail: discussion of a projected reconstruction at the National Maritime Museum, Greenwich

Torr, Cecil (1894) *Ancient Ships.* Cambridge (reprinted in the Argonaut Library of Antiquities, Chicago 1964)

Van Doorninck, F. J., Jnr (1982) 'Protogeometric long ships and the introduction of the ram', *IJNA* 11.4:277–85

Vermeule, C. C. (1964) 'The Dal Pozzo-Albani drawings of classical antiquity in the British Museum', *Transactions of the American Philosophical Society* NS 50.5:70, fig. 79 (fol. 171 no. 201)

Wallinga, H. T. (1982) 'The trireme and its crew', *Actus: Studies in Honour of H. T. W. Nelson.* Utrecht
(1984a) Review of B. Jordan (1975), *Mnemosyne* 37 Fasc. 1–2: 239–41
(1984b) 'The Ionian Revolt', *Mnemosyne* 37 Fasc. 3–4: 401–37

Walter, O. (1932) in *Festscrift für A. Rumpf.* Berlin

Weber, L. (1896) *Die Lösung des Trierenrätsel.* Danzig

Wieder, F. C. (1925–37) *Monumenta Cartographica.* 's Gravenhage

Williams, R. T. (1958) 'Early Greek ships of two levels', *JHS* 78:121–30
(1959) 'Addenda to ships of two levels', *JHS* 79:401–37

GENERAL INDEX

INDEX OF PASSAGES CITED